Behavior change in counseling
readings and cases

Century Psychology Series

Kenneth MacCorquodale,
Gardner Lindzey, and Kenneth E. Clark
Editors

BEHAVIOR CHANGE IN COUNSELING
Readings and Cases

Samuel H. Osipow & W. Bruce Walsh
BOTH OF THE OHIO STATE UNIVERSITY

New York

APPLETON-CENTURY-CROFTS
EDUCATIONAL DIVISION
MEREDITH CORPORATION

760-1

Library of Congress Card Number: 74–111884

ACKNOWLEDGMENTS

pp 4–13 from: Callis, R. Toward an integrated theory of counseling. *The Journal of College Student Personnel*, 1960, *1*, 2–9. Copyright 1960 by the American Personnel and Guidance Association and reproduced by permission.

pp 14–20 from: Krumboltz, J. D. Behavioral counseling: rationale and research. *Personnel and Guidance Journal*, 1965, *44*, 383–387. Copyright 1965 by the American Personnel and Guidance Association and reproduced by permission.

pp 21–29 from: Krumboltz, J. D. Behavioral goals for counseling. *Journal of Counseling Psychology*, Vol. 13, 1966, 153–159. Copyright 1966 by the American Psychological Association and reproduced by permission.

pp 30–34 from: Phillips, E. L. and Mattoon, C. U. Interference versus extinction as learning models for psychotherapy, *Journal of Psychology*, *61*, 1961, 399–403. Copyright 1961 by the Journal Press and reproduced by permission.

pp 45–54 from: Kanfer, F. J. Implications of conditioning techniques for interview therapy, *Journal of Counseling Psychology*, Vol. 13, 1966, 171–177. Copyright 1966 by the American Psychological Association and reproduced by permission.

pp 55–63 from: Lazarus, A. A. Learning theory and the treatment of depression, *Behavior Research and Therapy*, 1968, *6*, 83–89. Copyright 1968 by the Pergamon Press and reproduced by permission.

pp 64–74 from: Baer, D. N., Wolf, M. M., & Risley, T. R. Some current dimensions of applied behavior and analysis, *Journal of Applied Behavior Analysis*, 1968, *1*, 91–97. Copyright 1968 by the Society for the Experimental Analysis of Behavior Inc. and reproduced by permission.

pp 83–102 from: Ivey, A. E., Normington, Cheryl J., Miller, C. O., Morrill, W. H., & Haase, R. E. Microcounseling and attending behavior: an approach to prepracticum counselor training. *Journal of Counseling Psychology Monograph Supplement*, vol. 15, 1968, 1–12. Copyright 1968 by the American Psychological Association and reproduced by permission.

pp 103–126 from: Paul, G. L. Insight versus desensitization in psychotherapy two years after termination, *Journal of Consulting Psychology*, Vol. 31, 1967, 333–348. Copyright 1967 by the American Psychological Association and reproduced by permission.

pp 127–132 from: Lazarus, A. A. Behavior reversal versus non-directive therapy versus advice in effecting behavior change. *Behavior Research and Therapy*, 1966, 4, 209–212.

pp 133–145 from: Ryan, T. Antoinette and Krumboltz, J. D. Effect of planned reinforcement counseling on client decision-making behavior. *Journal of Counseling Psychology*, vol. 11, 1964, 315–323. Copyright 1964 by the American Psychological Association and reproduced by permission.

pp 146–159 from: Krumboltz, J. D. and Thoresen, C. E. The effect of behavioral counseling in group and individual settings on information seeking behavior. *Journal of Counseling Psychology*, vol. 11, 1964, 324–333. Copyright 1964 by the American Psychological Association and reproduced by permission.

pp 160–167 from: Allen, K. Eileen, Henke, Lydia B., Harris, Florence R., Baer, D. M., & Reynolds, Nancy J. Control of hyperactivity by social reinforcement of attending behavior. *Journal of Educational Psychology*, vol. 58, 1967, 231–237. Copyright 1967 by the American Psychological Association and reproduced by permission.

pp 168–177 from: Katahn, M., Strenger, S., & Cherry, Nancy. Group counseling and behavior therapy with test anxious students. *Journal of Consulting Psychology*, vol. 30, 1966, 544–549. Copyright 1966 by the American Psychological Association and reproduced by permission.

pp 178–182 from: Suinn, R. M. The desensitization of test anxiety by group and individual treatment. *Behavior Research and Therapy*, 1968, *6*, 385–387. Copyright 1968 by the Pergamon Press and reproduced by permission.

pp 185–193 from: Leventhal, A. M. Use of a behavioral approach within a traditional psychotherapeutic context: a case study. *Journal of Abnormal Psychology*, vol. 73, 1968, 178–182. Copyright 1968 by the American Psychological Association and reproduced by permission.

pp 194–200 from: Katahn, M. Systematic desensitization and counseling for anxiety in a college basketball player. *Journal of Special Education*, 1967, 1, 309–314. Copyright 1967 by the Journal of Special Education and reproduced by permission.

pp 201–207 from: Geer, J. H. & Katkin, E. S. Treatment of insomnia using a variant of systematic desensitization: a case report. *Journal of Abnormal Psychology*, vol. 71, 1966, 161–164. Copyright 1966 by the American Psychological Association and reproduced by permission.

pp 208–213 from: Geer, J. H. and Silverman, I. Treatment of a recurrent nightmare by behavior-modification procedures: a case study *Journal of Abnormal Psychology*, vol. 72, 1967, 188–190. Copyright 1967 by the American Psychological Association and reproduced by permission.

pp 214–219 from: Keutzer, Carolin S. Use of therapy time as a reinforcer: application of operant conditioning techniques within a traditional psychotherapy context. *Behavior Research and Therapy*, 1967, 5, 367–370. Copyright 1967 by the Pergamon Press and reproduced by permission.

pp 227–231 from: Migler, B. and Wolpe, J. Automated self-desensitization: a case report. *Behavior Research and Therapy*, 1967, 5, 133–135. Copyright, 1967 by Pergamon Press and reproduced by permission.

Preface

To quote one of the contributors to this volume, John Krumboltz, "there is a revolution in counseling" occurring. This book of readings and case studies deals with that revolution. The papers in this book represent some of the basic underpinnings of the behavioral approach to counseling. The volume is intended to be a companion to our text, *Strategies in counseling for behavior change*, though either book can be used independently of the other. It is our hope that this collection will focus attention on behavioral counseling and thus further its progress.

We wish to gratefully acknowledge the willingness of the authors to reprint their work in this volume. Even more, we appreciate the basic nature of their contributions to counseling psychology represented, in part, by their papers. It should be noted that several of the papers have never been published before, and some were especially written for this volume. We must also express our thanks to the American Psychological Association, the Pergamon Press, the American Personnel and Guidance Association, the Society for Applied Behavior Analysis, and the *Journal of Special Education* for their permission to reprint material copyrighted by them.

S.H.O. *and* W.B.W.

Contents

Page

Preface   v

Part I: Rationale

Callis, R.   Toward an integrated theory of counseling   4

Krumbolt, J. D.   Behavioral counseling: rationale and research   14

Krumboltz, J. D.   Behavioral goals for counseling   21

Phillips, E. L. and Mattoon, C. U.   Interference versus extinction as learning models for psychotherapy   30

Ullmann, L. P.   Beyond the reinforcement machine   35

Kanfer, F. H.   Implications of conditioning techniques for interview therapy   45

Lazarus, A. A.   Learning theory and the treatment of depression   55

Baer, D. N., Wolf, M. M. and Risley, T. R.   Some current dimensions of applied behavior analysis   64

Osipow, S. H.   Some ethical dilemmas involved in behavioral and client centered insight counseling   75

Part II: Research

Ivey, A. E., Normington, Cheryl J., Miller, C. D., Morrill, W. H. and Haase, R. E.   Microcounseling and attending behavior: an approach to prepracticum counselor training   83

Paul, G. L.   Insight versus desensitization in psychotherapy two years after termination   103

Lazarus, A. A.   Behavior reversal versus non-directive therapy versus advice in effecting behavior change   127

Ryan, T. Antoinette and Krumboltz, J. D.   Effect of planned reinforcement counseling on client decision-making behavior   133

Krumboltz, J. D. and Thoreson, C. E.   The effect of behavioral counseling in group and individual settings on information seeking behavior   146

Contents

Page

Allen, K. Eileen, Henke, Lydia B., Harris, Florence R., Baer, D. M. and Reynolds, Nancy J. Control of hyperactivity by social reinforcement of attending behavior   160

Katahn, M., Strenger, S. and Cherry, Nancy. Group counseling and behavior therapy with test anxious college students   168

Suinn, R. M. The desensitization of test anxiety by group and individual treatment   178

Part III: Cases

Leventhal, A. M. Use of a behavioral approach within a traditional psychotherapeutic context: a case study   185

Katahn, M. Systematic desensitization and counseling for anxiety in a college basketball player   194

Geer, J. H. and Katkin, E. S. Treatment of insomnia using a variant of systematic desensitization: a case report   201

Geer, J. H. and Silverman, I. Treatment of a recurrent nightmare by behavior-modification procedures: a case study   208

Keutzer, Carolin S. Use of therapy time as reinforcer: application of operant conditioning techniques within a traditional psychotherapy context   214

Burgess, Elaine. Applications of behavior modification in a student counseling center   220

Migler, B. and Wolpe, J. Automated self-desensitization: a case report   227

Ford, D. H. Introduction to planned behavior change   232

Urban, H. B. Verbal procedures in the modification of subjective responses   235

Wall, H. W. and Campbell, R. E. The alteration of overt instrumental responses by verbal methods   243

Osipow, S. H. and Grooms, R. R. Behavior modification through situational manipulation   248

Name Index   253

Subject Index   257

PART I

Rationale for Behavioral Counseling

Professional viewpoints in counseling psychology wax and wane. In the 1930's the "directive" viewpoint held sway. That view of counseling emphasized rational, cognitive processes and strived to help people solve their problems and reach decisions largely through the use of their intellectual resources. Though emotional aspects of living were neither ignored nor denied, proponents of "directive" counseling maintained that the greatest hopes for human progress in counseling lay in man's increased ability to use his problem solving capacities efficiently. Perhaps the emphasis was overdrawn and did not take into sufficient account the individual with emotional problems.

As a reaction to this lack of attention, the directive ideas gave way in the 1940's and 1950's to a considerable degree to a point of view which stated that the proper concern of counseling is with the individual's emotional life, specifically, the correction of distorted perceptions about himself and the world. The proponents of the new viewpoint suggested that intellectual, cognitive techniques merely feed such emotional problems. What was needed, they said, was a move away from evaluative, cognitive counseling toward the creation of a supportive, accepting, permissive counseling atmosphere which would free the client from threat and permit his natural problem solving abilities to emerge and growth to occur. Perhaps, at its extreme, this emphasis was overdrawn as much as the directive approach, excluding the proper care of those individuals presenting what are essentially cognitive concerns.

Once again, there arose a concern among some in counseling that the pendulum had again swung too far. Out of this concern and in an effort to avoid another excess has grown a new, behavioral cognitive approach to counseling, which has the effect of both moderating excesses in the affective "wing" of counseling as well as offering alternative methods and concepts for use where appropriate. The papers that follow in this first

1

section of this book represent some basic ideas underlying the new, behavioral mood.

The Callis paper catches the mood well, and sets the stage for the theme of the entire book. Callis chastizes counselors for their doctrinaire beliefs and practices, and works toward a counseling model which allows differential counseling for different kinds of problems. He suggests we match counseling techniques with client needs, rather than apply an available, universal catch-all technique to all comers.

The two Krumboltz papers which follow Callis' work continue in the same direction, but more concretely and specifically and with a slightly different emphasis. Krumboltz calls for a greater explicitness in the setting of goals in counseling, these goals ideally to be individually tailored. Krumboltz justifies these proposals in terms of the initial reason for providing counseling services, that is, the provision of individually oriented means to help people solve problems, make decisions, and generally get along better.

The next five papers each illustrate some special aspect of behaviorally oriented counseling. Kanfer's paper deals with the use of conditioning procedures in counseling. He suggests that there are really two broad categories of counseling procedures—*behaviorally oriented treatment* involving helping individuals develop new ways of dealing with events, and *friendship therapies* which provide warmth and support for those who need an extra boost at some point in their lives but who do not need or desire to change specific behaviors.

Baer, Wolf, and Risley describe some practical criteria for judging the adequacy of socially relevant behavior analysis to which, in their view, behavioral analysts must pay attention in order to fulfill self-assigned objectives. In his paper, Lazarus deals with making the term "depression" operational and shows how an S-R type of analysis can lead to therapeutic possibilities of various sorts. Phillips and Mattoon provide a similar analysis showing how a sophisticated learning based analysis of behavior can lead to greater precision in developing the most appropriate case strategy to be followed. In his paper entitled "Beyond the reinforcement machine", Leonard Ullmann argues that the behavior therapist is not mechanistic, as many opponents of behavior therapy charge, nor interested in taking over the life of the client. Instead, the behavioral counselor tries to teach the client how to analyze his behavior in its context in order to identify alternative behaviors to use, these to be applied ultimately outside the interview. It is the ability to analyze and implement alternatives that is the desired outcome of behavioral counseling.

In the last paper in Part I, Osipow has pointed out the fallacy in the oft mentioned criticism of behavioral counseling as being more controlling, and thus less ethical, than insight oriented client centered counseling approaches. The dilemma of control that exists in all types of counseling is illustrated and a tentative solution put forth to protect clients while at the same time permitting counselors to be effective professionally.

These nine papers have been selected to give the reader a taste of the conceptual basis of behavior approaches to counseling. In the sections that follow Part I the reader will also have an opportunity to get the flavor of case work and research representing the behavioral vantage point.

Toward an Integrated Theory of Counseling[1]

Robert Callis

Introduction

We need to organize our knowledge (theories and facts) in such a manner that the result is a consistent and unified guide to counseling thought, research and practice. We need a theory that is useful in our day-by-day practice; one that is not just a rag-bag collection of unrelated constructs, but a unified theory with high internal consistency. This paper is an attempt to take a step in that direction.

The definition of a theory is an organized set of ideas which will explain a maximum amount of the phenomena with which we are concerned. The test of a theory is—will it work? A good theory will work more often and in a greater variety of situations than a poor theory. Actually, there is no dichotomy between theory and practice. If a theory is adequate it is practical.

This paper is organized around three questions:

1. *What energizes behavior?* What causes the human organism to move, to act, to respond, to behave?
2. *How does the human organism develop a behavioral repertoire?* When is one's behavior repertoire adequate or inadequate? What is the nature of the inadequacies?
3. *How can the several kinds of inadequacies in behavior repertoire be corrected?* Which counseling method is most effective in correcting which inadequacy in behavior repertoire?

WHAT ENERGIZES BEHAVIOR?

Perhaps first we should state what appears to be a basic law of behavior: *The primary goal of an organism is to behave in such a fashion that he is able to extract from his environment the satisfaction of his needs not only at the moment but in a sustained manner in the future.* Most behavioral scientists agree that the

[1]Reprinted by permission of the author and the *Journal Of College Student Personnel*, 1960, *1*, 2-9.

stuff that energizes behavior is the need of the organism. Thus, if we are to understand behavior, we must understand the needs that the organism is trying to satisfy. Let us assume that needs and drives have to energize behavior.

Various authors have developed lists or needs. Maslow (1954) has ordered these needs into a hierarchy according to their power or priority relative to each other. This order is typical but individual variation from it can be observed. The following list is a modification of Maslow's list. It contains seven needs: two biological and five psycho-social. These are presented in order of their power or priority with the most powerful one first.

1. *Self-preservation.* This drive to survive physically has been rather well established in all forms of life. Immediately, we can think of instances in which some other need supersedes this supposedly most basic and powerful one. Suicide, for example, violates this basic drive. It seems that in the human organism we must introduce an additional construct here in order to understand self-preservation. Biologists describe self-preservation as a drive for physical survival. However, as we grow and develop, we develop a psychological self as well as a physical self. Somehow these two selves get intertwined. If we consider this drive for self-preservation to encompass both the physical and the psychological self, we can take it to be the highest priority and most powerful drive. Take, for example, the soldier who throws himself on a live grenade to protect his buddies from certain death; knowing full well that in doing so he will be killed. Some need more powerful than that to survive physically has motivated him. We can explain this act of heroism by invoking the notion of preservation of the psychological self and postulating that the soldier was acting in accordance with a concept of himself as a good soldier, one loyal to his buddies and one willing to risk his life to protect them.

2. *Reproduction of the species.* This is the second most powerful drive which biologists have identified. It also seems to be biologically inherited. The absence or malfunction of either the drive to physical survival or the drive to reproduce the species will cause the particular genetic strain to die out. We are here today only because our ancestors possessed these two drives in sufficient quantity. The genetic argument is perhaps the most powerful argument for these two biological drives being considered first in priority in relation to all the other drives. This puts preservation of the psychological self in second place. Dead heroes do not reproduce themselves.

3. *Security.* Security is a widely used term and perhaps loosely so at times. Security here has to do with a feeling of confidence within the individual that he will be able to satisfy his needs now and continuously in the future. When this security need is not satisfied, the person is fearful and apprehensive that he will not be able to interact with his environment in such a way that his needs will be satisfied. The magnitude of this fear may reach catastrophic proportions producing extreme anxiety and panic.

4. *Respect for self.* Each person needs to feel that he is worthy of dignity and respect. This is an attitude toward self; an approval of oneself. It is not necessarily associated with social or economic status. It is a need of everyone regardless of his status in life.

5. *Acceptance by others.* This includes heterosexual love, family and other close friendships, and general gregariousness. In adolescence acceptance by peers is highlighted.

6. *Self expression and accomplishment.* We have a need to use our abilities in manners suggested by our interests to create or accomplish something. Ability in itself has drive properties. This expression may take occupational forms or it may take recreational and hobby forms. Ability here is not restricted to intellectual ability.

7. *Esthetic experiences.* The need for esthetic experience accounts for the existence of art, music, drama, and the like.

Maslow's hierarchy principle states that in general until the most basic need has been satisfied in our perception or expectation, but not necessarily in reality, we cannot attend to the higher order but less powerful needs. The implications for the counselor are two-fold: (1) at what need level is the client functioning or having difficulty functioning? and (2) at what level is the counselor functioning and is the counselor able to distinguish between his own need level and that of his client? When the counselor understands at what need level the client is having difficulty, he is able to see more clearly the goal of counseling and is able to choose an appropriate counseling method in this case.

Once we have satisfied our more basic needs, we are then able to attend to our higher order needs. When the satisfaction of these lower order needs is threatened, we attend to them instead.

If we can accept the notion that needs motivate our behavior, we are ready to consider the behavior repertoire that we have at our command which we can use to interact with our environment for the purpose of satisfying our needs.

HOW DOES ONE DEVELOP HIS BEHAVIOR REPERTOIRE?

Needs provide the motivating force which energizes behavior and sets the goal to be attained as well. But what sort of behavior does one employ in attempting to satisy his needs? What patterns of behavior response does he have at his command; i.e., what repertoire of behavior responses does he have available for use? How does he choose a single course of action from among the several that may be in his repertoire? What happens if the choice is wrong? What happens if the behavior repertoire cupboard is bare? Where does counseling fit into such a scheme? These are a few of the questions which must be answered. Pepinsky and Pepinsky (1954) have dealt with several of these questions at length, and my treatment of the questions has been influenced by them.

We can define behavior repertoire as the total of all behavior responses that the individual is capable of making. We start with our inherited capacities and through maturation and experience build a behavior repertoire. Our behavior repertoire changes or is subject to change with each new experience. Thus, experience becomes the first level in a schematic diagram (Figure 1) which we can construct to represent behavior repertoire.

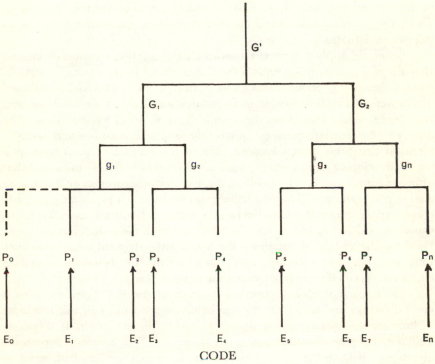

CODE

E– Experience; P– Perception; g– First Order Generalization; G– Second Order Generalization; G'– Third Order Generalization

FIGURE 1 Schematic Diagram of Behavior Repertoire Showing the Relationship of Experience, Perception and Generalization

For our purposes here, the unit of experience can be conceived of as being of any size. Experience is an objective occurrence external to the "psyche."

The second element is *perception*. Perception is the individual's interpretation of the experience or that which is interiorized by the individual.

The third element is *generalization*. We seem to have a natural tendency to group perceptions which appear to us to be of a similar kind and draw one rule of generalization from the whole class of events. We use this generalization to guide our behavior at any time in the future when we encounter an event perceived to be of the same class of events as those about which the generalization was drawn. For example, if we go into a strange room which is dark and wish to turn on the light, where would we look for the light switch? Most of us have had experiences with light switches and from these experiences and our perceptions of them, we have concluded or generalized that usually the light switch is located on the wall adjacent to the door frame a little above waist high. We have also learned, that is, concluded or generalized that light switches are not to be found on the floor or ceiling. Thus, the generalization based on past experience guides our behavior in this present situation.

Before we apply a generalization to a new situation we must determine that the new situation is identical for our purposes to the class of situations from which our generalizations came. Thus, if the dark room mentioned above were in a rustic log cabin in an isolated wooded area we would suspect that there would be neither lights nor light switches in the room. The ability to differentiate between apparently identical situations and actually identical situations must be admitted into the scheme of thinking which we are developing here. Dollard, Auld and White (1953) have indicated that improvement in accuracy of differentiation and discrimination is a major goal in psychotherapy. They describe instances in which psychiatric patients try to apply generalizations developed out of childhood experiences to situations which they encounter as adults. Although the generalizations were valid for the childhood situations the apparently identical adult situations were in reality not identical, and, consequently, the behavior repertoire employed was ineffective in satisfying the patients' needs.

The constellation of all generalizations developed out of past experience gives direction and selectivity to our behavior tendencies in our attempts to interact with present environment to satisfy present needs. If this constellation of generalization which we have labelled behavior repertoire directs our behavior in such a way that our needs are satisfied, we can consider it adequate.

When a client comes to a counselor saying, "I have a problem. I would like you to help me with it," he is, in effect, saying, "My behavior repertoire is inadequate. Will you help me correct the inadequacies?" No matter what language he uses, in the model we are developing here, that is the translation.

There are three general classes of inadequacies: (1) lack of experience, (2) distortions in perception, and (3) errors in generalization.

Lack of experience simply means that we have not had the kind of experience necessary to develop generalizations appropriate for the situation with which we are confronted. This includes lack of information about ourselves as well as our environment. Most counseling effort devoted to increasing understanding of self and of the world of work is attacking this first kind of inadequacy. (See E_O in Figure 1.)

Distortion in perception can occur even though our experience or exposure is adequate. For example, our need to regard ourselves highly may be so pressing that we distort or deny all evidence or experience which suggests that we may not be as intelligent or popular as our current self-concept suggests. Generalizations based on distorted perceptions are apt to be invalid and will direct us into behavior which will not satisfy our needs.

Errors in generalization are more difficult to describe in concrete terms. We could say that they are faulty logic but this is not very helpful. Errors in grouping perceptions from which we draw a generalization would produce a faulty generalization, but, also, there can be errors in actual generalization itself. The process of creating an idea resists definition and description. We can test the validity of an idea, hypothesis or generalization once it has been invented, but we know very little about how these inventions were produced. In our model, we must include errors in generalization even if we cannot describe exactly how they occur.

In addition to the three types of inadequacies, there is a fourth notion that needs mentioning. That is the *spread of effects of errors*. Lack of experience or distortion in perception does not stop there. They cause, in turn, erroneous generalization based this time on the original error. One is reminded here of the children's ditty: "For the lack of a nail, the shoe was lost. For the lack of a shoe, the horse was lost. For the lack of a horse, the rider was lost. For the lack of the rider, the battle was lost."

Let us return to our client who has said to us (translated), "My behavior repertoire is inadequate. Will you help me correct the inadequacies?" It seems that the problem calls for two discoveries: (1) discovery of the error, and (2) discovery of a way to correct the error. Who is to make the discoveries? We have two choices – the counselor or the client. Or, to say it another way, there are two general methods of counseling – (1) client self discovery and (2) counselor discovery followed by interpretation.

WHICH COUNSELING METHOD IS MOST EFFECTIVE IN CORRECTING WHICH INADEQUACY IN BEHAVIOR REPERTOIRE?

This question suggests that the counselor's behavior repertoire should include more than one counseling method. Is there any justification for a counselor's being competent in and using more than one counseling method? Or, is some one counseling method sufficient to solve all client problems, as many counselors contend?

Suppose that you move to a new town and shortly thereafter you develop a severe head cold. You consult a physician and he gives you a shot of penicillin. You get well. You conclude that he is a good physician. Later on you break your arm. You go back to your physician. He gives you a shot of penicillin and starts to dismiss you. You say, "But Doc, how about this broken bone? Aren't you going to set it?" He replies, "I don't believe in bone setting. I'm a penicillin man." Do you still consider him a good physician? If not, why not? Because he is a one-tool physician. He refuses to vary his treatment according to the problem. Should we not also condemn counselors for this one-tool attitude?

Suppose your car has blown a head gasket. You take it to a garage for repair. The mechanic starts banging on the head bolts with a screwdriver. You say, "Why don't you use a wrench on these head bolts?" and he replies, "Oh, I couldn't do that, you see I'm a screwdriver man." Would you judge him to be a competent mechanic? If not, why not? Would you really condemn him for being a one-tool mechanic? He has strong *faith* in his screwdriver and such strong *conviction* that it is proper to limit himself to only one tool. Isn't faith and conviction a sufficient basis for determining one's professional behavior? Since it seems to be a sufficient basis for many counselors, it would seem only fair that we also permit physicians and mechanics the same privilege of restricting their tools on the basis of faith and conviction.

Many counselors restrict themselves to the client-self discovery method solely. Suppose we instruct every third grade teacher that he is to employ the self-discovery method solely, and, in addition, we set the standard that every third grader must know the multiplication tables before he can go on to the fourth grade. How many grey-bearded third graders would we have hobbling around in our schools because they had not yet discovered the multiplication tables? Of course, someone did discover the multiplication tables years ago, but it was not a third grader. However, millions of third graders have learned the multiplication tables by having them interpreted to them. Many a client has learned within a few hours, through interpretation, the occupational groups that match his interests. Most of these would expend hundreds of hours to acquire the same understanding of themselves by self-discovery method.

I have tried to show that a single counseling method cannot solve all types of problems, and that client self-discovery method of counseling cannot solve certain client problems and will be grossly inefficient with others. But, how about the converse? Can counselor discovery and interpretation be effective in all instances? Let us return to our discussion of distortion in perception. It has shown that distortion in perception can occur even though the client has had adequate and appropriate experience or exposure. Certainly, interpretation by the counselor is an experience or exposure for the client. Therefore, it is quite possible and conceivable that the client may distort or reject a counselor's interpretation which would in turn produce an erroneous generalization. An erroneous generalization is an inadequacy in behavior repertoire, so the client is still unable to satisfy his needs. Counseling has failed.

We now come to the major point in this paper. Clients consult counselors because they have found that their behavior repertoire is inadequate. Inadequacies in behavior repertoire can be of three different kinds and counseling methods are basically of two kinds, neither of which can be effective with all kinds of inadequacies. Therefore, it is absolutely necessary that counseling include differential diagnosis which will form the basis for differential choice of treatment, i.e., counseling method. The one-tool counselor must go. He is just as unscientific, unprofessional, unethical and immoral as the penicillin physician or the screwdriver mechanic. The only instance in which a counselor would be justified in restricting himself to one method, would be for him to limit his practice to one type of inadequacy. Even then he would have to engage in diagnosis to determine if this particular client is the type of case he would accept. Diagnosis in counseling is not a new topic, nor is it a completely forgotten one. (See Apostal and Miller, 1959; Berezin, 1957; Bordin, 1946; Pepinsky, 1948; Weiner, 1959; Williamson and Darley, 1937).

In spite of all the important contributions Rogers (1931, 1939, 1942, 1951) has made, he has damaged the field quite significantly by making most of us feel guilty about diagnosis, and yet if you read his works carefully this should not have happened. Rogers limits his methods to certain kinds of cases and makes the determination (diagnosis) at the outset that the case is appropriate to this method (client self-discovery) before accepting the case. I have a bone to pick with the pseudo-Rogerians, not Rogers himself.

If the word diagnosis makes you feel squeamish, if it rankles you, I believe we can avoid that very nicely by substituting "working hypothesis" for "diagnosis." Of course, we are still talking about the same thing, but "working hypothesis" may be more palatable to many counselors. Each counselor, whether he admits it or not, draws generalizations (working hypotheses) about his client on a moment-to-moment basis throughout the entire counseling process. On the basis of these hypotheses the counselor determines what his behavior will be, what method he will employ at the next moment. In reality, every counselor employs differential diagnosis and differentially chooses his treatment method accordingly. My plea, simply, is to make these operations explicit so that we can begin to think about and conduct some research on the effectiveness of various counseling methods in correcting the several kinds of inadequacies in behavior repertoire.

As a starting point for this line of investigation, let me propose two hypotheses. Earlier three kinds of inadequacies in behavior repertoire were described: (1) lack of experience, (2) distortion in perception and (3) erroneous generalization. I will deal here with the first two only. Also, I will not attempt to distinguish between the two kinds of discoveries to be made. However, I suspect that the following hypotheses are more appropriate to discovery of a way to correct an inadequacy than to discovering the inadequacy in the first place.

Hypothesis A. Lack of experience is most effectively dealt with by the method of counselor discovery and interpretation.

Hypothesis B. Distortion in perception is most effectively dealt with by the method of client self-discovery.

There are several arguments to support these two hypotheses as a starting point. Lack of experience includes lack of information about self and the environment. Experience can be direct or vicarious. The client is motivated by his needs to obtain the result of the experience which he is lacking. Typically the counselor is able to obtain the necessary information, understandings and insights by virtue of his superior knowledge of human behavior, his superior knowledge of the environment, and his superior methods of assessing psychological characteristics. The counselor can supply the client with the proper information (experiences) and the client can correct his inadequacies in a straightforward learning situation. However, if the client is unable to utilize the counselor discoveries, the problem is not one of lack of experience but one of distorted perceptions. The client does not need more information or experience to distort. He needs to correct his distortions. Since his distortions are in part a defense against encroachment from the outside, he cannot accurately utilize information from the counselor. Therefore, he must discover for himself. The counselor can aid by creating a situation in which the client need not spend all of his attention and energy defending himself against his environment but can attend to the things in his own make-up which are causing him trouble. The counselor can provide a safe situation in which the client can work on material he already has on hand.

To summarize very briefly, I have suggested a theoretical model for counseling which includes the following points:

1. Biological and psycho-social needs are the energizers of behavior.

2. Behavior repertoire is made up of three elements—experience, perceptions and generalizations.

3. Behavior repertoire may be inadequate for any of three reasons—lack of experience, distortion in perception or erroneous generalizations.

4. The goal of counseling is to discover and correct inadequacies in behavior repertoire.

5. These discoveries can be made by either client or counselor. Therefore, counseling methods can be grouped under general methods: client self-discovery, and counselor discovery accompanied by interpretation.

6. Any one counseling method will not be equally effective in discovering and correcting all types of inadequacies in behavior repertoire.

7. There is an urgent need for attention to the problem of differential diagnosis leading to differential choice of treatment. Two attractive research hypotheses as a start on the problem are: (a) lack of experience can be most effectively dealt with by counselor-discovery. (b) Distortions in perceptions can be most effectively dealt with by client self-discovery.

REFERENCES

Apostal, R. A., & Miller, J. G. A manual for the use of a set of diagnostic categories. Columbia: University of Missouri Testing and Counseling Service Report No. 21, 1959.

Berdie, R. F. Counseling principles and presumptions. *J. Counsel. Psychol.*, 1959, *6*, 175-182.

Berezin, Annabel G. The development and use of a system of diagnostic categories in counseling. Unpublished doctoral dissertation, University of Missouri, 1957.

Bordin, E. S. Diagnosis in counseling and psychotherapy. *Educ. Psychol. Measmt.*, 1946, *6*, 169-184.

Dollard, J., Auld, F. W., & White, Alice M. *Steps in psychotherapy*. New York: Macmillan, 1953.

Maslow, A. H. *Motivation and personality*. New York: Harpers, 1954.

Pepinsky, H. B. The selection and use of diagnostic categories in clinical counseling. *Psychol. Monogr.*, 1948, No. 15.

Pepinsky, H. B. and Pepinsky, Pauline N. *Counseling: Theory and Practice*. New York: Ronald, 1954.

Rogers, C. R. *Test of personality adjustment*. New York: Association Press, 1931.

Rogers, C. R. *The clinical treatment of the problem child*. Boston: Houghton Mifflin, 1939.

Rogers, C. R. *Counseling and psychotherapy*. Boston: Houghton Mifflin, 1942.

Rogers, C. R. *Client-Centered therapy*. Boston: Houghton Mifflin, 1951.

Weiner, I. B. The role of diagnosis in a university counseling center. *J. Counsel. Psychol.*, 1959, *6*, 110-115.

Williamson, E. G., & Darley, J. G. *Student personnel work*. New York: McGraw-Hill, 1937.

Behavioral Counseling: Rationale and Research[1]

John D. Krumboltz

In order to focus on the purpose of counseling, I have elected to use the term "behavioral counseling." The adjective "behavioral" does not imply that there are other kinds of counseling that should be categorized as "non-behavioral counseling." I use the term "behavioral counseling" only as a reminder that all counseling is designed to affect the behavior of the client. I know of no counselor or psychotherapist of any school of thought who would deny that he hopes to influence the behavior of his client. In this sense, all counseling is behavioral counseling, although occasionally counselors appear to forget this fact.

RAISON D'ÊTRE

Why do counselors exist? What is the central purpose for which the profession of counseling has been established? Occasionally, in reading the professional literature, one gets the impression that the central purpose of counseling has been forgotten in our attention to tangential issues. The central purpose of counseling is not to keep information from falling into the wrong hands. It is not to make interpretations of psychological tests. It is not to make hypotheses about a client's past or future behavior. It is not to induce the client to talk about his feelings and let him know that he is understood. While all of these activities may at one time or another be involved in counseling, they do not constitute its central purpose.

The central reason for the existence of counseling is based on the fact that people have problems that they are unable to resolve by themselves. They come to counselors because they have been led to believe that the counselor will be of some assistance to them in resolving their problems. The central purpose of counseling, then, is to help each client resolve those

[1]Reprinted from the *Personnel and Guidance Journal*, 1965, *44,* 383-387, with permission of the author and the American Personnel and Guidance Association.

problems for which he requests help. If a client terminates his contact with a counselor and is still bothered by the same problem that brought him to the counselor in the first place, that counselor has failed. If, on the other hand, the client has either solved the problem he brought to the counselor or planned a course of action that will eventually lead to a resolution of his problem, then the counselor has succeeded. Within limits, it is each client's wishes that dictate the criteria of success for that client.

Some people may be offended by the notion that we should permit the wishes of our clients to determine the criteria of our success and would prefer to establish universal criteria applicable to all clients. It should be remembered that all professional groups and all professional persons are ultimately evaluated by the extent to which they bring about the conditions desired by their clientele. When a client requests his lawyer to write out a last will and testament, the client expects the lawyer to write that document in such a manner that the client's requests will eventually be executed in precisely the manner that he wishes. In like manner a physician is successful if, let us say, a patient with a broken leg can walk normally again as he desires.

In the case of both the lawyer and the physician there come times when the professional man cannot carry out the wishes of his client either because the request is not within the scope of his interests, or because it is beyond his powers, or because it violates his ethical standards. In such cases the professional man explains the reasons why he cannot carry out the specific request of the client, perhaps indicating alternate courses of action including referrals when appropriate. When a professional man does accept a client, however, he is implicitly agreeing to exert whatever efforts he can to accomplish what his client requests. The use of clients' requests as a basis for generating the criteria of success is as appropriate for counselors as it is for lawyers and physicians. In the case of counselors it means that the same criterion measures cannot be applied to evaluate all counseling contacts.

REQUESTING ENDS, NOT MEANS

The client's request must be in terms of some end condition or result, not the means to achieve that end. A professional person agrees to try to accomplish certain goals for his client but does not permit the client to dictate the precise manner and means of accomplishing that goal. The lawyer who agrees to his client's request to try to obtain an acquittal accepts full responsibility for the means used to obtain that acquittal. Similarly a physician does not allow his patient to supervise his manner of treatment or his method of operating. Both may consult their clients or patients, advising them of the consequences of alternative courses of action, but it is the client's or patient's request for what outcomes he ultimately desires that provides the basis for the professional man's decision as to exactly which means are best suited to that end. Similarly, in counseling the client's request provides the basis for determining the success of counseling with that client. If a client requests of a counselor, "I would like to reach a decision as to what career I should follow," and the counselor agrees to help the client with this problem, then it becomes the counselor's responsibility to launch his client on a course of action that will ultimately enable that client to reach a well-considered decision. If the client requests of the counselor, "I want you to tell me what occupation I should enter," then the counselor, unless he is omniscient, has an obligation to tell his client, in effect, "I am not able to tell you what occupation you should enter, but I can lead you to consider a number of alternatives and factors that you can explore to increase the likelihood that your ultimate decision will be a wise one."

A DEFINITION OF COUNSELING

On the basis of the foregoing discussion I should like to offer the following definition of counseling:

> Counseling consists of whatever ethical activities a counselor undertakes in an effort to help the client engage in those types of behavior which will lead to a resolution of the client's problems.

The critical feature of this definition is that the counselor's methods are not specified, but what he is trying to accomplish is. Accomplishment of clients' goals, not adherence to specified procedures, should be the mark of a successful counselor.

A COUNSELOR'S LIMITATIONS ON CLIENT REQUESTS

This definition does not imply that a counselor would agree to work on whatever problems a client presents. There are three types of limitations a counselor might invoke.

Interest Limits

Each counselor must decide for himself what types of problems he is interested in helping to solve. If the client asks for help in deciding which used car to buy, many counselors would wish to refer his problem to other authorities. Some counselors, on the other hand, might be willing to help with this problem on the grounds that (a) the process of making a wise decision about used cars may well transfer to making wise decisions about other matters, or (b) the "used car" problem is merely a preliminary to problems of more concern to both the counselor and the client.

The day is coming when the counseling function will be even more specialized than it is today. Just as lawyers and physicians select clients on the basis of their specialized interests, so we may find counselors who have special interests. Some may only be willing to work with clients who have phobias of various types. Other counselors may specialize in working with clients who have problems of vocational indecision. The interests of each individual counselor are one factor in determining whether or not a client's requests will be used to establish the criteria of success for that counselor working with that client on that problem.

Competency Limits

Clients sometimes present requests that go beyond the powers of any human being to help. Requests such as "I would like you to increase my IQ," or "I would like you to decide for me whether I should get married or not," or "I want everybody to love me," are examples of problems that most counselors would find beyond their competency to accomplish as requested. On the other hand, each problem represents an area of concern where some progress could be made in remedying the specific problem bothering the client. Although a person's "IQ" may not be readily increased, it may be possible to help that person to learn some study skills which will enable him to perform a little bit more competently in his academic tasks. Though a counselor may not be competent to decide whether or not another person should get married, he may be able to help his client consider a number of factors which would enable the client to arrive at a proper decision. And although no counselor may be able to help his client to be loved by everybody, he may be able to help his client change certain behavioral mannerisms or reactions which antagonize his friends, relatives, or employers. It would seem incumbent on an ethical counselor to make clear the limits of his capabilities at the outset of the counseling process so that the client would not labor under a mistaken notion that his unrealistic requests will be attained.

Ethical Limits

A counselor must also evaluate his client's requests in terms of his own ethical standards. Just as physicians and lawyers have ethical limits to the kinds of things they will undertake (e.g., abortions, or illegal means of collecting evidence), so also do good counselors establish ethical limits on their activities. I shall not attempt to spell out the possible kinds of unethical requests that might be made of counselors, but would only like to mention that requests must be screened on the basis of each counselor's own ethical standards. Requests that might be unethical to some counselors might be quite ethical to others. Problems in the area of religion and sexual adjustment are examples of areas in which conflicting standards might exist.

USEFUL COUNSELOR ACTIVITIES

Counselors may be understandably reluctant to accept client wishes as a basis for judging their own success if they are not familiar with techniques or procedures that would be useful in bringing about what the client requests.

Indeed the literature of our field is sadly lacking in descriptions of specific techniques or procedures that will lead to specific outcomes with known degrees of probability. However, research in this direction is under way, and I should like to summarize briefly some few findings based on experimental studies conducted at Stanford University. I shall formulate several questions and then give the answers suggested by the research to date. These answers will be stated as unqualified generalizations, although it should be obvious that further experimental confirmation is necessary. These studies were all based on a limited number of subjects under particular environmental circumstances, and replication of these findings will be required to strengthen the generalizations.

A. *What can a counselor do to get vocationally undecided students to begin exploring some possible alternatives?* One technique consists of systematic reinforcement of information-seeking responses during an interview. Studies by Krumboltz and Schroeder (1965), and Krumboltz and Thoresen (1964) both confirm that the counselor's warm approval and support of certain types of client statements during the interview will result in the client voluntarily engaging in a number of information-seeking behaviors after leaving the interview situation.

Another technique consists of presenting a 15-minute tape-recorded interview as a model of information-seeking activities. Such a tape-recorded model results in marked exploratory behavior relevant to career decisions when the model chosen is appropriate for the client. The use of male models was proved effective with male subjects (Krumboltz & Schroeder, 1965; Krumboltz & Thoresen, 1964) and a video tape of a female client and counselor has proved effective with female clients (Varenhorst, 1964).

B. *What can a counselor do for unsophisticated students who are puzzled and confused by multiple-choice tests even though they claim they know the right answers?* By means of a 20-minute presentation a counselor can increase the "test-wiseness" of students lacking this skill. A study by Gibb (1963) clearly demonstrated that subjects given instruction designed to make them sensitive to secondary cues in tests made markedly higher scores on a test of test-wiseness than subjects not given this instruction.

C. *When a client expects his test scores to be quite different from what they really are should the counselor begin by reporting the most discrepant or the least discrepant score first?* If a counselor wishes a client to accept a series of test scores in which the client's expectations are markedly discrepant from the actual test scores, then the counselor should begin by reporting the most discrepant test score first rather than the least discrepant test score first. An experiment performed by MacQuiddy (1964) showed that parents with markedly discrepant expectations of their children's test scores would change their opinions toward accepting the test scores more readily when the greatest discrepancies were presented first as compared with parents who received the least discrepant scores first.

D. *What can a counselor do to help children overcome their shyness?* A counselor can increase the social participation of shy children in the classroom by systematically reinforcing any verbal behavior in small therapy groups outside the classroom. A study by Johnson (1964) with elementary school children showed that five half-hour sessions during a two-week period of time, during which the counselor provided warmth, praise, and support for any verbal participation whatsoever, markedly increased the amount of verbal participation in the therapy session, and that this increase transferred to the classroom environment.

E. *Can a counselor influence the degree to which clients will deliberate over a decision?* By systematically reinforcing "deliberation" responses during the interview the counselor can increase the extent to which the client will continue to deliberate in the interview. Ryan and Krumboltz (1964) showed that both "deliberation" and "decision" types of statements could be increased during counseling interviews in as little as six to 10 minutes, and that, in the case of the group reinforced for "decision" responses, a tendency to make decisions could be detected later in a projective type of problem test in a classroom setting.

F. *What can the counselor do to encourage students to reconsider "unrealistic" decisions?* The presentation of specific probabilities of success in various colleges can be used to modify the planning of students who are making unrealistic college decisions. A study by Gelatt (1964) showed that the use of a programmed booklet in which students would systematically determine their own probability of success in various types of colleges on the basis of their previous high school grade-point average was effective in modifying the college choices of at least some of these subjects.

Conclusion

It should be clear that there are things that counselors can do that have marked effects on the behavior of clients after leaving the counselor. We have scarcely begun to determine what some of these activities might be and how they might be most effectively employed. The evidence from these studies done at Stanford University within the last few years indicates at least some things that have proved effective in promoting career planning, in improving test-wiseness, in increasing social participation, in increasing deliberating and decision behavior, in promoting acceptance of test results, and in modifying unrealistic decisions. The techniques that have been tried out may not be necessarily the most effective techniques possible. Continued experimentation will be necessary to determine additional techniques and the circumstances under which each kind of technique might help each type of client to produce the effects that the client desires. As we learn more about what activities can be used to bring about the types of behavior changes that clients request, then we as counselors will be better able to fulfill our professional responsibilities.

REFERENCES

Gelatt, H. B. The influence of outcome probability data on college choice. Unpublished doctoral dissertation, Stanford Univ., 1964.

Gibb, B. G. Test-wiseness as secondary cue response. Unpublished doctoral dissertation, Stanford Univ., 1963.

Johnson, C. J., Jr. The transfer effect of treatment group composition on pupils' classroom participation. Unpublished doctoral dissertation, Stanford Univ., 1964.

Krumboltz, J. D., and Schroeder, W. W. Promoting career planning through reinforcement and models. *Personnel Guidance Journal*, 1965, *44*, 19-26.

Krumboltz, J. D., and Thoresen, C. E. The effect of behavioral counseling in group and individual settings on information-seeking behavior. *Journal of Counseling Psychology*, 1964, *11*, 324-333.

MacQuiddy, R. H. The effect of alternative methods of reporting objective test results to parents in reducing cognitive dissonance. Unpublished doctoral dissertation, Stanford Univ., 1964.

Ryan, T. Antoinette, and Krumboltz, J. D. Effect of planned reinforcement counseling on client decision-making behavior. *Journal of Counseling Psychology*, 1964, *11*, 315-323.

Varenhorst, Barbara B. An experimental comparison of non-verbal factors determining reinforcement effectiveness of model-reinforced counseling. Unpublished doctoral dissertation, Stanford Univ., 1964.

Behavioral Goals for Counseling[1]

John D. Krumboltz

I shall argue that stating the goals of counseling in terms of observable behavior will prove more useful than stating goals in terms of such inferred mental states as "self-understanding" and "self-acceptance." Self-understanding and self-acceptance are frequently listed among the goals of counseling although definitions of these terms lack precision. Let me make perfectly clear that I am not opposed to people having self-understanding and being self-accepting. Counselors who use these terms probably want the same kind of outcomes which I would want. But with terms as abstract as these, it is impossible to tell whether agreement exists and whether the goals are ever attained.

It is my contention that it would be far more useful to state the goals of counseling in terms of overt behavior changes. Ultimately counselors of all persuasions look to client behavior changes as justification for their procedures. Self-understanding and self-acceptance constitute intermediate mental states which some people assume make possible these ultimate modifications in behavior patterns. It is assumed that if clients can attain some degree of self-understanding and/or self-acceptance, they will be "freed" to change their overt behavior. Whether or not this assumption is justified is an empirical question, the evidence on which is discussed in Krumboltz (1966).

Disavowal of subjective states as goals of counseling is not new. Recently Brayfield (1962) argued that counseling psychologists had placed undue emphasis on egocentric self-regarding internal states and should instead use a performance criterion which would stress dependability, accountability, obligation and responsibility. Similarly, Samler (1962) cited three instances in which problems of prejudice, self-pity and poor workmanship were brought to the counselor. In each case, Samler argued, the important objective was

[1]Reprinted from the *Journal of Counseling Psychology*, 1966, *13*, 153-159, with permission of the author and the American Psychological Association.

that the client change his behavior in relevant ways whether or not his subjective feelings changed. Such logic finds a foundation in the concept of efficiency as advocated by Wishner (1955) and the concept of competence which was brilliantly developed by White (1959).

Why have objective statements of behavior change not already replaced subjective states as counseling objectives if they are superior? Subjective states are appealing because their very abstractness enables them to be interpreted to suit individual preferences. "Self-fulfillment" commands the same instant acceptance from some counselors as "patriotism" does from some politicians. It is only when attempts are made to specify concrete actions that dissension occurs. With abstract goals real differences between people may still exist but may not be discovered. The resulting harmony is reinforcing to many.

The fundamental obstacle to formulating behavioral objectives has been the assumption that we must write one list of objectives which applies to all counselees. It has been hoped that once we discover exactly what constitutes the "good life" we could analyze and list its elements as counseling objectives. Such attempts quickly bog down when it becomes apparent that what's good for GM is not good for MG. Hence, any list of behavioral objectives, if taken as desirable behavior for *all* clients, is justifiably vulnerable to criticism.

CRITERIA FOR COUNSELING GOALS

Any set of goals for counseling should meet each of the following criteria:

1. *The goals of counseling should be capable of being stated differently for each individual client.* One set of statements cannot apply to all clients. The unique feature of counseling is the individualization it provides. If we take seriously the assertion that each client is entitled to our respect as an individual, then we should be willing to work toward different goals with each of our clients. The common goals that our society holds for all individuals are partially met by the regular instructional program in our schools and colleges. Helping different individuals attain their different goals provides a unique opportunity for counselors to be of service. If this is true, there may be a virtually unlimited number of goals toward which counselors might help their clients strive. The goals of one client might be in direct contradiction to the goals of another client. For example, one client might wish to learn how to become more assertive in his social responses, while another might wish to learn how to become less assertive. A counselor could legitimately work with both of these clients, helping each one to achieve the particular type of behavior he desired.

2. *The goals of counseling for each client should be compatible with, though not necessarily identical to; the values of his counselor.* To use an extreme example, a boy who wanted help in becoming a more effective bank robber would find few counselors willing to help him attain that particular goal. However,

if the boy indicated a desire to consider the possible consequences of a bank robbing career in relation to other career possibilities, then probably many more counselors would be willing to help him think through the alternatives.

This second criterion implies that each counselor has some responsibility for evaluating the particular goals of his clients. This is not to say that he would necessarily attempt to change the goals of his clients, but he must make a judgment of whether or not he would be willing to help a client attain his particular goal. There might be goals acceptable to some counselors but not to others. For example, a client might ask a counselor for help in strengthening (or abandoning) his religious practices. It is quite conceivable that some counselors working in certain settings would be willing to help attain this goal while other counselors in different settings would not accept the assignment. The counselor's own interests, competencies and ethical standards should place limitations on what he is, and is not, willing to help his client accomplish (Krumboltz, 1965b).

3. *The degree to which the goals of counseling are attained by each client should be observable.* Some means must be available so that competent judges, regardless of their theoretical preferences, can agree that a particular goal has or has not been attained. This means that some overt indication of the client's behavior provides the basis for the judgment. Behavior, of course, is interpreted broadly to include any verbal or written statement, any responses that can be seen or heard, and any other responses that can be assessed reliably through some type of instrumentation.

THREE TYPES OF BEHAVIORAL GOALS

There are three types of goals which meet the criteria listed above and which clearly fall within the scope of counselors' responsibilities. The three categories are not intended to be mutually exclusive or even all inclusive but may provide a convenient framework for organizing the tasks a counselor may accomplish.

Under each category illustrative examples of goals are listed. Clearly all possible goals of counseling can never be listed if we use the above criteria. Any type of behavior change desired by a client and agreed to by his counselor could be listed as an illustrative counseling goal.

1. *Altering Maladaptive Behavior.* Many clients are unhappy because they are engaging in a pattern of behavior which does not lead to the satisfactions they desire. Of course, many are not able to identify the maladaptive behavior pattern to the counselor, especially at first, but instead report their subjective feelings which result from the inappropriate behavior. For example, a client may report "I am lonely" while his typical behavior pattern is to spend all his spare time alone in his own room. Or if he spends time with other people, he may not have learned how to interact with them in a meaningful way.

In any event it is the counselor's job to help the client translate his problem into a behavioral goal that the client wants to attain and that the counselor believes will contribute to the welfare of his client. Considerable skill on the part of the counselor is required to make this translation. Listed below are some illustrative behavioral goals concerned with altering maladaptive behavior.

Increasing socially assertive responses

Decreasing socially assertive responses

Increasing social skills necessary in meeting new people

Decreasing fear responses to examinations

Increasing ability to concentrate for longer periods of time on school work

Decreasing the frequency of stealing

Increasing participation in school activities

Learning how to initiate social contacts with members of the opposite sex

Learning to assume responsibility for a task and carry it through to completion

Decreasing aggressive responses to smaller children

Increasing aggressive responses to abusive peers

Learning to respond calmly to hostile remarks

Decreasing quarreling behavior with other members of the family

Increasing ability to complete work on time

Decreasing the frequency of reckless and fast driving

Increasing the sharing of possessions with friends

Decreasing excessive sharing with friends and acquaintances

Increasing ability to say "no" to salesmen

Increasing ability to return unsatisfactory articles to stores

Decreasing threatening or violent behavior

Learning to discriminate between insults and friendly teasing

Decreasing weeping behavior in social situations

Increasing ability to communicate with friends and acquaintances

2. *Learning the Decision Making Process.* Another major category of problems concerns decision making. Again the client may not present his problem as a behavioral goal in decision making but instead may simply indicate that a decision must be made, e.g., "What shall I do next year?" "Give me some tests that tell me what I'm good at." "I can't make up my mind between law and engineering." "I don't have the slightest idea of what I want to be." "Shall I get married now or wait until after graduation?"

Counselors seem universally agreed that they cannot provide ready-made solutions for such problems. Instead the counselor must help launch the client on a course of action that will increase the probability that the client will ultimately be satisfied with his own decision. His decision will probably be more satisfactory if he engages in some or all of the illustrative counseling goals listed below.

Generating a list of all possible courses of action

Gathering relevant information about each feasible alternative course of action

Estimating the probability of success in each alternative on the basis of the experience of others and projections of current trends

Considering the personal values which may be enhanced or diminished under each course of action

Deliberating and weighing the facts, probable outcomes and values for each alternative

Eliminating from consideration the least favorable courses of action

Formulating a tentative plan of action subject to new developments and opportunities

Generalizing the decision making process to future problems

3. *Preventing Problems*. The highest priority in the counseling profession should involve the prevention of problems. The development of a polio vaccine was far more beneficial than the treatment of persons who had already become victims of the disease. Similarly, developing educational programs that will prevent certain kinds of maladaptive behavior and inadequate decision making should deserve high priority. It is far easier to prevent a problem than to remedy it after it has occurred. Many of the problems that come to counselors need never have arisen if teachers had been more skillful, if parents had been wiser, and if administrators had established more effective programs. It is not necessary, desirable or helpful, however, to blame others for the problems that come to counselors. Instead counselors need to ask what they can do to prevent such problems from arising in the future.

The most valuable and ethical behavior of professional persons consists of eliminating the need for their own services. At the present time we do not know just what programs and systems would prove effective in reducing the incidence of misery, discouragement and waste. Research designed to explore new possibilities should be encouraged. A few general examples may indicate the direction these efforts might take.

Developing a school marking system so that even the poorest student in each class can be encouraged by seeing the extent of his own progress

Implementing a system of helping young men and women select compatible marriage partners

Planning an educational program in child rearing techniques for parents

Helping to construct a curriculum more useful and effective for the students in it

Evaluating the effectiveness of preventive and remedial programs

CONSEQUENCES OF BEHAVIORAL STATEMENTS
OF COUNSELING GOALS

Why should stating goals behaviorally in this manner be more useful than stating internal mental states as goals? The consequences of shifting to a more behavioral orientation would be the following in my judgment.

1. *Counselors, clients and citizens could more clearly anticipate what the counseling process could, and could not, accomplish.* Counselors and clients would formulate tentative statements of desired behavior changes early in the counseling process. The very process of stating the goals in unambiguous language might have therapeutic effects. The clarification of goals would result in better public relations and public support. In the long run I can see no benefits from having a mystified clientele.

2. *Counseling psychology would become more integrated with the mainstream of psychological theory and research.* By conceiving of their professional problems as problems in behavior, counseling psychologists would be in a position to generate testable hypotheses from the research and theory in learning, perception, developmental and social psychology. The testing of such extrapolations in counseling settings would have important implications for all of psychology.

3. *The search for new and more effective techniques of helping clients would be facilitated.* With a variety of possible counseling goals, it seems safe to assume that no one counseling procedure would be universally applicable. Work is just beginning on alternative approaches. I have discussed elsewhere some of the philosophic objections to certain experimental guidance procedures (Krumboltz, 1964). It would seem to me that the professional responsibility of each counselor is to seek whatever ethical methods most effectively and efficiently bring about the desired behavior changes. When we are clear on the behavioral goals we are trying to attain, when we have developed adequate procedures for assessing each goal, when our ingenuity has generated a number of alternative procedures which seem likely to attain each goal, then we can test and evaluate the effectiveness of each procedure and determine experimentally what methods produce which results best with what type of clients (Krumboltz, 1965a).

4. *Different criteria would have to be applied to different clients in assessing the success of counseling.* Outcomes would be evaluated in terms of the extent to which each individual had changed his own behavior in the desired direction. Investigators of counseling outcomes would not be able to state one single criterion (e.g., grade point average) which every client would be expected to increase. The reason that some evaluations of counseling have not produced more significant results may be that the criteria chosen were not equally appropriate for all members of the sample. For example, half the counseled students might have wished to increase their assertive responses while the other half wished to become less assertive. Even if counseling were successful in every single case, the average "assertiveness score" of the

experimental group would still be equal to the average "assertiveness score" of the control group. Unless some provision is made for taking into account the different goals of different clients, evaluations of counseling are likely to continue to produce negative results.

A precedent for considering the individual goals of clients has been provided by Pascal and Zax (1956). Although their study may be questioned on certain methodological grounds, it nevertheless makes an important contribution by showing how each subject's own goals and prior behavior can be the baseline for evaluating whether or not changes in the desired direction occur. Bijou (in press) has shown how this can be done by counting the frequency of responses in certain categories. Brayfield (1963) also stressed this point when, in anticipating the present article, he stated, " . . . it remains now for someone to suggest that the counselee set the goals and that evaluation be undertaken in that context" (p. 341).

DISCUSSION

In discussing these ideas informally with groups of counselors, psychologists and counselor educators, a number of questions have arisen. I shall attempt to restate some of the most frequent questions and try to answer them.

I do not regard the views I have expressed here as any final commitment. Questions and comments from my colleagues have been most helpful to me in clarifying my own views, and I hope that continued questioning and discussing will lead us all to a progressive refinement of our notions as to what counselors should accomplish.

Question: Are you saying that counselors have been wrong all these years in stating goals of counseling like self-actualization, self-fulfillment, self-understanding and self-acceptance?

Answer: Not at all. These would be fine goals if each were accompanied by a list of illustrative behaviors to define what it might mean for different clients. These abstract goals are not wrong; they are just not as useful as more specific statements would be.

Question: Don't people have feelings and isn't it important for counselors to be sensitive to these feelings?

Answer: Without doubt, people have feelings, and many have learned an extensive vocabulary for describing such feelings. I am not against people feeling they understand and accept themselves; I favor such feelings just as I favor people loving justice, truth and beauty. My point is that, stated as goals of counseling, such subjective feelings will not prove as useful as more objective statements of behavior. Being sensitive to the feelings of a client is certainly a necessary attribute for any counselor. That it is sufficient is questionable (Krumboltz, in press).

Question: But don't people act the way they do because of their feelings, insights and self-perceptions?

Answer: It seems more plausible that positive feelings are the by-product, not the cause, of competent behavior and the rewards it brings. As Hobbs (1962, p. 742) puts it,

> It seems to me that the traditional formulation of the relationship between self-understanding and effective behavior may be backwards. I suggest that insight is not a cause of change but a possible result of change. It is not a source of therapeutic gain but one among a number of possible consequences of gain.

Hence, if we succeed in helping people to act more competently, they will receive more positive feedback from their friends, relatives and employers; then their feelings about themselves will improve as a matter of course.

Question: What would be done about the large number of clients who come to the counselor reporting feelings of dissatisfaction and unhappiness but having no idea about what behavior they could change?

Answer: The possible causes of unhappiness are infinite. An understanding listener is all some people require. Others need help in formulating and implementing plans. The counselor's job is to help the client formulate more concrete goals and take appropriate action.

Question: Aren't behavioral goals pretty superficial? Don't they imply habitual action without comprehension? Wouldn't we be overlooking permanent personality changes? Aren't there some things we can't observe or measure that are nevertheless very important? Don't "self-understanding" and "self-acceptance" really imply much more than can be expressed in words?

Answer: These questions deserve more of an answer than space permits. Undoubtedly, many complicated behavior patterns have not yet been categorized and described, but an affirmative reply to these questions would imply that we should give up without trying.

To those who say there is "something more" than behavior (defined broadly) I would ask these questions: (a) Can you point to any individual who exhibits the "something more" trait? (b) Can you point to any individual who fails to exhibit this trait? (c) What does the first individual do or say differently than the second individual under what circumstances that leads you to conclude that he possesses the "something more" trait? (d) Why don't we list what he does or says under which circumstances as another possible behavioral goal?

The task of stating behavioral goals is hard work and the job has scarcely begun. But only when our goals are clearly stated and communicated will we be able to engage in the service and experimentation which will ultimately benefit clients, counselors and citizens alike.

REFERENCES

Bijou, S. W. Implications of behavioral science for counseling and guidance. In J. D. Krumboltz (Ed.), *Revolution in counseling: implications of behavioral science*. Boston: Houghton Mifflin, in press.

Brayfield, A. H. Counseling psychology. In P. R. Farnsworth, Olga McNemar, and Q. McNemar (Eds.), *Annual review of psychology*. Vol. 14. Palo Alto, Calif.: Annual Reviews, 1963, pp. 319-350.

Brayfield, A. H. Performance is the thing. *J. counsel. Psychol.*, 1962, *9*, 3.

Hobbs, N. Sources of gain in psychotherapy. *Amer. Psychologist*, 1962, *17*, 741-747.

Krumboltz, J. D. The agenda for counseling. *J. counsel. Psychol.*, 1965, *12*, 226. (a)

Krumboltz, J. D. Behavioral counseling: rationale and research. *Personnel guid. J.*, 1965, *44*, 383-387. (b)

Krumboltz, J. D. Parable of the good counselor. *Personnel guid. J.*, 1964, *43*, 118-124.

Krumboltz, J. D. Promoting adaptive behavior: new answers to familiar questions. In J. D. Krumboltz (Ed.), *Revolution in counseling: implications of behavioral science*. Boston: Houghton Mifflin, in press.

Krumboltz, J. D. *Stating the goals of counseling*. Monograph published by the California Counseling and Guidance Association, 1966.

Pascal, G. R., and Zax, M. Psychotherapeutics: success or failure. *J. consult. Psychol.*, 1956, *20*, 325-331.

Samler, J. An examination of client strength and counselor responsibility. *J. counsel. Psychol.*, 1962, *9*, 5-11.

White, R. W. Motivation reconsidered: the concept of competence. *Psychol. Rev.*, 1959, *66*, 297-333.

Wishner, J. A concept of efficiency in psychological health and in psychopathology. *Psychol. Rev.*, 1955, *62*, 69-80.

Interference versus extinction as learning models for psychotherapy[1]

E. Lakin Phillips and Creighton U. Mattoon

Studies of psychotherapy and theories as to its nature leave some puzzling doubts. Within the confines of a single article, an author may now take one viewpoint, now another. Emphasis on uncovering the repressed childhood origins of personality disturbances as necessary for successful therapy may be found along with statements that psychotherapy is a social re-learning process much like any other learning.

As a result of a lack of differentiation between various premises as to the nature of both psychotherapy and psychopathology, a lack of precise formulation of the behavioral processes exists. Effort is extended in this paper to develop a simple, logical analysis of the re-learning problem associated with overcoming psychopathology (Phillips, 1960).

ASKING THE RIGHT QUESTION

The effort begins by asking what are the minimum conditions under which behavior change may occur. (Reference is not made to change resulting from neurological or structural alterations, from atrophy or disuse.)

It is hypothesized that one can change behavior only on three non-neurological grounds: by interference, by extinction, or by skill acquisitions (as with conventional definitions of learning). Our interest here is not in the usual problems of skill acquisition but with re-learning in connection with modifying psychopathology. Attention is therefore drawn to the similarities and differences between extinction and interference as models for psychotherapy.

More specifically, the purpose of this paper is to argue that extinction reduces to interference.

Learning, or skill acquisition in the conventional sense, is based on

[1]Reprinted from the *Journal of Psychology*, 1961, *51*, 399-403, with permission of the senior author and the Journal Press.

discriminations where the learned behavior increases in probability of occurrence, and the errors decrease, under a given set of conditions. One can be said to interfere with errors by discriminating them more clearly, by precluding their development. The Beta hypothesis of Dunlap illustrates this point: The learner deliberately types "hte" in order to correct this frequent error in typing the article, "the", by bringing under more direct motor control the previously poor discriminations. One thereby deliberately interferes with errors by increasing discriminatory acuity; with practice, this discrimination allows for skill increase of a greater or lesser degree.

EXPERIMENTAL EXTINCTION AND CLINICAL UNCOVERING

The situation with extinction—or "uncovering," as psychotherapists are prone to call it—is similar. The learning theory equivalent to catharsis or uncovering is the desensitization process of presenting in a new context (the therapist's office) the old stimuli that evoked anxiety or tension responses; this permits non-reinforcement, leading to extinction of the old, neurotic behavior, and a building up of a new set of discriminations that are relatively non-pathological (Phillips, 1957a; 1957b).

What the psychotherapist has failed to realize, we hypothesize, is that the process of extinction is fundamentally an interference process. Consider the classical conditioning and extinction studies of Pavlov, Watson, Jones, and others. In these studies, in broad outline, the negative or noxious (fear producing) stimulus was presented just prior to or simultaneous with the neutral object (the rabbit) which, in time, came to produce fear, anxiety and withdrawal responses to the rabbit. When extinction came back into the picture, the experimenter was able to systematically present the conditioned, noxious stimulus in milder, controlled stages without evoking the full intensity of the unconditioned stimulus (loud noise). In time, the conditioned fear object lost its noxious value and the fear to this object was said to have been extinguished.

AN ALTERNATIVE VIEWPOINT

This paradigm has led to the assumption on the part of psychotherapists that some original fear or anxiety provoking situation or situations have to be found, uncovered, extinguished by the simultaneous talking and re-living, which seem parallel to the conditioned fear and experimental extinction conditions. Hence, the relatively long time necessary in real life, and in psychotherapy, traditionally felt to be necessary in order to lift the repression which buried the originally potent fear-and-anxiety conditioned experiences.

An alternative view is possible which, we feel, is simpler, more heuristic, more experimentally and clinically typical of life circumstances.

The alternative view states that extinction is a controlled and greatly simplified version of a broader-based interference. In the absence of knowing exactly what produced a fear or anxiety condition, one cannot be sure of the points-to-be-extinguished, as was possible in the classical conditioning experiments. In fact, in life situations and in typical clinical situations, the practical approach seems to search for *on-going processes* for their rehabilitative value; not for what was allegedly originally repressed, with eventual uncovering and extinction in mind.

EXTINCTION VERSUS INTERFERENCE WITH COMPLEX SKILLS

Take for example the situation of wanting to change from a standard keyboard system of typing to another system. One would not set out to extinguish the old system of typing; one would, rather, set about to develop new discriminations. By the same token new languages, new sets of pronunciations, new systems of communication, or any new, complex skill acquisition would seem to follow a discriminatory or interference model rather than an extinction model.

Consider another common, but more "emotionalized" situation: The overcoming of fears of the dark or of water, as with children. The problem here is how to gradually introduce more controls over the fear-producing situation by the frightened one. Such a situation does not call for an uncovering therapy—"What is to be uncovered?" but for the judicious handling of controls and opportunities for new discriminations—in short, for interference with old processes.

CLINICAL SITUATIONS MORE "EMOTIONAL"

The depth therapist would say that the therapeutic problem is more overladen with motivational and anxiety complications than is the development of new skills or even the overcoming of specific fears. It would be contended that the original motivating circumstances and the subsequent "neurotic" defenses would be the relevant features when discussing psychotherapy. The depth theorist would also say that the conditioned fear and extinction model from Pavlov was relevant for the therapeutic situation in that both derive from an original trauma, both receive protective "defensive maintenance," and both were overcome via an extinction route.

The main difference, however, from the interference viewpoint, between the simple conditioning and extinction processes, and the complex situation in the therapist's office, is that in the former instances the precise nature of the anxiety-provoking stimuli were known and could be brought under direct control. The elements of clear knowledge and direct control over what is known are relatively lacking in the therapeutic situation. Also, in the fear-of-darkness or fear-of-water circumstances one knows, or can know, to a considerable extent what elements have to be brought under control.

KNOWLEDGE MEANS CONTROL

If one knows what the fear or anxiety provoking conditions are, they can then be brought under more or less direct control. If full knowledge is not available, control becomes indirect; judicious handling is required if results are to be constructive. This is precisely the point where the depth or uncovering therapists have said, in effect: "We must search for the original causes so that they can be uncovered and extinguished." Perhaps the non-directive therapist would assert that the "inner meaning" or the "phenomenological world" of the patient had to be revealed first. Both the psychoanalytic and non-directive positions stress the "inner" or "hidden" aspects of the problem which, one way or another have to be uncovered. The interference position, on the other hand, stresses the availability of *overt behavioral controls* which can be managed or shaped to meet rehabilitative or therapeutic goals.

Thus if a childhood behavior disorder (enuresis, for example) is the pathological behavior in question, the interference position is that of teaching broadbased responsibilities to the child, of interfering with his too self-centered approach to living, by bringing under control many aspects of his daily routine. In contrast, the psychoanalytic or non-directive positions would attempt to uncover origins (historical, cognitive) and regard such strategies as revealing the "cause" of the disturbance.

In summary, in the interference position a search is instituted to find effective means of control over the pathological processes. The older extinction studies did not have to seek origins; the origins were already known. The psychotherapist can now see that the extinction experiments were important in offering means of control, and should serve in this capacity as a model for learning theory applications to psychotherapy, rather than being placed under the too narrow interpretation involving extinction and uncovering. The cybernetic formulation of "controlling the effects" (DeLatil, 1957; Phillips, 1958); or the learning theory formulations concerned with controlling reinforcing conditions (Phillips, 1959; Phillips, 1960; Phillips, Wiener, and Haring, 1960); or the decision theory formulations of recent origin (Luce, 1959)[2] might all be interpreted as supporting larger scale theoretical and logical issues emphasized in the interference theory position.

[2]Following some implications of Luce's formulations, the question of past relevance for present decisions and actions is based not on what did happen, but what *can* (be made to) happen (Luce, 1959, pp. 92-95).

REFERENCES

DeLatil, P. *Thinking by machine*. New York: Houghton Mifflin, 1957.

Luce, R. D. *Individual choice behavior*. New York: Wiley, 1959.

Phillips, E. L. Contributions to a learning theory account of childhood autism. *Journal of Psychology*, 1957, *43*, 117-124. (a)

Phillips, E. L. Some neglected aspects of learning theory applied to psychotherapy and psychopathology. *American Psychologist*, 1957, *12* (abstract). (b)

Phillips, E. L. Diagnosis in terms of effects. *American Psychologist*, 1958, *13* (abstract).

Phillips, E. L. The role of structure in psychotherapy. *American Psychologist*, 1959, *14* (abstract).

Phillips, E. L. Parent-child psychotherapy: a follow-up study comparing two techniques. *Journal of Psychology*, 1960, *49*, 195-202.

Phillips, E. L., Wiener, D. N., and Haring, N. G. *Discipline achievement and mental health*. Englewood Cliffs, N.J.: Prentice-Hall, 1960.

Beyond the Reinforcement Machine[1]

Leonard P. Ullmann

At conventions I often meet fellow therapists whose company I thoroughly enjoy until, in an excess of good fellowship and alcohol, they say something like, "Behavior therapy may well be effective, but it's simply too mechanistic for me." The major purpose of this paper is to respond to such comments. Doing so will also provide the opportunity to offer some remarks on the practice of behavior therapy in counseling settings.

The development of the stereotype of behavior therapy as mechanistic is understandable. There are a number of reasons that might lead a person who had not observed a behavior therapist or practised behavior therapy himself to presume that behaviorists are unthinking applicators of techniques. The first is that some of the original impetus for the development of behavior therapy was a reaction against a procedure that was as unrigorous as it was ineffective: "Psychotherapy is an undefined technique applied to unspecified problems with unpredictable outcome. For this technique we recommend rigorous training." (Raimy, 1950, p. 93.)

In particular, the reaction was a challenge to psychoanalytic thinking, the official psychiatric nosology, and the attempts of the medical profession to restrict the practice of psychotherapy. Behavioral scientists eschewed concepts of people and the manner in which they could be changed that had been developed in clinical settings and took as their starting point methods of behavior change that had been validated in psychological experiments. The early work in behavior therapy drew its major inspiration from animal learning. The language of behavior therapy still remains that of reinforcement theory although at times the word reinforcement seems to be used in so many ways that it is becoming almost as nonspecific a term as anxiety (Ullmann, 1967a).

The central concept of behavior therapy is that behavior may be altered *directly* without recourse to underlying personality dynamics. The current

[1]This paper was prepared especially for the volume, *Behavior change in counseling: readings and cases*.

model is essentially an educational model: a person is taught to make different responses to situations that had previously led to difficulties for himself or others. As with the teaching of number facts, the person's ability to do the task, his recognition of the correct time and place for the act, his indulging in the necessary practice, and, finally, his reward for making the act must all be taken into consideration. A grade school teacher may be very interested in a student's prior educational history: such information may make reasonable the present difficulties and alert the teacher both to methods that have failed and methods that have succeeded. The change in arithmetic skills, however, is a task of the present, not the past.

This analogy may be pursued further. Goldiamond (1965) has noted that a person may seem stupid when he is deficient in behaviors that he is presumed to have. Teachers diagnose to find if such deficits are present. When they are found, training is given to make up the deficit, not "to work it through." In college counseling a boy may not have developed, much less practised, date-obtaining behavior. He may currently avoid asking girls for dates because this activity has been followed by unpleasant events, i.e., rejection. The behavior therapist will deal only superficially with the parents' attitudes that were associated with sex or the boy's lack of money in high school that kept him from asking girls for dates. The behavior therapist will, on the other hand, give information about and encouragement for the development of dating skills.

Reaction to evocative procedures and movement to a learning, psychological, or educational model followed the same pattern as the development of any new and, at that time, deviant behavior (Ullmann, 1969). Notably, as with social movements, the leaders pointed out difficulties in the present situation, the need for change, and the reasons why their ideas provided a solution. The behaviorists in this early phase emphasized the differences between their ideas and those of the traditionalists. A number of examples can be given. One is Eysenck's (1959) slogan "Get rid of the symptom and you have eliminated the neurosis." In context, Eysenck meant that the overt behavior rather than some underlying unconscious cause was the appropriate focus for treatment. Unfortunately, out of context this has led to the notion of behavior therapists as treaters of symptoms when their genuine objective is not the elimination of a behavior but the development and maintenance of alternative behaviors. Another example is alluded to in the title of this paper. Krasner (1962) called his germinal article "The therapist as a social reinforcement machine." Like Eysenck, Krasner was reacting to the status of therapy at that time and was pointing out how the therapist might help others more effectively.

A related reason for the development of a stereotype of behavior therapy as mechanistic, stems from the research published by behavior therapists. A great strength in behavior therapy is that the procedures permit evaluation and that behavior therapy attracted people with the training and orientation to complete precise experiments. Research demands that to as great an extent as possible the particular therapist and his technique be separated rather than confounded. An example is the classic work of Paul (1966). In order to be able to specify the role of the different techniques used (evocative therapy, systematic desensitization, and placebo), therapists in the systematic desensitization group were constrained in the extent to which they used behavior that might have been rationalized away as "merely suggestion." This is one of the strengths of Paul's research. It is, however, misleading if the reader presumes that in clinical practice the therapist will not use a number of influence techniques concurrently or in sequence as the client's level of preparation and the present social situation demand. The aims of research and clinical treatment differ: the former has the objective of evaluating a specific element so that a decision may be made as to its future use. The latter, clinical practice, has as its first objective helping a particular person. Any other objective, such as proving a method of therapy or the skill of the therapist, is at least subsidiary and, if it runs counter to the best interests of the client, improper.

The most common research design in psychology today compares two or more groups that receive different treatment in terms of a dependent variable or outcome measure. The stereotype of mechanistic application may be fostered when meeting the demands of such designs. The dependent variable is some overt target behavior. A large number of people, for example 40 if there are to be 20 in the experimental group and 20 in the control group, must be similar in regard to the target. The experimental procedure focuses on the alteration of the target behavior. For purposes of replication, the target behavior and the experimental procedures are as clearly specified and closely followed as possible. This constitutes reasonable and appropriate research, but it is misleading to think that the practitioner must follow the same constraints.

Another set of reasons why the stereotype may have developed deals with the training of behavior therapists. Because no distinction is made between normal and abnormal behavior as to the development and maintenance of the behavior itself, all careers, whether they be labeled "schizophrenic" or "mental healer," follow the same principles (Ullmann & Krasner, 1969). Some of the previous remarks in this paper reflect this theoretical view. The effect is that concepts of modeling, shaping, and the like are used in describing the training of future behaviour therapists (Ullmann, 1967b). It should be explicit that this is a direct deduction from an educational model. Further, thinking of therapists in the same manner as clients is not derogatory unless one derogates clients.

In regard to training, the very increase in popularity of behavioral techniques has created a problem. Using the word reinforcement or the technique of systematic desensitization no more makes a person a behavior therapist than using a maze and studying animals makes a person a scientist.

There are some people who would like a technique to take the place of ideation. Because some behavior modification procedures have been carefully spelled out, there has been an application of the form without the substance. An example of what is meant occurred one of the times I tried to stop smoking. Like other smokers, I wanted a technique to do the work for me. I decided to use aversive conditioning. I thought of a stimulus that I had never grown accustomed to and hence would avoid adaptation effects. I chose reading psychological journals. During treatment, I did not smoke at other times, so that smoking a cigarette would be followed exclusively by the horrendous consequence of at least one hour of journal reading per cigarette. I sat down, opened a journal, and just before starting to read, lit up. The result was that my journal reading increased. Psychoanalysts might say this is an illustration of symptom substitution while a behavior therapist would say that this is an illustration of sloppy application of learning principles.

Behavior therapy manipulates the present environment to alter the person's behavior. The greater control the therapist has over the environment, the less he will make use of concepts such as the individual's personality. For a behaviorist the role of personality is not *explanatory* as in medical analogues such as the American Psychiatric Association's (1952) diagnostic manual where ". . . a psychoneurotic reaction may be defined as one in which the personality, in its struggle for adjustment to internal and external stresses, utilizes the mechanisms listed above to handle the anxiety created" (page 13). " 'Anxiety' in psychoneurotic disorders is a danger signal felt and perceived by the conscious portion of the personality. It is produced by a threat from within the personality. . ." (page 31).

For a behavior therapist a person is what he does. If a *description* of the frequency, amplitude, and latency of types of responses to stimuli is "personality," then behaviorists might be said to use the concept. Since, however, the behaviors are the object, the term "personality" adds nothing. On a different level, if a treatment attains as high a rate of success as systematic desensitization did in Paul's (1966) work, there is no variance left to be accounted for by measures of personality. Because they do not use the concept of personality as an explanation, at times it seems as if the behaviorist has taken something from people.

Given these considerations, the development of a stereotype of behavior therapy as mechanistic is understandable, but it should also be clear that the notion is not accurate either in theory or practice. In the last half of this paper I want to focus on some practical issues illustrating the non-mechanical applications of behavior therapy techniques.

It should be explicit that the therapist neither possesses complete knowledge of all antecedent and current relevant material (i.e., he works in a complex world and in the face of varying degrees of uncertainty) and that he is steadily learning, that is, being changed by his experiences. If something works, the behavior therapist is likely to repeat the act in future similar circumstances. Behavior therapists are similar to clients in this regard: they are not mechanical, but they are fundamentally mammalian.

When working with an adult outpatient in the typical counseling situation, the behavior therapist is likely to explain in detail both his formulation of the difficulty and the rationale of his procedure. For example, if systematic desensitization is used—that is, increasingly difficult images of a social situation are paired with deep muscle relaxation—the procedure depends on information from the subject for the construction of the hierarchy, the client's performing the relaxation-inducing exercises, the client's imaging the scenes as presented, and the client's signaling when he becomes uncomfortable. The therapist can make these acts more likely, but only the client can perform them. The more the client understands the reasons for these activities, the more likely he is to engage in them. This may be put in other words: the client must be taught the behaviors that will help him.

The person cannot be treated in the manner that a passive patient may be treated by a physician. If the person is uncomfortable, the discomfort may be paired with the treatment. For example, if care is not taken, the negative practice or reactive-inhibition technique for the treatment of tics (Yates, 1958) may lead to an increase in the target behavior. Rather than exhaustion and extinction, the therapist may be providing new experiences in which a tic is emitted in response to an unpleasant or incomprehensible situation.

Almost by definition, learning experiences are not static. The objective of treatment is change. As the client changes, the therapist's behavior should also change. In research a target is selected and a limited experimenter behavior is evaluated. The experimenter does the same thing with each subject, and especially in short duration experiments, the same thing all the time with each subject. This is not the case in therapy. Further, a behavior therapist does not cure, he makes alternative behavior more likely. The test of behavior therapy is what the person does in the extra-therapy situation. What maintains the alternative behavior is not what the behavior therapist did in the counseling hour but the response the new behavior receives from teachers, parents, employers, friends, and other significant people.

With this goal in mind, the object of the behavior therapist is to make himself unnecessary. Elsewhere (Ullmann, 1968) I have indicated that the behavior therapist teaches the person, frequently through modeling, to be his own therapist. The therapist may start by asking questions about specific areas and offering alternative solutions to the ones the client currently uses. At the start, the behavior therapist may reinforce every favorable response. Over time, however, the behavior therapist will shape, that is, will reinforce selectively, acts that attain an increasingly high standard. The therapist may start by reinforcing responses to his questions, but he may shift to reinforcing the person for asking himself first in the therapy, and later outside it, the sort of questions the therapist had asked. In this manner, the person in the target situation is already making a new response, that is, looking for a new type of information. When behavior changes in the target situation, the significant others may react differently. When the client reports changes, the therapist asks what conditions may have led to the changes by either the client or people responding to him. There is a matter of discrimination training. There is also reinforcement at this point for what the client did in the situation rather than discussion of what he might do. That is, the therapy has moved from possibilities of new behavior to reinforcement of actual behavior. The role of the therapist has changed.

It is possible to conceptualize the behavior therapist's interview techniques as prompting and then a fading of prompts, until the client is being his own therapist or controlling his own behavior as he analyzes situations and contingencies for himself. To repeat, the behavior therapist may alter what he reinforces (shaping), may prompt and fade, and may stretch-out either the time between, or the ratio of, his own reinforcing behavior. These procedures are in response to changes in the client and provide techniques for reducing the client's dependence on the therapist as a "social reinforcement machine." Again, above all else, it is the response of significant others to the client that maintains the new behavior. In an educational setting, reading is taught in progressively more difficult assignments; but what is most crucial is that reading on the proper occasions is a behavior that is useful to the one-time student.

Within this scheme the therapist must respond to specific situations when only general principles have been established. In an experiment every person can start out at the same point and be exposed to similar experiences. In therapy the interaction between the client and therapist differs from person to person. What has gone before is uncontrolled. The question is not whether a particular maneuver is "good" but rather whether that particular maneuver is "good" after what has preceded. The therapist must make this decision rapidly. While a properly programmed machine certainly might make the decision, the time required to collect the data and program the machine would in itself alter the nature of the proper decision. If we say the therapist is a reinforcement machine, we must realize that he is not only a reinforcing stimulus, he is also the scheduler of the delivery of the reinforcing stimulus. The therapist must decide when and what to reinforce. In shaping, for example, the therapist's timing runs dangers between satiation and extinction. The therapist must go neither too fast nor too slow; he does not run, he jogs.

A major area of decision-making lies with what to reinforce. At a first level, this is a matter of diagnosis or functional analysis of situations: what is the person doing, what should he be doing, what skills are required to emit the acts he should be making, and the like. The answers to these "what" questions frequently are complex. A shy male, for example, may have difficulty in dating girls. This difficulty may be but one aspect of a series of responses to social situations that might be labeled "lack of self-assertion." This lack of self-assertion may, in turn, be associated with "avoidance of rejection." The problem is not so much which technique to apply as where to start. This question may be rephrased as to what is the most effective and rapid program of therapeutic maneuvers. Increasing effective dating behavior is likely to increase the client's confidence both in himself and in his therapist. The changed relationship to girls is likely to lead to changes in the way the client labels his own capabilities and, acting on these self-produced cues, his behavior in non-dating situations may change. Because of his success, the client may more readily undertake new activities in the manner suggested by the therapist and learn one of the most important lessons of therapy, namely, that he can be different. In short, there may be generalization to both the more pervasive difficulties and to the methods of changing behavior. On the other hand, dealing with the more pervasive difficulties may lead to gains in a wide variety of situations of which dating may be one. The point to be made is that the therapist is faced with decisions and there is little prior data that will make the decision for him. In this context it is worth noting that Stevenson and Wolpe (1960) reported on cases in which training in assertion in not directly sexual situations helped men towards heterosexuality. I and other behavor therapists with whom I have compared notes have observed the converse: men successfully changing to greater heterosexuality frequently become more poised and assured in non-sexual situations.

In general, when faced with a complex of difficulties I choose to start with one of the relatively easier areas. I do so for the reasons cited above and for two additional ones. The first is that changed behavior requires a social situation. To benefit from a change, the person must experience the change. This implies a specific social situation. Verbalizations may well change in the therapy hour, but the pay-off for such attitude change is the response of others to overt behavior. On the one hand nothing succeeds like success, and on the other, there is learning to learn.

The other reason that I am inclined to work from specific, relatively limited situations to more pervasive difficulties, is clinical. I have had a number of people who first presented circumscribed difficulties. When these problems had been successfully dealt with they re-negotiated the therapeutic contract and moved on to more pervasive and socially difficult topics. Success in changing an aspect of their own behavior generated that complex, self-produced discriminative stimulus that people who do not make their living lecturing to college classes call "hope." When in doubt, as a clinician, I prefer to do what people do naturally and, as an academician, I can conceptualize the process as successive tasks undertaken in a manner analogous to shaping.

The matter of selection of a target area from among the number presented leads back to the general model of people and personality. Psychoanalysts think of symptoms as "over-determined," that is, the overt behavior provides as much indirect gratification of a number of underlying conflicts as possible. To the psychoanalyst, personality is a unity and every problem is dynamically and integrally related to every other problem. One can deduce from the psychoanalytic position the hypothesis of symptom substitution and the concept that specific changes should not be made without first dealing with the pervasive or "deeper levels." In contrast, behaviorists argue that a person may learn different disadvantageous behaviors in different situations and that difficulties need not be dynamically associated. Wolpe (1964) has utilized multiple hierarchies and Yates (1958) has dealt with one tic at a time in an individual with multiple tics.

In outpatient adults, behaviors may be separately changed just as components of a system may be separately changed. In both instances, the changes may influence other parts of the system, but this does not mean that a change in one component may not be made without first changing the entire system. I think that individuals are not born with an innate tendency toward consistency, but they are taught that being consistent is a virtue. Consistency here may be generalization of learned behavior but it may also be the learning of acts that make it possible for other people to predict the individual's behavior. Such prediction is a major help in social situations and the vast majority of cultures train individuals to be consistent. That is, telling the truth is not innate, but it is a form of consistency that is generally encouraged.

The behavior therapist does not label the individual by his difficulty like the psychoanalyst who talks about his patients as homosexuals, phobics, or schizophrenics, but deals with his client as a person who under certain circumstances emits behavior that people call homosexual, phobic or schizophrenic. Both diagnosis and treatment are aimed at behavior in specific situations. The genuine respect for the individual manifested by thinking of him as a person behaving in situations rather than as a type of sick personality is as crucial in treatment as it is in theoretical formulations.

As the behaviorist works in the interview he is constantly asking himself questions such as "what should my client be doing?" and "what can I do to help him do it?" Some of the answers may be in terms of techniques, some in terms of targets. An integral part of what a behaviorist can do to help an individual involves decisions as to methods of delivery. This was touched on earlier when it was noted that the client must understand the reasons for a procedure or else the procedure might be paired with discomfort and therefore backfire. The therapist engages in activities that will increase the chances of the client's liking and trusting him, that is, feeling comfortable. Feelings of comfort on the part of the client, or associated target behaviors to be increased in the client such as likelihood of trying new behaviors, are overtly measurable. They may become dependent variables for testing the different conditions that foster them. An example of an effort in this direction is by Ullmann *et al.* (1968). Rapport may be operationally defined and once defined be the subject of experiments. The better one specifies the behaviors that lead to rapport, the less one will talk about rapport and the more one will focus on specific actions. This is similar in form to the decreased use of the concept of personality, and as with personality, may seem mechanistic.

The pairing of relaxation with visualization of a difficult situation has its parallel in the interview. One aspect of the answer to the question the therapist asks himself in terms of what he can do to help the client is the language of his remarks to the client. The new behavior is more likely to be emitted if it is presented in a manner consistent with the client's values. No matter how "right" the therapist is, if he presents his rationale in a language, such as textbook jargon, that is aversive or incomprehensible to the client, he will be wrong operationally, that is, he will have an effect of increasing rather than decreasing discomfort. When working with spouses, for instance, the object is not to fix blame or unravel motivations. The object is to improve a situation by making each partner's behavior more pleasant for the other. Previous behavior may be accepted as stemming from good intentions and understandable contingencies. Within the context of good intentions, prior behavior simply did not work out and new behaviors are suggested that more directly and effectively serve the purpose. To be more concrete, when working with lack of sexual satisfactions, one partner may be asked to delay his (frigidity) or her (impotence) gratification for a period of time. The procedure may be presented as courting. One of the greatest practical difficulties is that the partner for whose benefit the delay is suggested will often think that delaying the other spouse's pleasure is "wrong." With capitalistic Americans, the procedure may be phrased as one of making an investment, of giving up a small immediate gratification for a long-term gain.

In summary, the idea that behavior therapists are mechanistic is understandable in terms of the history of the procedure, the demands of experimentation, and the theoretical orientation that spells out and manipulates rather than accepts as given concepts such as personality and rapport. It was pointed out that, while understandable, the idea that behaviorists are mechanistic is a stereotype and does not accord with actual practice. Of crucial import is that the behavior therapist is not only a reinforcing stimulus, but is also the decision maker as to the timing, target, and manner of reinforcement. The therapist has general principles that he applies to particular instances. The therapist is changed by the consequences of his own behavior. While in principle a computer might have these characteristics, the relative complexity and uniqueness of the specific case and the necessary speed of response required of a therapist, make it unlikely and uneconomical to program a machine to do the job save in cases where masses of people have the same problem. If one will, one can think of the therapist as the cheapest high grade computer one can rent: he is the only 160 pound billion channel computer that is manufactured by unskilled labor. There are machines and there are machines. *Vive la différence!*

REFERENCES

American Psychiatric Association. *Diagnostic and statistical manual: mental disorders.* Washington, D.C.: A.P.A., 1952.

Eysenck, H. J. Learning theory and behaviour therapy. *Journal of Mental Science,* 1959, *105,* 61-75.

Goldiamond, I. Self-control procedures in personal behavior problems. *Psychological Reports,* 1965, *17,* 851-868.

Krasner, L. The therapist as a social reinforcement machine. In, H. H. Strupp and L. Luborsky (Eds.) *Research in psychotherapy.* Washington, D.C.: American Psychological Association, 1962, volume 2, 61-94.

Paul, G. L. *Insight vs. desensitization in psychotherapy.* Stanford, Calif.: Stanford University Press, 1966.

Raimy, V. C. (Ed.) *Training in clinical psychology.* Englewood Cliffs, N.J.: Prentice-Hall, 1950.

Stevenson, I., and Wolpe, J. Recovery from sexual deviations through overcoming non-sexual neurotic responses. *American Journal of Psychiatry,* 1960, *116,* 737-742.

Ullmann, L. P. Abnormal psychology without anxiety. Paper read at Western Psychological Association Convention, 1967 (a).

Ullmann, L. P. The major concepts taught to behavior therapy trainees. Paper read at American Psychological Association Convention, 1967 (b).

Ullmann, L. P. Making use of modeling in the therapeutic interview. Paper read at Association for the Advancement of the Behavioral Therapies Convention, 1968.

Ullmann, L. P. Behavior therapy as social movement. In, C. M. Franks (Ed.) *Assessment of the behavioral therapies and associated developments.* New York: McGraw-Hill, 1969, 495-523.

Ullmann, L. P., Bowen, M. E., Greenberg, D. J., Macpherson, E. C., Marcum, H. B., Marx, R. D., and May, J. S. The effect on rapport of experimenters' approach and avoidance responses to positive and negative self-references. *Behaviour Research and Therapy,* 1968, *6,* 355-362.

Ullmann, L. P., and Krasner, L. *A psychological approach to abnormal behavior.* Englewood Cliffs, N.J.: Prentice-Hall, 1969.

Wolpe, J. Behaviour therapy in complex neurotic states. *British Journal of Psychiatry,* 1964, *110,* 28-34.

Yates, A. J. The application of learning theory to the treatment of tics. *Journal of Abnormal and Social Psychology,* 1958, *56,* 175-182.

Implications of Conditioning Techniques for Interview Therapy[1]

Frederick H. Kanfer

Current psychological research makes it clear that effective alterations in human behavior can be produced directly by control of the environment, by the use of drugs to regulate the biochemical state of the organism or by change of the consequences of a response. Traditional psychotherapy, on the other hand, has relied most heavily on indirect methods, using as a mediating link the patient's self-examining and self-regulatory behaviors. Insight and verbalizations are expected to modify the patient's subjective experiences, his thoughts and emotions. In turn, these changes in central processes are relied upon to increase the patient's effectiveness in his daily interpersonal and motor responses. Some dynamic interview therapies go even further and describe the reconstruction of personality as the only object of therapy, denying the relevance of limited changes in specified behaviors. In fact, success in therapy has often been described only in terms of changes in the patient's verbal report about his inner experiences and insights, even when his daily living patterns remain unaffected.

TO INTERVIEW OR TO CONDITION?

The cost of traditional psychotherapy, its effectiveness, and its lack of validated theory has given rise to discontent and resulted in intensified efforts to find new techniques.[2] In this climate of growing disenchantment with conventional psychotherapies and rising social pressures for cheaper and more effective treatment, the demonstrations of the effectiveness of drug therapies and of conditioning methods have been accepted by many psychologists as sufficiently persuasive evidence for the abandonment of

[1] Reprinted from the *Journal of Counseling Psychology*, 1966, *13*, 171-177 with permission of the author and the American Psychological Association.
[2] The issues and innovations have been summarized by many authors including London (1964), Schofield (1964), Wolpe, Salter and Reyna (1964) and others.

traditional interview therapy. The high recovery rates reported for conditioning therapies by Lazarus (1963); Rachman (1963); and Wolpe,
Salter and Reyna (1964) have further served to increase skepticism about
interview therapies.

The new methods have additional advantages. Environmental controls,
programmed changes in response-reinforcement contingencies, discrete
conditioning trials in the laboratory or biochemical agents do not require
deep personal involvement of the therapist with a patient. They permit more
rigorously planned procedures and more objective evaluation of treatment
outcome. The non-dynamic techniques also are more easily described in
operational terms. They can be taught more rapidly to intelligent non-
professional personnel and they do not require prolonged contact with a
verbally fluent patient. In contrast to interview therapies, behavior therapy
or drug therapy also promises to free the therapist from his own uneasiness
about the vagaries of language and from the ever present problem of finding
validations for his interpretations of the patient's verbal responses. Thus it
would seem that the traditional "talking therapies" would not be of interest
to the practicing clinician when he defines his goals in terms of changing
individual behavior, eliminating symptoms and reinstating social effectiveness. As the clinician's repertoire of non-verbal and impersonal techniques
increases he might strive to conduct the entire therapeutic enterprise by
precise application of highly reliable operations with predictable outcome
and with little direct personal contact. The loss of intimate and prolonged
contact with patients may deprive some clinicians of their personal satisfactions in therapy, but this is surely not sufficient grounds for perpetuating a
fascinating but inefficient relationship under the guise of treatment.

While the issues have been intentionally over-stated, the foregoing
considerations have strengthened the very vigorous claim by conditioning
therapies for a secure position among schools of psychotherapy. Even though
this approach is only in its rudimentary stage, many clinicians have widely
proclaimed the virtues of conditioning therapies, while others have busied
themselves in demonstrating that learning principles have always formed an
integral part of the actual operations of traditional psychiatric treatment.
The proponents of these new methods do not represent a hard core of
clinicians whose "school" grew out of collaborative efforts. They work in
different settings, they accept different learning theories, and many are
academicians and researchers rather than practitioners. Although there may
be good grounds for this wide-spread enthusiasm, it is probably based as
much on the short-comings of the past methods as it is on the new documented accomplishments of the new. Therefore, it may be too early and too
easy to be swept up by fervor, the faith and the freshness of this approach and
to proclaim conditioning therapies as the panacea for all mental ills.

Even at this early stage of research it is clear that both psychophar-
macological methods and conditioning techniques have their limitations.

Our problem in the area of psychotherapy is not to decide whether conditioning therapies will replace interview methods, but to ask how the best elements of both techniques can be combined for maximum utility.

CONDITIONING WITHIN THE INTERVIEW

There are two distinct areas in which conditioning response has offered its products, the mechanics of the interview process, and the operations for symptom removal. With regard to the first, research on verbal conditioning and the microscopic analysis of the dyadic therapy interactions seems to hold excellent promise for providing rules of conduct for the interview itself. It has been shown repeatedly that conditioning of verbal behavior occurs during psychotherapy and that the therapist's behavior affects the patient in a systematic manner. Extensive research has been reported showing that particular variables related to the therapist's strategy, the patient's behavioral history and the conditions of treatment affect this learning process in the therapy-dyad. There are many recent reviews of the relevant research findings and their implications, e.g.: Krasner (1961), Marsden (1965), Williams (1964), Ulrich and Trumbo (1965), Gardner (1964) and others. From numerous laboratories have come studies which contain suggestions for optimizing the effectiveness of interview procedures both for eliciting information and for bringing about attitude changes. Many careful studies have shown the relationship between therapist operations and momentary verbal and autonomic responses of the patient. Studies of the verbal interchange by Lennard and Bernstein (1960), and Pope and Siegman (1962), Matarazzo and Saslow (1961) and numerous others have contributed to our knowledge of the details of the dyadic process. Strupp (1960) and others have documented the contributions of the therapist's personality to the treatment process.

These research findings may help therapists to become more aware of the impact of their own behavior on the patient, in a broad sense. But to date, we have found reports from only one group, headed by Ewen Cameron, which suggest serious and consistent efforts to apply control over therapist's verbal responses in actual treatment of patients (Cameron *et al.*, 1964). In contrast to the wealth of information available in the literature, the behavior of interviewing therapists and the format of the interview therapy seems to be essentially unaffected by these findings and continues to follow closely the framework of the traditional dynamic theories of personality. This lag of utilization of research findings in the revision of therapy techniques makes doubtful that the impact of research on verbal conditioning, on the reinforcing effects of various therapist operations, or on the anxiety reducing function of some therapist operations, will find extensive applications in interview therapy until a general theory of behavior provides also firmer guidelines for the over-all strategies in psychotherapy. Deliberate utilization of verbal operations to produce predictable patient reactions may also have to wait until we decide what goals are appropriate for whom, and what techniques are most effective.

CONDITIONING AS TREATMENT

We turn to a second implication of conditioning techniques for psychotherapy. It is based on the premise that the major consequences of the increasing use of the conditioning methods in the psychotherapy is not a minor revision in the method but a *drastic* change in the relative importance of interview procedures as therapeutic instruments. Improvement in conditioning techniques may eventually relegate interview therapy to the status of an adjunct for behavioral modification techniques. As psychologists make increasing use of the same direct methods of modifying behavior in psychotherapy as they use in the laboratory, they should become more effective in treating patients with debilitating symptoms. With the focus on social behavior, understanding the patient's thinking becomes less important and treatment should require fewer interviews in a less intimate personal relationship.

Some day soon we may publically differentiate two types of services which we can offer to the people in trouble: (1) *Behavior therapy* for the treatment of socially crippling behavior disorders, associated with symptoms of specifiable socially inadequate responses or deficits; and (2) *friendship therapy* for the counsel and guidance of the uncertain, confused but generally socially adequate person. To classify patients with regard to their probable responsiveness to the two different approaches, the highly sophisticated, socially and financially successful neurotic patient, who often consults a private psychoanalyst in a metropolitan area and whose problems consist of confusions and difficulties in self-appraisal, sometimes described as Quest for Identity, Weltangst, Dasein-query, or general dissatisfaction with life, may require the type of interview relationships prescribed by psychoanalytic and other dynamic approaches, and characterized by Schofield (1964) as a special kind of purchasable friendship. On the other hand, the majority of patients coming to clinics and seeking relief from crippling emotional and interpersonal problems, or from difficulties with particular circumscribed symptoms, may be better helped by variations of conditioning therapy. A focus on the specific behavior problem suits their needs much better than an effort toward re-orientation of their entire life patterns to a new philosophy.

It is interesting to note that broad eclectic approaches may attempt to work toward both goals and can accomplish each of these sub-goals at different stages. For example, Frank *et al.* (1959) have reported that outpatients in psychiatric treatment show rather quick improvement in subjective complaints after a few interviews. Their social behaviors change much more slowly. Parenthetically, these differences in goals may be one reason why attempts to compare psychotherapeutic success ratios across different techniques are usually not meaningful, since they do not take into account the differences in goals posited by different techniques.

TOWARD AN INTEGRATION

The progress toward broader applications of learning principles in psychotherapy and toward construction of a technology of behavior therapy has been seriously impeded by the failure to combine interview and conditioning techniques. This combination appears essential because conditioning provides a methodological approach for the process of treatment. It has few guidelines to offer for selecting the content of treatment. Most traditional interview methods permit the collection of life-history data and simultaneously provide the opportunity for observation of interactional behaviors. Although Wolpe (1958), Eysenck (1960) and other behavior therapists use interviews for observations and for gathering of information, they have stressed almost exclusively those features and techniques which are most comparable to laboratory conditioning procedures.

Those who see clinical psychology of the future in the hands of "behavioral engineers" aspire toward a time when complete sets of therapeutic programs will be available to a therapist, not only fragments of the treatment procedure. This Utopia envisions a time when a therapist will select a set of procedures with predictable effects for use on a patient with specific symptoms and assets, to accomplish a clearly defined goal. The therapist would then serve as a behavioral engineer whose major skill lies in the proper choice of known instruments for the change of behavior, and who programs his own behavior and that of other people and events in the patient's environment. In fact, the actual details of carrying out the program might be left to a technician with lesser skill and shorter training than that of current psychotherapists.

But the translation of such dreams into reality requires that each of the separate steps of the therapeutic interaction be studied, understood and integrated into a coherent sequence. An important step preceding therapy is the diagnostic process, the patient's assessment and the choice of the particular behavior to be treated. Extensive revision of our current approach to diagnosis is needed to fit this step into the total clinical enterprise. Proper diagnostic assessment must have relevance for the proper choice of treatment techniques, and for definition of treatment criteria (Kanfer & Saslow, 1965). The task of matching patients and treatments is especially difficult because research efforts have been bogged down by the problems in adopting statistical designs to use with individual patients, and because we do not yet know the most relevant dimensions of patient behaviors to be selected for measurement. Yet, the ultimate utility of a new look in psychotherapy lies in its applicability to the individual case. And for individual diagnosis, interview methods may continue to be important clinical tools. For the purpose of fitting the individual to the norms, some more rigorous form of the common interview will remain invaluable, not as a curative agent but as an evaluative tool.

There are other valuable functions of the interview in the therapeutic process. Application of conditioning techniques *per se* does not circumvent the need for providing the most efficient structure of therapist and patient roles. Prior to use of conditioning methods the patient's expectations must also be considered and modified to promote treatment effectiveness (Goldstein, 1962). Methods for the evaluation of treatment progress and for making decisions about changes in treatment also require careful investigation in a domain distinct from conditioning methodology.

In our own recent attempts to combine interview and conditioning methods, we have been impressed with the need for the development of standardized techniques in the implementation of a basic conditioning approach in actual clinical practice. Conditioning procedures can be applied only when specific responses are selected, idiosyncratically appropriate reinforcing stimuli are found and some control over the patient's social or physical environment is obtained. Provisions must also be made in the treatment plan for continuing evaluation of progress and for alternate procedures, in case failure is encountered. These activities, as well as the constant examination of goals represent steps in treatment equal in opportunity, equal in importance to the therapeutic technique itself. For instance, we have found that continued changes had to be made in the original program for behavior therapy because patients progressed at a different rate than expected, because reinforces changed in efficacy during treatment, because extra-therapy experiences changed the patient's behavior in the therapy sessions, and because profound behavior changes occur in patients which are not directly related to the response class which is conditioned. These problems suggest the primitive state of our current repertoire for behavioral therapy. The same careful testing of techniques will be necessary for the construction of inventories and tests, and in the design of experimental laboratory procedures.

A combination of interview and conditioning therapy lies in a technique which we have called Instigation Therapy. This approach rests heavily on the utilization of the patient's verbal repertoire and his self-regulatory behaviors. The approach is similar to that reported by Ferster *et al.* (1962) in his treatment of obese nurses, and Goldiamond (1963) in treatment of a marital problem. In essence, it consists of teaching the patient to arrange optimal conditions for his own behavior change in his daily environment. We have used this method with severely neurotic patients, with psychotics in remission, and with behavioral problems in children. This approach depends heavily on interviews as well as conditioning sessions. In an extension of instigation therapy, behavior changes have also been obtained, not by direct contact with the patient himself, but by working with people who can regulate the patient's environment for him. For example, in a case of functional invalidism in a bed-ridden hysteric adolescent girl, changes were obtained not by direct intervention with the patient's fatigue and rest, but by programming the patient's parents to carry out specific response-reinforcement contingencies in a systematic program. In working with a schizophrenic woman in remission, similar methods were used with initially modest goals of helping the patient toward independent living, vocational adjustment and eventually toward establishment of social relationships with others.

Brief mention of these problems is intended to suggest that we are only at the threshold of potential applications of learning principles to the area of psychotherapy. Not only do we need exploration of new techniques, but also additional basic research on learning mechanisms in humans and on other psychological processes of greater complexity than have been explored in the laboratory to date. There is also the possibility that many techniques suggested by other schools of psychotherapy can be fitted into a behavioral approach, once their specific effects have been explored.

THE EXPANDED SCOPE OF THERAPY

There is one final consequence of the introduction of conditioning techniques into psychotherapy which merits attention. With the rapid departure of treatment methods from the "talking therapies," the clinician has ventured out of his office and there has been an expansion of his field of activity. Unlike his predecessor, the behavioral engineer may find that he can be most effective in the patient's home, in his work environment or in the schoolroom. But traditional methods have set up some very difficult and unreasonable social demands of the therapist. Psychiatrists and psychologists are expected to change people by talking to them. In addition, the community only vaguely alludes to the desired end-product of treatment in terms of better mental health or improved adjustment. While making these large demands, there is also an implicit social and moral restriction on the methods to be used for producing behavioral changes. Even with psychotic patients, society limits the mode of treatment to talk, to physical restraints, and to drugs. The locus of treatment is further limited to the hospital or to the professional office. Although there is increasing recognition that the patient's behavioral disorder may be a result of the particular social environment in which he lives, therapists are rarely admitted to observe, and even less frequently permitted to change the conditions in which the patient habitually lives. These restrictions have forced the therapist to work mainly on verbal and interpersonal behaviors which can be observed or reported in the office, and which are amenable to changes only by those techniques applicable in these restricted treatment settings. Consequently, therapeutic strategies often aim at accomplishing changes which are unrelated to the patient's problem.

The increased use of direct modification techniques will more sharply bring into focus the clinician's dilemma. The availability of new approaches should also result eventually in a clearer definition of the types of interventions which are accepted by society in the treatment of behavior disorders. It may also require more explicit safeguards against misuse of such increased control for purposes other than restoration of adequate individual functioning.

In a recent APA symposium, George Kelly (1964) made a plea for training the clinical psychologist to be "a real man. . . an actual person. . . one who is willing to take the pains to try to understand Man intimately." But listening and understanding impose a heavy moral burden on the listener. They obligate him to action. Recent developments in the field of psychotherapy suggest that in addition to warmth, understanding and compassion we should also train the clinician so that he possesses the technical skills to do something about the patient's misery. The use of conditioning techniques alone may not turn out to be the answer to the mental health movement's prayer. However, unless we constantly search for new and better treatment methods, the clinician could easily become a handholding prophet of false truths, rich in understanding but poor in therapeutic effectiveness.

REFERENCES

Cameron, D., Levey, L., Ban, T., and Rubenstein, L. Automation of Psychotherapy. *J. Amer. Psychopath. Assn*, 1964, *5*, 1-14.

Eysenck, H. J. *Behavior therapy and the new neuroses.* New York: Pergamon Press, 1960.

Ferster, C. B., Nurnberger, J. I., and Levitt, E. The control of eating. *J. Mathetics*, 1962, *1*, 87-109.

Frank, J. D., Gliedman, L. H., Imber, S. D., Stone, A. R., and Nash, E. H. The patients' expectancies and relearning as factors determining improvement in psychotherapy. *Amer. J. Psychiat.*, 1959, *115*, 961-968.

Gardner, G. Gail. The psychotherapeutic relationship. *Psychol. Bull.*, 1964, *61*, 426-437.

Goldiamond, I. Justified and unjustified alarm over behavioral control. In, O. Milton (Ed.), *Behavior disorders: perspectives and trends.* Philadelphia: J. B. Lippincott, 1965. Pp. 237-261.

Goldstein, A. P. *Therapist-patient expectancies in psychotherapy.* New York: Macmillan, 1962.

Kanfer, F. H., and Saslow, G. Behavioral analysis: an alternative to diagnostic classification. *Arch. Gen. Psychiat.*, 1965, *12*, 529-538.

Kelly, G. A. Training for professional obsolescence. Paper presented to the Conference of Chief State Psychologists at Los Angeles, California in September 1964.

Krasner, L. The therapist as a social reinforcement machine. In, H. H. Strupp, and L. Luborsky (Eds.), *Research in psychotherapy.* Vol. II. Baltimore: French-Bray, 1962.

Lazarus, A. A. The results of behavior therapy in 126 cases of severe neurosis. *Behav. Res. and Ther.*, 1963, *1*, 69-80.

Lennard, H. L., and Bernstein, A. *The anatomy of psychotherapy.* New York: Columbia Univer. Press, 1960.

London, P. *The modes and morals of psychotherapy.* New York: Holt, Rinehart and Winston, 1964.

Marsden, G. Content-analysis studies of therapeutic interviews: 1954 to 1964. *Psychol. Bull.*, 1965, *63*, 298-321.

Matarazzo, J. D., and Saslow, G. Differences in interview interaction behavior among normal and deviant groups. In, I. A. Berg, and B. M. Bass (Eds.), *Conformity and Deviation.* New York: Harper & Bros., 1961.

Pope, B., and Siegman, A. W. The effect of therapist verbal activity level and specificity on patient productivity and speech disturbance in the initial interview. *J. Consult. Psychol.*, 1962, *26*, 489.

Rachman, S. Introduction to behavior therapy. *Behav. Res. and Ther.*, 1963, *1*, 3-16.

Schofield, W. *Psychotherapy: the purchase of friendship.* Englewood Cliffs, N.J.: Prentice-
    Hall, 1964.
Strupp, H. H. *Psychotherapists in action.* New York: Grune and Stratton, 1960.
Ulrich, L., and Trumbo, D. The selection interview since 1949. *Psychol. Bull.*, 1965,
    63, 100-116.
Williams, Juanita H. Conditioning of verbalization: a review. *Psychol. Bull.*, 1964,
    62, 383-393.
Wolpe, J. *Psychotherapy by reciprocal inhibition.* Stanford: Stanford Univer. Press, 1958.
Wolpe, J., Salter, A., and Reyna, L. J. *The conditioning therapies.* New York: Holt,
    Rinehart and Winston, 1964.

Learning Theory and the Treatment of Depression[1]

Arnold A. Lazarus

Depression, according to Hathaway and McKinley (1951) "is the most ubiquitous of the patterns seen in psychological abnormality." Yet apart from exploratory studies on conditionability (e.g. Ban *et al.*, 1966) behavior therapists have tended to ignore the subject or have dealt with it mainly *en passant*. Psychoanalysts, by contrast, have invested much energy in attempting to unravel the putative inconscious dynamics involved. The general psychiatric literature on the topic of depression, although extremely vast, is disappointingly inconsistent. For instance, there does not seem to be an acceptable system of classification or a standard nomenclature. Even the broadest nosological divisions are open to criticism. The validity of the numerous sub-divisions such as "involutional melancholia" in contrast to the "manic-depressive reaction," as distinct from "schizo-affective disorders" as opposed to "agitated depressions," etc. certainly does not hold up well under statistical scrutiny (e.g., Stenstedt, 1959). The main difficulty as Blinder (1966) points out, is that the current nosology and taxonomy of depression is based upon the old Kraepelinian classification of mental disorders as definite disease entities.

Despite the perennial dispute which centers around the distinction between endogenous and exogenous (reactive) depressions, there is little doubt, as Maddison and Duncan (1965) point out, that many depressions are based entirely on *physiological* factors (i.e., some genetic, enzymatic, metabolic, endocrine, or other biochemical disturbance). The picture is further complicated by "mixed depressions" and so-called "masked depressions" (in which the patient initially complains only of atypical somatic symptoms). Faced with these diagnostic difficulties it is well worth inquiring whether learning theory can bring the field into clearer focus.

In general, where a therapist finds himself unable to account for a

[1]Reprinted from *Behavior Research and Therapy*, 1968, 6, 83-89, with permission of the author and Pergamon Press, Ltd.

55

persistent response pattern in terms of contiguous associations, drive reduction, stimulus generalization, positive or negative reinforcement, or any other principle of learning, he is best advised to consider the likelihood of organic pathology. This is by no means a cut-and-dried matter, but one cannot ascribe to learning, response patterns which have no logical antecedents. Learned responses do not mysteriously well up from unconscious depths. They have a discernible history and, for this reason, a careful S-R analysis is considered indispensable for adequate diagnosis and therapy.

The main purpose of this paper is to present some of the many and complex variables involved in understanding, assessing, and treating "psychogenic" or "reactive" depressions. It is perhaps necessary first to try and define the subject matter under discussion.

Problems of definition

Depression is exceedingly difficult to define (let alone measure!) and it is clear that many diverse phenomena have been lumped together under this term. It is difficult to evoke "depression" in experimental subjects, and even more difficult to isolate and maintain this response in a "pure" state. Yet, the temptation to deny depression status as a subject matter for scientific consideration must be resisted—if for no reason other than the fact that clinicians daily are consulted by thousands of people who say they feel depressed. Literature, art, drama, and psychiatric reports are replete with descriptions of depression which are often at variance with each other.

Shall we define depression as a subjective experience involving inner dejection, despair, misery, despondency, futility, or perhaps in such terms as nuclear unworthiness or implosive aggression? Or should we avoid the snares of subjectivity and like Skinner (1953), simply define depression as a general weakening on one's behavioral repertoire? But as Ferster (1965) points out: "Whether a man who moves and acts slowly is 'depressed' or merely moving slowly is not easily or reliably determined by observing his behavior alone."

If we compile a catalogue of operant responses, we might establish a base rate of frequent weeping, decreased food intake, frequent statements of dejection and self-reproach, psychomotor retardation, difficulties with memory and concentration, insomnia or a fitful sleep pattern, and general apathy and withdrawal. Descriptively, depressed patients primarily express a pool of gloomy feelings and pessimistic thoughts, and are relatively refractory to various kinds of stimulation, while displaying one or more of the above-mentioned operant responses.

Some theorists separate depression from what Freud (1925) termed "the normal emotion of grief" which he felt one would never regard as a morbid condition in need of therapeutic intervention. In fact, he stated that "we look upon any interference with it as inadvisable or even harmful." From a behavioral point of view, this separation seems to have no therapeutic usefulness. What criteria can be utilized to differentiate "normal grief" from intense or protracted grief, which is indistinguishable from "depression?"

Dengrove (1966) has in fact successfully treated grief reactions, whether due to the death of a loved one, separation, or desertion, by systematic desensitization. He commences by having the patient visualize the person or the "lost object" in a series of formerly happy and pleasant contexts. Then, under conditions of deep muscle relaxation, he slowly moves forward in time gradually progressing to the events of the funeral. He adds that if fear of death or reactions of guilt are present, these are included in the hierarchy.

Depression and anxiety

It is sometimes difficult to separate depression from "anxiety." While it is true that depression is often a consequence of "anxiety that is unusually intense or prolonged" (Wolpe and Lazarus, 1966, p. 162), it is important to separate anxiety from depression and to stress that they usually have different antecedents.

Fundamentally, anxiety may be viewed as a response to noxious or threatening stimuli, and depression may be regarded as a function of inadequate or insufficient reinforcers. In Skinnerian terms, this would probably result in a weakened behavioral repertoire. A depressed person is virtually on an extinction trial. Some significant reinforcer has been withdrawn. There is loss and deprivation—loss of money or love, status or prestige, recognition or security, etc. More subtle factors are sometimes involved, e.g. loss of youth or a particular loss of body functioning. Clinicians are sometimes puzzled by depressions which have their onset when an individual finally attains a pinnacle of success. One reason for these depressive patterns is perhaps the loss of striving.

Ferster (1965) describes how diverse factors such as (a) sudden environmental changes, (b) punishment and aversive control, and (c) shifts in reinforcement contingencies give rise to depression. For him, the essential characteristic of a depressed person is "a reduced frequency of emission of positively reinforced behavior."

The essence of therapy in overcoming anxiety is to remove the noxious elements and/or change the patient's responses towards them. Depressed patients require a different schedule of reinforcement and/or need to learn a way of recognizing and utilizing certain reinforcers at their disposal.

Where depression is secondary to anxiety, it may prove helpful to deal with the anxiety component (e.g. by means of relaxation, desensitization, assertive training, aversion-relief, feeding responses, galvanic stimulation, etc.). In this paper, the section on therapy will consider the treatment of those cases in whom the depressive component is uppermost and in whom the removal of attendant anxieties is unlikely to dislodge the debilitating depressive reaction.

Clinical assessment

One pragmatic rule is that when the depressive verbalizations, such as nihilistic statements and complaints of helplessness and hopelessness, do not center around stressful or other provoking emotional experiences, endogenous (i.e. physiological) factors must receive diagnostic priority. The treatment of depressions which are primarily physiological in nature usually calls for drugs and/or ECT (Maddison and Duncan, 1965), possibly in a supportive psychotherapeutic setting. The converse is true when treating depressions in which psychological features predominate. Here, intensive psychological techniques are called for, and the use of medication (if any) is mainly palliative.

An adequate life history remains an indispensable aid towards a valid and reliable assessment of the patient's condition. Consider the following case: Miss B. D., a 29-year-old unmarried female developed persistent feelings of depression following a prolonged bout of viral influenza. She felt most depressed in the early morning hours but was seldom depressed in the evenings. She fell asleep readily but kept waking up intermittently, and would usually fail to go back to sleep after 3 a.m. at which time she experienced perseverating morbid thoughts. She ate poorly since her illness, had lost weight and was constipated. She accused herself of indolence and had lost her *joie de vivre*. A family history revealed that the patient's mother had been treated for a "puerperal depression."

To the writer's surprise, several clinicians ventured to make differential diagnoses based on the scanty material outlined above. Learning theory demands a detailed and precise description of S-R patterns before problem identification can be attempted. Presented with the syndrome described in the case of Miss B. D. (a physiological precipitant, diurnal variation, characteristic sleep pattern, weight loss, statements of self-recrimination, and a family history of depression), too many clinicians might be inclined to label the problem "endogenous" without further inquiry. A more detailed behavior analysis revealed that the patient had been unhappy for some time with her work situation, that her fiancé had been acting in an inconsistent manner, that her mother had become increasingly demanding, and that she was concerned about some financial reversals her family had suffered in recent months. Furthermore, her depressive content and her perseverating thoughts were always focused on her specific problem areas. A program of assertive training resulted in a new work situation, a new boyfriend, a contrite mother and an efficient accountant. Not surprisingly, she no longer complained of depression and has withstood a 3-yr follow-up inquiry.

Specific methods of treatment

The generic conception of depression as a consequence of inadequate or insufficient reinforcement requires elaboration. The obvious withdrawal of a reinforcer (such as loss of money, work, or friendship) followed by a pattern of misery and gloom, calls for very little diagnostic ingenuity. The clinician is taxed most by those patients who show no obvious loss to account for their depression. Some very subtle features are sometimes operative. For instance, an expected loss or any anticipation of a non-reinforcing state of affairs may precipitate various intensities of depression. These cases are sometimes too hastily classified as "endogenous depressions." Furthermore, depression which may have had physiological origins and/or obvious history of rein-forcement-deprivation, may be maintained by operant consequences. The patient when "blue" finds people who cheer-him-up and they thus reinforce his depressive behavior. Therapy must take cognizance of both antecedent factors and the consequences of behavior.

Most therapists, when confronted by depressed patients, prescribe anti-depressant medication and a combination of reassurance and supportive therapy. Let us turn to some more specific therapeutic strategies.

Environmental manipulation has an obvious place in those cases where depression appears to be a consequence of inimical life situations—an un-satisfactory job, an unhappy marriage, social isolation, etc. These non-rewarding circumstances are often altered by a touch of assertiveness and by some therapeutic ingenuity in fostering recreational pursuits, meaningful friendships, hobbies and other constructive activities. As already mentioned, when depression is secondary to anxiety, the elimination of the latter (by means of the usual behavioral techniques) is often enough of a rewarding contingency to break through the depressive condition. Three specific anti-depressive behavioral techniques will now be outlined for those cases in whom "reactive" depression is the primary complaint.

1. *Time projection with positive reinforcement*

The truism "time heals" ignores the fact that the passage of time *per se* is not therapeutic, but that psychological healing occurs because time permits new or competing responses to emerge. Generally, an event which causes intense annoyance or distress can be viewed with indifference or detachment after say a lapse of 6 months or a year. The therapeutic utility and application of this observation is illustrated by the following case history:

Miss C. H., a 23-year-old art student, became acutely depressed when her boyfriend informed her that he intended marrying one of her classmates. She became sleepless, anorexic, restless, and weepy. Previously she had been a most talented and enthusiastic student; now she was unable to con-centrate on her work, had stopped attending classes, and had become apath-etic and listless. After 10 days, her parents persuaded her to consult a psychiatrist who prescribed amphetamines and barbiturates, whereupon she made a suicidal attempt by swallowing all her pills. Fortunately, the dose was not lethal. She refused to seek further psychiatric help, but her family physician nevertheless requested the writer to conduct a home visit.

It was difficult to establish rapport but the patient was finally responsive to emphatic statements of sympathy and reassurance. She agreed to see the writer at his consulting room on the following day. A behavioral inquiry revealed that prior to her unrequited love relationship, she had enjoyed painting, sculpting, and practicing the guitar. She also went horse-riding and displayed some interest in symphony concerts. During the 10 months of her love affair, she had exchanged all of these activities for "stock-car racing, amateur dramatics and a few wild parties."

As the patient proved highly susceptible to hypnotic techniques, a trance state was induced and the following time projection sequences were applied:

"It is almost 3:15 p.m. on Wednesday, April 14, 1965. (This was the date of the actual consultation.) Apart from sleeping, eating, etc., how could you have occupied these 24 hours? You could have gone horse-riding for a change, or taken your guitar out of mothballs . . . (5-second pause) . . . Let's push time forward another 24 hours. You are now 48 hours ahead in time. Enough time has elapsed to have started a painting and done some sculpting. You may even have enjoyed a ride in the country and attended a concert. Think about these activities; picture them in your mind; let them bring a good feeling of pleasant associations, of good times . . . (5-second pause) . . . Let's advance even further in time. A whole week has gone by, and another, and yet another. Now these past three weeks into which you have advanced have been busy and active. Reflect back for a moment on three weeks of enjoyable activity . . . (10-second pause) . . . Now you move further forward in time. Days are flying past; time advances; days become weeks; time passes; weeks become months. It is now 6 months later. It's the 14th of October, 1965. Look back on the past 6 months, from April to October. Think about the months that separate April from October. What have you done during May, June, July, August, and September? (Pause of 5 seconds) . . . Now six months ago, going back to April, you were very upset. In retrospect, how do you feel? Think back; reflect over an incident now more than 6 months old. If it still bothers you, signal to me by raising your left index finger."

As the patient did not raise her finger, she was told that she would recall the entire time projection sequence and return back in time to April 14, feeling as she did during October. She was then dehypnotized and asked to recount her feelings. (If she had signalled, the time projection sequence would have been continued, up to 2 years ahead.) She stated: "How can I put it in words? Let me just explain it in three ways. First, I feel kind of foolish; second, there are lots of pebbles on the beach; and number three, there's something inside that really wants to find an outlet on canvas. Does that make sense?"

Miss C. H. was interviewed a week later. She reported having enjoyed many productive hours, had regained her appetite, and had been sleeping soundly. There were some minor episodes of "gloom" which responded to self-induced imagery, similar to the therapeutic time-projection sequence. She cancelled her subsequent appointments, stating that she had completely overcome her depression. This impression was confirmed by her parents and the referring physician. A follow-up after a year revealed that she had been exposed to a series of disappointments which often led to temporary bouts of depression (none, however, as severe as that which had led her to therapy).

Some patients have responded well to this technique when neither hypnosis nor relaxation was employed. All successful cases, however, were able to picture vivid images. Although depressed patients are usually deaf to advice and guidance, the cognitive effects of this procedure are similar to the old "pull-yourself-together-sufficiently-to-do-something-creative-and-then-you-will-feel-better" doctrine. Once the patient can imagine himself sufficiently freed from his oppressive inertia to engage in some enjoyable (or formerly enjoyable) activity, a lifting of depressive affect is often apparent. This may be sustained by insuring that the patient thereupon experiences actual rewarding activities.

The time projection sequence has been used with 11 patients. Six cases responded excellently, two improved moderately, and three were un-improved. These results refer to one-session trials.

2. *Affective expression*

Reference has already been made to the notion that depressed patients are relatively refractory to most forms of stimulation. Yet almost any stimulus which shatters this web of inertia may also vanquish their depression—temporarily at least. The writer recalls witnessing a severely depressed patient evince an extreme startle reaction followed by panic at a false fire alarm. Both his subjective report and his overt behavior revealed the absence of depression for many hours thereafter. It is hypothesized that when an individual feels or expresses anger, depressive affect is often undermined. This idea was bolstered when a patient who grew angry at the writer for asking too many personal questions remarked: "I was feeling very depressed when I walked in here, but now I feel fine." *In general the writer submits that anger (or the deliberate stimulation of feelings of amusement, affection, sexual excitement, or anxiety) tends to break the depressive cycle.* The clinical utility of this principle is suggested by a patient who was exceedingly depressed about the end of a love affair. He became furious when he discovered that his ex-girl-friend had spread false rumors about him, whereupon his depression immediately (and lastingly) disappeared. The writer has several cases on record in which the development of "righteous indignation" rather than "self-blame" appeared to coincide with the elimination of depression and suicidal feelings.

3. *Behavioral deprivation and re-training*

The schema of depression elaborated in the previous sections is that a chronic and/or acute non-reinforcing state of affairs can result in a condition where the person becomes relatively refractory to most stimuli and enters a state of "depression." A period of deliberate or enforced "sensory deprivation" and inertia, may, however, make the depressed patient more susceptible to incoming stimuli, so that positive reinforcement may take effect. This is in keeping with the practices of "Morita Therapy" (Kora, 1965) where the patient is subjected to a 5- to 7-day period of absolute bed rest, without access to any external stimuli (i.e. no reading, writing, smoking, visitors, or other distractions are permitted). At the end of this period, most people find positive reinforcement value in almost *any* external stimulus. After leaving bed, patients are gradually exposed to a graduated series of tasks commencing with "light work" for 1 week (a form of occupational therapy) and eventually progress from "heavy work" to "complicated work."

Although Morita Therapy is not advocated by its practitioners specifically for the treatment of depression (they have applied it with success to cases of so-called neurasthenia, anxiety states and obsessional disorders), the writer has had some encouraging preliminary results when applying it to depressed patients in a less stringent manner.

The well-known methods of narcosis or sleep therapy (e.g. Loucas and Stafford-Clark, 1965; Andreev, 1960) might also have a place in this schema. It must be emphasized again that, from the behavioral viewpoint, the rationale for these methods is that they render persons more amenable to a wider range of positive reinforcers.

To recapitulate, therapy for psychological depressions requires the introduction of sufficiently powerful reinforcers to disrupt the "emotional inhibitions" which characterize the behavior of depressed patients. If the patient is enabled merely to contemplate future positive reinforcements, depressive responses usually diminish or disappear. The time-projection sequence described above makes use of this observation. Any change in emotional tone in which excitatory rather than inhibitory affect predominates (whether due to positive or negative reinforcement) is also likely to impede depressive reactions. When depressed patients are highly refractory to the usual range of positive reinforcers, they are sometimes rendered more amenable to stimulation after undergoing a general régime of stimulus deprivation. The three methods discussed above are merely a small sample of the many and varied techniques which can be advanced within a general behavioral framework.

REFERENCES

Andreev, B. V. (1960) *Sleep Therapy in the Neuroses*. Consultant's Bureau, New York.

Ban, T. Z., Choi, S. M., Lehmann, H. E. and Adamo, E. (1966) Conditional reflex studies in depression. *Can. psychiat. Ass. J.*, *11*, S98-S104.

Blinder, M. G. (1966) The pragmatic classification of depression. *Am. J. Psychiat.*, *123*, 259-269.

Dengrove, E. (1966) *Treatment of Non-phobic Disorders by the Behavioral Therapies*. Lecture to the Association for Advancement of the Behavioral Therapies, in New York on 17 December.

Ferster, C. B. (1965) Classification of behavioral pathology. In *Research in Behavior Modification*. (Eds. Krasner, L. and Ullmann, L. P.). Holt, Rinehart and Winston, New York.

Freud, S. (1925) Mourning and melancholia. In *Collected Papers*, Vol. IV. Hogarth, London.

Hathaway, S. R. and McKinley, J. C. (1951) *Manual of the M.M.P.I.* The Psychological Corporation, New York.

Kora, T. (1965) Morita therapy. *Int. J. Psychiat.*, *1*, 611-640.

Loucas, K. P. and Stafford-Clark, D. (1965) Electronarcosis at Guy's. *Guy's Hosp. Reps.*, *114*, 223-237.

Maddison, D., and Duncan, G. M. (1965) (Eds.) *Aspects of Depressive Illness*. Livingston, Edinburgh.

Skinner, B. F. (1953) *Science and Human Behavior*. Macmillan, New York.

Stenstedt, A. (1959) Involutional melancholia. *Acta Psychiat. Scand.*, *34*, Suppl. 127, 1-71.

Wolpe, J. and Lazarus, A. A. (1966) *Behavior Therapy Techniques*. Pergamon Press, Oxford.

Some Current Dimensions of Applied Behavior Analysis[1]

Donald M. Baer, Montrose M. Wolf, and Todd R. Risley

The analysis of individual behavior is a problem in scientific demonstration, reasonably well understood (Skinner, 1953, Sec. 1), comprehensively described (Sidman, 1960), and quite thoroughly practiced (*Journal of the Experimental Analysis of Behavior*, 1957—). That analysis has been pursued in many settings over many years. Despite variable precision, elegance, and power, it has resulted in general descriptive statements of mechanisms that can produce many of the forms that individual behavior may take.

The statement of these mechanisms establishes the possibility of their application to problem behavior. A society willing to consider a technology of its own behavior apparently is likely to support that application when it deals with socially important behaviors, such as retardation, crime, mental illness, or education. Such applications have appeared in recent years. Their current number and the interest which they create apparently suffice to generate a journal for their display. That display may well lead to the widespread examination of these applications, their refinement, and eventually their replacement by better applications. Better applications, it is hoped, will lead to a better state of society, to whatever extent the behavior of its members can contribute to the goodness of a society. Since the evaluation of what is a "good" society is in itself a behavior of its members, this hope turns on itself in a philosophically interesting manner. However, it is at least a fair presumption that behavioral applications, when effective, can sometimes lead to social approval and adoption.

Behavioral applications are hardly a new phenomenon. Analytic behavioral applications, it seems, are. Analytic behavioral application is the process of applying sometimes tentative principles of behavior to the improvement[2] of specific behaviors, and simultaneously evaluating whether or not any changes noted are indeed attributable to the process of application—

[1]Reprinted from the *Journal of Applied Behavior Analysis*, 1968, *1*, 91-97, with permission of the authors and the Society for the Applied Analysis of Behavior.

and if so, to what parts of that process. In short, analytic behavioral application is a self-examining, self-evaluating, discovery-oriented research procedure for studying behavior. So is all experimental behavioral research (at least, according to the usual strictures of modern graduate training). The differences are matters of emphasis and of selection.

The differences between applied and basic research are not differences between that which "discovers" and that which merely "applies" what is already known. Both endeavors ask what controls the behavior under study. Non-applied research is likely to look at any behavior, and at any variable which may conceivably relate to it. Applied research is constrained to look at variables which can be effective in improving the behavior under study. Thus, it is equally a matter of research to discover that the behaviors typical of retardates can be related to oddities of their chromosome structure and to oddities of their reinforcement history. But (currently) the chromosome structure of the retardate does not lend itself to experimental manipulation in the interests of bettering that behavior, whereas his reinforcement input is always open to current re-design.

Similarly, applied research is constrained to examining behaviors which are socially important, rather than convenient for study. It also implies, very frequently, the study of those behaviors in their usual social settings, rather than in a "laboratory" setting. But a laboratory is simply a place so designed that experimental control of relevant variables is as easy as possible. Unfortunately, the usual social setting for important behaviors is rarely such a place. Consequently, the analysis of socially important behaviors becomes experimental only with difficulty. As the terms are used here, a non-experimental analysis is a contradiction in terms. Thus, analytic behavioral applications by definition achieve experimental control of the processes they contain, but since they strive for this control against formidable difficulties, they achieve it less often per study than would a laboratory-based attempt. Consequently, the rate of displaying experimental control required of behavioral applications has become correspondingly less than the standards typical of laboratory research. This is not because the applier is an easy-going, liberal, or generous fellow, but because society rarely will allow its important behaviors, in their correspondingly important settings, to be manipulated repeatedly for the merely logical comfort of a scientifically skeptical audience.

[2]If a behavior is socially important, the usual behavior analysis will aim at its improvement. The social value dictating this choice is obvious. However, it can be just as illuminating to demonstrate how a behavior may be worsened, and there will arise occasions when it will be socially important to do so. Disruptive classroom behavior may serve as an example. Certainly it is a frequent plague of the educational system. A demonstration of what teacher procedures produce more of this behavior is not necessarily the reverse of a demonstration of how to promote positive study behaviors. There may be classroom situations in which the teacher cannot readily establish high rates of study, yet still could avoid high rates of disruption, if she knew what in her own procedures leads to this disruption. The demonstration which showed her that would thus have its value.

Thus, the evaluation of a study which purports to be an applied behavior analysis is somewhat different from the evaluation of a similar laboratory analysis. Obviously, the study must be applied, behavioral, and analytic; in addition, it should be technological, conceptually systematic, and effective, and it should display some generality. These terms are explored below and compared to the criteria often stated for the evaluation of behavioral research which, though analytic, is not applied.

Applied

The label applied is not determined by the research procedures used, but by the interest which society shows in the problems being studied. In behavioral application, the behavior, stimuli, and/or organism under study are chosen because of their importance to man and society, rather than their importance to theory. The non-applied researcher may study eating behavior, for example, because it relates directly to metabolism, and there are hypotheses about the interaction between behavior and metabolism. The non-applied researcher also may study bar-pressing because it is a convenient response for study; easy for the subject, and simple to record and integrate with theoretically significant environmental events. By contrast, the applied researcher is likely to study eating because there are children who eat too little and adults who eat too much, and he will study eating in exactly those individuals rather than in more convenient ones. The applied researcher may also study bar-pressing if it is integrated with socially important stimuli. A program for a teaching machine may use bar-pressing behavior to indicate mastery of an arithmetic skill. It is the arithmetic stimuli which are important. (However, some future applied study could show that bar-pressing is more practical in the process of education than a pencil-writing response.[3])

In applied research, there is typically a close relationship between the behavior and stimuli under study and the subject in whom they are studied. Just as there seem to be few behaviors that are intrinsically the target of application, there are few subjects who automatically confer on their study the status of application. An investigation of visual signal detection in the retardate may have little immediate importance, but a similar study in radarscope watchers has considerable. A study of language development in the retardate may be aimed directly at an immediate social problem, while a similar study in the MIT sophomore may not. Enhancement of the reinforcing value of praise for the retardate alleviates an immediate deficit in

---

[3]Research may use the most convenient behaviors and stimuli available, and yet exemplify an ambition in the researcher eventually to achieve application to socially important settings. For example, a study may seek ways to give a light flash a durable conditioned reinforcing function, because the experimenter wishes to know how to enhance school children's responsiveness to approval. Nevertheless, durable bar-pressing for that light flash is no guarantee that the obvious classroom analogue will produce durable reading behavior for teacher statements of "Good!" Until the analogue has been proven sound, application has not been achieved.

his current environment, but enhancement of the reinforcing value of 400 Hz (cps) tone for the same subject probably does not. Thus, a primary question in the evaluation of applied research is: how immediately important is this behavior or these stimuli to this subject?

Behavioral

Behaviorism and pragmatism seem often to go hand in hand. Applied research is eminently pragmatic; it asks how it is possible to get an individual to do something effectively. Thus, it usually studies what subjects can be brought to do rather than what they can be brought to say; unless, of course, a verbal response is the behavior of interest. Accordingly a subject's verbal description of his own non-verbal behavior usually would not be accepted as a measure of his actual behavior unless it were independently substantiated. Hence, there is little applied value in the demonstration that an impotent man can be made to say that he no longer is impotent. The relevant question is not what he can say, but what he can do. Application has not been achieved until this question has been answered satisfactorily. (This assumes, of course, that the total goal of the applied researcher is not simply to get his patient-subjects to stop complaining to him. Unless society agrees that this researcher should not be bothered, it will be difficult to defend that goal as socially important.)

Since the behavior of an individual is composed of physical events, its scientific study requires their precise measurement. As a result, the problem of reliable quantification arises immediately. The problem is the same for applied research as it is for non-applied research. However, non-applied research typically will choose a response easily quantified in a reliable manner, whereas applied research rarely will have that option. As a result, the applied researcher must try harder, rather than ignore this criterion of all trustworthy research. Current applied research often shows that thoroughly reliable quantification of behavior can be achieved, even in thoroughly difficult settings. However, it also suggests that instrumented recording with its typical reliability will not always be possible. The reliable use of human beings to quantify the behavior of other human beings is an area of psychological technology long since well developed, thoroughly relevant, and very often necessary to applied behavior analysis.

A useful tactic in evaluating the behavioral attributes of a study is to ask not merely, was behavior changed? but also, whose behavior? Ordinarily it would be assumed that it was the subject's behavior which was altered; yet careful reflection may suggest that this was not necessarily the case. If humans are observing and recording the behavior under study, then any change may represent a change only in their observing and recording responses, rather than in the subject's behavior. Explicit measurement of the reliability of human observers thus becomes not merely good technique, but a prime criterion of whether the study was appropriately behavioral. (A study merely of the behavior of observers is behavioral, of course, but probably irrelevant to the researcher's goal.) Alternatively, it may be that only tчe experimenter's behavior has changed. It may be reported, for example, that a certain patient rarely dressed himself upon awakening, and consequently would be dressed by his attendant. The experimental technique to be applied might consist of some penalty imposed unless the patient was dressed within half an hour after awakening. Recording of an increased probability of self-dressing under these conditions might testify to the effectiveness of the penalty in changing the behavior; however, it might also testify to the fact that the patient would in fact probably dress himself within half an hour of arising, but previously was rarely left that long undressed before being clothed by his efficient attendant. (The attendant now is the penalty-imposing experimenter and therefore always gives the patient his full half-hour, in the interests of precise experimental technique, of course.) This error is an elementary one, perhaps. But it suggests that in general, when an experiment proceeds from its baseline to its first experimental phase, changes in what is measured need not always reflect the behavior of the subject.

Analytic

The analysis of a behavior, as the term is used here, requires a believable demonstration of the events that can be responsible for the occurrence or non-occurrence of that behavior. An experimenter has achieved an analysis of a behavior when he can exercise control over it. By common laboratory standards, that has meant an ability of the experimenter to turn the behavior on and off, or up and down, at will. Laboratory standards have usually made this control clear by demonstrating it repeatedly, even redundantly, over time. Applied research, as noted before, cannot often approach this arrogantly frequent clarity of being in control of important behaviors. Consequently, application, to be analytic, demonstrates control when it can, and thereby presents its audience with a problem of judgment. The problem, of course, is whether the experimenter has shown enough control, and often enough, for believability. Laboratory demonstrations, either by over-replication or an acceptable probability level derived from statistical tests of grouped data, make this judgment more implicit than explicit. As Sidman points out (1960), there is still a problem of judgment in any event, and it is probably better when explicit.

There are at least two designs commonly used to demonstrate reliable control of an important behavioral change. The first can be referred to as the "reversal" technique. Here a behavior is measured, and the measure is examined over time until its stability is clear. Then, the experimental variable is applied. The behavior continues to be measured, to see if the variable will produce a behavioral change. If it does, the experimental variable is discontinued or altered, to see if the behavioral change just brought about depends on it. If so, the behavioral change should be lost or diminished (thus the term "reversal"). The experimental variable then is applied again, to see if the behavioral change can be recovered. If it can, it is pursued further, since this is applied research and the behavioral change sought is an important one. It may be reversed briefly again, and yet again, if the setting in which the behavior takes place allows further reversals. But that setting may be a school system or a family, and continued reversals may not be allowed. They may appear in themselves to be detrimental to the subject if pursued too often. (Whether they are in fact detrimental is likely to remain an unexamined question so long as the social setting in which the behavior is studied dictates against using them repeatedly. Indeed, it may be that repeated reversals in some applications have a positive effect on the subject, possibly contributing to the discrimination of relevant stimuli involved in the problem.)

In using the reversal technique, the experimenter is attempting to show that an analysis of the behavior is at hand: that whenever he applies a certain variable, the behavior is produced, and whenever he removes this variable, the behavior is lost. Yet applied behavior analysis is exactly the kind of research which can make this technique self-defeating in time. Application typically means producing valuable behavior; valuable behavior usually meets extra-experimental reinforcement in a social setting; thus, valuable behavior, once set up, may no longer be dependent upon the experimental technique which created it. Consequently, the number of reversals possible in applied studies may be limited by the nature of the social setting in which the behavior takes place, in more ways than one.

An alternative to the reversal technique may be called the "multiple baseline" technique. This alternative may be of particular value when a behavior appears to be irreversible or when reversing the behavior is undesirable. In the multiple-baseline technique, a number of responses are identified and measured over time to provide baselines against which changes can be evaluated. With these baselines established, the experimenter then applies an experimental variable to one of the behaviors, produces a change in it, and perhaps notes little or no change in the other baselines. If so, rather than reversing the just-produced change, he instead applies the experimental variable to one of the other, as yet unchanged, responses. If it changes at that point, evidence is accruing that the experimental variable is indeed ineffective, and that the prior change was not simply a matter of coincidence. The variable then may be applied to still another response, and so on. The experimenter is attempting to show that he has a reliable experimental variable, in that each behavior changes maximally only when the experimental variable is applied to it.

How many reversals, or how many baselines, make for believability is a problem for the audience. If statistical analysis is applied, the audience must then judge the suitability of the inferential statistic chosen and the propriety of these data for that test. Alternatively, the audience may inspect the data directly and relate them to past experience with similar data and similar procedures. In either case, the judgments required are highly qualitative, and rules cannot always be stated profitably. However, either of the foregoing designs gather data in ways that exemplify the concept of replication, and replication is the essence of believability. At the least, it would seem that an approach to replication is better than no approach at all. This should be especially true for so embryonic a field as behavioral application, the very possibility of which is still occasionally denied.

The preceding discussion has been aimed at the problem of reliability: whether or not a certain procedure was responsible for a corresponding behavioral change. The two general procedures described hardly exhaust the possibilities. Each of them has many variations now seen in practice; and current experience suggests that many more variations are badly needed, if the technology of important behavioral change is to be consistently believable. Given some approach to reliability, there are further analyses of obvious value which can be built upon that base. For example, there is analysis in the sense of simplification and separation of component processes. Often enough, current behavioral procedures are complex, even "shotgun" in their application. When they succeed, they clearly need to be analyzed into their effective components. Thus, a teacher giving M & M's to a child may succeed in changing his behavior as planned. However, she has almost certainly confounded her attention and/or approval with each M & M. Further analysis may be approached by her use of attention alone, the effects of which can be compared to the effects of attention coupled with candies. Whether she will discontinue the M & M's, as in the reversal technique, or apply attention with M & M's to certain behaviors and attention alone to certain others, as in the multiple baseline method, is again the problem in basic reliability discussed above. Another form of analysis is parametric: a demonstration of the effectiveness of different values of some variable in changing behavior. The problem again will be to make such an analysis reliable, and, as before, that might be approached by the repeated alternate use of different values on the same behavior (reversal), or by the application of different values to different groups of responses (multiple baseline). At this stage in the development of applied behavior analysis, primary concern is usually with reliability, rather than with parametric analysis or component analysis.

Technological

"Technological" here means simply that the techniques making up a particular behavioral application are completely identified and described. In this sense, "play therapy" is not a technological description, nor is "social reinforcement." For purposes of application, all the salient ingredients of play therapy must be described as a set of contingencies between child response, therapist response, and play materials, before a statement of technique has been approached. Similarly, all the ingredients of social reinforcement must be specified (stimuli, contingency, and schedule) to qualify as a technological procedure.

The best rule of thumb for evaluating a procedure description as technological is probably to ask whether a typically trained reader could replicate that procedure well enough to produce the same results, given only a reading of the description. This is very much the same criterion applied to procedure descriptions in non-applied research, of course. It needs emphasis, apparently, in that there occasionally exists a less-than-precise stereotype of applied research. Where application is novel, and derived from principles produced through non-applied research, as in current applied behavior analysis, the reverse holds with great urgency.

Especially where the problem is application, procedural descriptions require considerable detail about all possible contingencies of procedure. It is not enough to say what is to be done when the subject makes response R_1; it is essential also whenever possible to say what is to be done if the subject makes the alternative responses, R_2, R_3, etc. For example, one may read that temper tantrums in children are often extinguished by closing the child in his room for the duration of the tantrums plus ten minutes. Unless that procedure description also states what should be done if the child tries to leave the room early, or kicks out the window, or smears feces on the walls, or begins to make strangling sounds, etc., it is not precise technological description.

Conceptual Systems

The field of applied behavior analysis will probably advance best if the published descriptions of its procedures are not only precisely technological, but also strive for relevance to principle. To describe exactly how a preschool teacher will attend to jungle-gym climbing in a child frightened of heights is good technological description; but further to call it a social reinforcement procedure relates it to basic concepts of behavioral development. Similarly, to describe the exact sequence of color changes whereby a child is moved from a color discrimination to a form discrimination is good; to refer also to "fading" and "errorless discrimination" is better. In both cases, the total description is adequate for successful replication by the reader; and it also shows the reader how similar procedures may be derived from basic principles. This can have the effect of making a body of technology into a discipline rather than a collection of tricks. Collections of tricks historically have been difficult to expand systematically, and when they were extensive, difficult to learn and teach.

Effective

If the application of behavioral techniques does not produce large enough effects for practical value, then application has failed. Non-applied research often may be extremely valuable when it produces small but reliable effects,

in that these effects testify to the operation of some variable which in itself
has great theoretical importance. In application, the theoretical importance
of a variable is usually not at issue. Its practical importance, specifically its
power in altering behavior enough to be socially important, is the essential
criterion. Thus, a study which shows that a new classroom technique can
raise the grade level achievements of culturally deprived children from D—
to D is not an obvious example of applied behavior analysis. That same study
might conceivably revolutionize educational theory, but it clearly has not
yet revolutionized education. This is of course a matter of degree; an increase
in those children from D— to C might well be judged an important success
by an audience which thinks that C work is a great deal different than D
work, especially if C students are much less likely to become drop-outs than
D students.

In evaluating whether a given application has produced enough of a
behavioral change to deserve the label, a pertinent question can be, how much
did that behavior need to be changed? Obviously, that is not a scientific
question, but a practical one. Its answer is likely to be supplied by people
who must deal with the behavior. For example, ward personnel may be able
to say that a hospitalized mute schizophrenic trained to use 10 verbal labels
is not much better off in self-help skills than before, but that one with 50
such labels is a great deal more effective. In this case, the opinions of ward
aides may be more relevant than the opinions of psycholinguists.

Generality

A behavioral change may be said to have generality if it proves durable
over time, if it appears in a wide variety of possible environments, or if it
spreads to a wide variety of related behaviors. Thus, the improvement of
articulation in a clinic setting will prove to have generality if it endures into
the future after the clinic visits stop; if the improved articulation is heard at
home, at school, and on dates; or if the articulation of all words, not just the
ones treated, improves. Application means practical improvement in important behaviors; thus, the more general that application, the better, in
many cases. Therapists dealing with the development of heterosexual behavior may well point out there are socially appropriate limits to its generality
once developed; such limitations to generality are usually obvious. That
generality is a valuable characteristic of applied behavior analysis which
should be examined explicitly apparently is not quite that obvious, and is
stated here for emphasis.

That generality is not automatically accomplished whenever behavior
is changed also needs occasional emphasis, especially in the evaluation of
applied behavior analysis. It is sometimes assumed that application has
failed when generalization does not take place in any widespread form. Such
a conclusion has no generality itself. A procedure which is effective in
changing behavior in one setting may perhaps be easily repeated in other

settings, and thus accomplish the generalization sought. Furthermore, it may well prove the case that a given behavior change need be programmed in only a certain number of settings, one after another, perhaps, to accomplish eventually widespread generalization. A child may have 15 techniques for disrupting his parents, for example. The elimination of the most prevalent of these may still leave the remaining 14 intact and in force. The technique may still prove both valuable and fundamental, if when applied to the next four successfully, it also results in the "generalized" loss of the remaining 10. In general, generalization should be programmed, rather than expected or lamented.

Thus, in summary, an applied behavior analysis will make obvious the importance of the behavior changed, its quantitative characteristics, the experimental manipulations which analyze with clarity what was responsible for the change, the technologically exact description of all procedures contributing to that change, the effectiveness of those procedures in making sufficient change for value, and the generality of that change.

REFERENCES

Journal of the Experimental Analysis of Behavior. Bloomington: Society for the Experimental Analysis of Behavior, 1957.

Sidman, Murray. *Tactics of scientific research*. New York: Basic Books, 1960.

Skinner, B. F. *Science and human behavior*. New York: Macmillan, 1953.

Some Ethical Dilemmas Involved in Behavioral and Client-Centered Insight Counseling[1]

Samuel H. Osipow

Counseling psychology has long been concerned with ethical questions regarding counselor-client interactions. Prime among the ethical issues raised have been concerns with client privacy, the maintenance of client autonomy, and the assurance of client freedom from undue professional manipulation. It is entirely appropriate and, given the nature of those individuals generally attracted to the practice of counseling, predictable that these matters should preoccupy the professional conscience. Counselors are usually democratically oriented and highly concerned with individual freedom and self-actualization. They typically respect other human beings and find the thought of one person controlling another's behavior to be repugnant. They are cautious about making the assumption that one individual's weakness and ineffectiveness justifies another person's assumption of control over him "for his own good."

At the same time, counselors often find that the conflict between social and client needs makes ethical procedures hard to clarify, and some ethical questions arise which are difficult to resolve. Questions of privacy are easy: the counselor discusses with his client what can and cannot be disclosed and stands by the decision. Many ethical matters are not so easily managed, however, since they have two or more conflicting but correct (from different vantage points) answers. These more difficult questions are likely to involve the client's openness to or freedom from counselor manipulation. Often, counselors have resolved their doubts by default, avoiding action if possible, apparently in the hope that the issue would work itself out. This has been one of the attractions of insight oriented client-centered counseling approaches. Such counselors are able to indulge their humanistic values through their work with clients, justifying their failure to intervene in the client's behalf or to manipulate his behavior (where counseling technology makes it possible to do so) on the grounds that "the ends do not justify the means." They

[1]Prepared specially for this volume and printed by permission of the author.

75

prefer that the client should be depressed, destroy his marriage, or flunk out of school than have his autonomy violated. Client-centered counseling has justified its passivity on the grounds that significant client growth does not occur as a result of counselor intervention, but rather as a consequence of client understanding. All the counselor appropriately does is to provide the conditions (love, empathy, positive regard, congruence, and transparency) for this understanding and growth to occur.

Where client concerns are identity problems, mild affective disorders, or transient situational reactions, such a strategy with its minimal intervention ethic is easy to tolerate and causes little dissonance for the counselor. But where the distress of the client is more acute, or where the consequences of his difficulty may be enduring (i.e., the stigma of flunking out of college, the aftermath of a broken marriage, the legal consequences of sexual deviation or narcotics use) the counselor may find it increasingly difficult to restrain himself from using what means he has to help his clients avoid their self-destruction. In a sense, life was easier for counselors when they had few potent techniques with which to change behavior. Now, however, there is increasing evidence that behavior change can be fostered directly through the introduction of such techniques as counter-conditioning, situational manipulation, relaxation and desensitization, etc. Once the counselor's potency as a behavioral controller becomes clearly established, the issue can no longer be avoided. The oft mentioned concern about the social consequences of advances in physical science has its parallel in the need for behavioral science to pay attention to the results of its technological advances.

Further compounding the ethical dilemma is the fact that clients are rarely asked their preferences about treatment and outcome, and often when they volunteer such information, their objectives are discounted and ignored as being uninformed. However, it should be noted that it is reasonable to assume that many clients would gladly eschew such goals as autonomy or self-actualization (at least during "treatment," as they do when they consult a physician) in order to be rid of their nagging behavioral discomforts. Would not the failing student welcome a way out of his academic disarray, or the exhibitionist prefer a more acceptable way to satisfy his desires without jeopardizing his other life goals? Do not counselors violate their own humanism and ethics about imposing their will on another when they fail to respond to client needs as directly as their technology permits them to? Is it not wrong for a counselor to assume that the proper goal for counseling is the client's self-actualization no matter how long it takes or what happens otherwise to his life when the client complains of misery in his marriage? Would not the client be justified in being indignant if he knew the counselor was manipulating the interview in order to discuss issues consistent with long range goals when his (the client's) concerns are immediate? Does the client not have even more justification for indignation when payment of fees directly to the counselor is involved? Would the client not be entitled to bring legal action against the counselor if he could demonstrate that the counselor ignored the client's objectives and implicitly imposed his own? The question of manipulation and imposing one's views on another is subtle, and poses a serious dilemma for any counselor.

Are there no answers? Probably no perfect one exists, but some guidelines can be developed. Perhaps the most significant fact to be kept in mind is that what is especially unsavory and unethical about counselor's controlling client behavior, is the counselor's greater potency vis-à-vis the client in the professional situation, and the possibility that he might be tempted to exploit the client in some manner by means of his professional position. It is really against the danger of such exploitation that the client needs the protection that ethical standards can provide.

A second significant factor in the ethical question is the recognition that counselors, in addition to accepting and working toward client goals, also behave in accordance with certain professional objectives. The levels of these professional objectives vary from counselor to counselor as a function of his theoretical orientation, the context or institution in which he works, his society, and his own personal background. Identifying the proper balance between professional and client goals contributes to the ethical dilemma in which the counselor finds himself.

At least two professional practices, if instituted, might reduce some of the problems involved in client protection from poor practice and undue counselor manipulation. The first is tied to counseling theory, the second to institutional practice. The clear specification of the goals of counseling with any particular client could, if routinely practiced, go a long way toward the resolution of the problem of client and counselor working toward different ends, each set of objectives seen as legitimate from their respective points of view. These objectives need not necessarily be stated in behavioral terms (though my bias would be to do so) but could range from broad goals (such as clarification of the self-concept, improvement of self-esteem, and fostering of empathy in the client), all the way to specific and concrete behaviors (such as an increased frequency of particular study responses, reduction in the frequency of aggressive interpersonal remarks, etc.). Were an early interview devoted to questions of middle and long range counseling objectives, much of the ethical dilemma would dissolve. Other professions do not exercise the "right" to impose their views and objectives on their clientele without permission and neither should counseling. At the same time, the *choice of method* used to attain goals, once agreed upon, does legitimately remain in the province of the professional, since, presumably, he is the one who is the expert in such matters.

A second procedure which could protect clients, lies in a greater willingness on the part of counselors to open their practices to professional scrutiny. This could be accomplished in a number of ways. Building in post-doctoral supervision requirements to licensing or certification laws, encouraging colleague supervision, or the creation of case review boards which would meet regularly and judge the *ethical* practices of their peers, would each be ways to monitor ethical behavior. For example, if the review boards were implemented, they might judge randomly selected cases or they might concern themselves only with cases brought to their attention as a result of some complaint or undesirable outcome. The boards themselves could either be a function of state or local professional associations, state licensing boards, or groups such as the American Board of Examiners in Professional Psychology. Such a move would contribute to greater public respect for psychological practice, as well as improve its quality, since as professional practice now stands in most states, psychologists work in private, and are often responsible to no one but themselves. How tempting it might be to the unscrupulous practitioner to dismiss questions raised about his professional practices as the psychotic ramblings of a former client.

In summary, it has been suggested that two contrasting kinds of ethical problems exist for counselors. The behavioral counselor runs the risk of succumbing to the temptation of excessively controlling the life of his client. Review boards such as were suggested might control that problem. At the same time, insight focused counselors run the risk of ignoring client goals and subtly imposing their own objectives on their clients. The regular practice of discussing case objectives with clients early in counseling might work to reduce the possibility of abuse in that quarter.

PART II

Research in Behavioral Counseling

The research reported in this section represents attempts to investigate the effectiveness of behavioral counseling. The first article (Ivey *et al.*, 1968), really a series of studies, explores the use of micro counseling training procedures with beginning counselors. The next two investigations (Paul, 1967; Lazarus, 1966) focus on counseling outcome and attempt to compare the effectiveness of different counseling approaches. The following three studies (Ryan & Krumboltz, 1964; Krumboltz & Thoresen, 1964; Allen *et al.*, 1967) attempt to investigate the effectiveness of reinforcement counseling. The final two articles (Katahn *et al.*, 1966; Suinn, 1967) focus on the treatment of test-anxiety using a behavioral counseling approach.

The first study by Ivey, Normington, Miller, Morrill, and Haase investigated the effects of microcounseling training procedures with beginning counselors. Microcounseling is a video method of training counselors in basic skills of counseling within a brief period of time. The major purpose of microcounseling is to provide prepracticum training for beginning counselors. The focus of the research was concerned with three different skills: attending behavior, reflection of feeling, and summarization of feeling. According to the authors, attending behavior involves being with the client both physically and verbally and reinforcing the client for being himself. Reflection of feeling is viewed as selectively attending to the emotional aspects of the client's responses and reinforcing only certain responses. Summarization of feeling involves the first two skills, but in addition requires the counselor to integrate and discuss common elements in diverse client responses. The authors found attending behavior to be central to all three of the studies. In general, the studies suggest that attending behavior and its related concepts of reflection and summarization of feeling may be described in behavioral terms meaningful to beginning counselors.

The next two articles attempt to study counseling effectiveness by comparing different therapeutic approaches. The major purposes of the Paul article were (a) to determine the effects of the different treatments from pre-treatment to a 2-year follow-up and (b) to investigate the relative stability of improvement from the 6-week follow-up (Paul, 1966) to the 2-year follow-up. A test battery assessing treatment effects was readministered to subjects previously assessed before treatment, at a 6-week follow-up, and at a 2-year follow-up. The groups included in the study had individually received systematic desensitization, insight-oriented psychotherapy, attention-placebo treatment or no treatment. The test battery included personality and anxiety scales (IPAT Anxiety Scale, Pittsburgh Social Extroversion-Introversion and Emotionality Scales, Interpersonal Anxiety Scales of the S-R Inventory of Anxiousness, and a scale of specific anxiety in a referenced speech performance). For the 2-year follow-up additional test data were collected in order to obtain the relevant frequency data. In general, the findings showed the relative gains in treatment effects found in the 6-week follow-up to be maintained over the 2-year follow-up. The subjects in the systematic desensitization group continued to show greater positive treatment effects than any other group. The insight-oriented psychotherapy group and the attention-placebo group both showed greater treatment effects than the un-treated control group. This type of study represents research likely to lead to development of a basis for differential treatment in counseling. Some problem categories may respond more effectively to certain specific treatments.

Lazarus investigated the relative effectiveness of behavior rehearsal compared to other treatments. The behavior reversal procedure serves to replace inadequate social responses with effective behavior patterns. The client practices the desired responses under the supervision of the counselor. The counselor plays the role of someone to whom the client frequently reacts with excessive anxiety or vice-versa. Behavior rehearsal is frequently employed with clients lacking in assertive responses. In the Lazarus study subjects received one of the following individual treatments: reflection-interpretation, direct advice, or behavior rehearsal. Four 30-minute sessions were devoted to each treatment condition. If there was no evidence of change within one month, the treatment was regarded as having failed. The criterion for success was objective evidence that the client was behaving adaptively in the previously defined problem area. The findings suggest that behavior rehearsal is more effective in resolving specific social and interpersonal problems than the other two procedures.

The next group of three studies examined the effectiveness of "reinforcement counseling." The Ryan and Krumboltz study focuses on the degree to which reinforcement counseling increased client decision-making and deliberation responses. The authors were also interested in the problem of generalization. Three treatment groups were used in the study. In the first group, decision responses were reinforced, in the second group, deliberation responses were reinforced, while in the control group neither decision nor deliberation responses were reinforced. During a 20-minute semi-structured interview counselors reinforced decision and deliberation responses. The transfer of the behavior was studied using a projective-type story completion task. The findings showed that counselor reinforcement of decision and deliberation responses increased the frequency of reinforced responses. In addition, the decision-making behavior was found to generalize to a non-counseling setting. Significantly, none of the subjects reported awareness of the response-reinforcement contingency.

The Krumboltz and Thoresen article investigates the effect of behavioral counseling in individual and group settings on information-seeking behavior. The task was to determine which behavior change technique would most effectively promote independent information-seeking behavior of students. The contrasting techniques used in the study were termed "reinforcement counseling" and "model-reinforcement counseling." The subjects were assigned to individual and group counseling settings in which three treatments were administered. In the individual and group reinforcement counseling groups verbal information-seeking behaviors were reinforced. In the model-reinforcement counseling groups a tape-recorded model interview was shown followed by reinforcement counseling. In the control film discussion groups a film was shown followed by a discussion. An inactive control group and a reserve pool of *Ss* received no treatment. The results showed that the model reinforcement and reinforcement counseling produced more external information-seeking behavior than control procedures. In general, group and individual settings were about equally effective.

The Allen, Henke, Harris, Baer and Reynolds investigation attempts to determine if systematic social reinforcement could effectively reduce the hyperactivity of a child by increasing the duration of the child's attending behavior. Attending behavior was defined as attention span, or the length of time the child persisted in one activity. The subject, James, a $4\frac{1}{2}$-year-old boy, was observed while moving from one play activity to another. The procedure for increasing the duration of time spent in any activity involved adult social reinforcement after James had remained with a single activity for one continuous minute. After this criterion had been met teachers emitted attention and approval responses for as long as James remained with the activity. The frequency of activity changes decreased within seven days. The reversal stage of this study reinstated the hyperactive behavior. When the social reinforcement was re-introduced, a decrease in the frequency of activity changes could again be observed. These data support the hypothesis that attending behavior can be effected by adult social reinforcement.

The final pair of studies focus on the behavioral treatment of test anxiety. The Katahn, Strenger, and Cherry study combined systematic desensitization and behavior-oriented discussion to treat test anxiety. The goal of the treatment group was to reduce behaviors which are maladaptive in the academic environment. The test-anxious students in the treatment group received group counseling and behavior therapy. Systematic desensitization was implemented to bring the students' anxiety under control and counseling was used to help the students develop academic skills. The treated group was compared to the volunteer controls and the non-volunteer controls on the variable of grade-point average and test anxiety. The results showed an increase in grade-point average for the treated group and a decrease in Test Anxiety Scale scores. In general, the students reported the counseling procedure (suggestion and advice) to have been the more important variable in effecting anxiety and academic performance.

Suinn investigates the effect of group and individual treatment (desensitization) on test-anxious subjects. Subjects in the treated group were involved in three group meetings and several individual sessions. The subjects in the control group were seen in a group in which they responded to the three scales. Five weeks later they reconvened for retesting. Subjects in the treatment group were tested before and immediately after treatment was completed. The three scales used in this study were the Suinn Test Anxiety Behavioral Scale, Sarason Test Anxiety Scale, and the Fear Survey Schedule. An analysis of the variation between mean score differences showed that the treated subjects' decreases on all scales were greater than the decreases shown by the control subjects. The results suggest that a combination of group and individual desensitization treatment is use fulin the treatment of test anxiety.

These studies examining the effectiveness of behavioral counseling indicate the positive value of the counseling treatment. The fact that the studies explore different facets of the counseling effectiveness problem is encouraging. The age-old criterion problem in the evaluation of counseling outcome was coped with by the use of a behavioral criterion in six of the studies. Behavior change was reported by the client or judged by an external observer(s). Three of the studies used an external criterion that measured changes that may have occurred as a consequence of counseling. In general, the research studies cited in this section show improved methods and increased sophistication in investigating the problem of counseling effectiveness.

The research in this section also suggests that behavioral techniques can be useful in the process of counselor training. In addition, findings suggest that behavioral counseling is as effective, if not more effective, than insight-oriented approaches. Furthermore, modeling and reinforcement were found to be effective and significant concepts in behavioral counseling.

Microcounseling and Attending Behavior: An Approach to Prepracticum Counselor Training[1]

**Allen E. Ivey, Cheryl J. Normington, C. Dean Miller,
Weston H. Morrill, and Richard F. Haase**

Teaching beginning counselors and therapists "how to counsel" is one of the more complex and challenging issues facing counseling psychology (Krumboltz, 1967; Matarazzo, Wiens, & Saslow, 1966; Wrenn, 1962). Most would agree that counselor training has not generally been efficient or economical of human resources. Beginning counselors frequently find their first interviews confusing. They often have trouble defining their own role in the interview and in simply getting the client "to talk."

This series of studies proposes that brief training, focused on the specific skills of counseling, can be useful in counselor education. A microcounseling approach is used which is based on the research of Allen and his associates (1967), who have used similar concepts of microteaching in teacher training. Microcounseling is a scaled-down sample of counseling, in which beginning counselors talk with volunteer "clients" during brief 5-minute counseling sessions which are video recorded. These scaled-down sessions focus on specific counseling skills or behavior. Microcounseling provides an opportunity for those who are preparing to counsel to obtain a liberal amount of practice without endangering clients. While microcounseling has other possible purposes and uses, its principal aim is to provide prepracticum training and thus, to bridge the gap between classroom theory and actual practice.

Recently there have been extensive efforts to train counselors in new models and in a briefer period of time. Lay counselors have been trained and research suggests that their work is effective (Beck, Kantor, & Gelineau, 1963; Poser, 1966; Rioch, Elkes, Flint, Usdansky, Newman, & Silber, 1963). Other studies (Carkhuff & Truax, 1965a, 1965b; Truax & Carkhuff, 1967) have indicated that trainees (graduate students in clinical psychology and lay personnel) can be brought to function at levels of effective therapy commensurate to more experienced therapists in less than 100 hours of

[1]Reprinted from the *Journal of Counseling Psychology*, *Monograph Supplement* 1968, *15*, 1-12, with the permission of the American Psychological Association and the authors.

training. Kagan, Krathwohl, and Farquhar (1965), through their inter-personal process recall, have demonstrated the value of video tape to aid in the understanding of counseling. They have further shown that video training can be useful in counselor education.

This research studies the effects of microcounseling training procedures upon three groups of beginning counselors. Three different skills, "attending behavior," reflection of feeling, and summarization of feeling, were the focus of research. Central to all studies was attending behavior which is the counseling skill of attending or listening to a client both verbally and non-verbally. These studies suggest that attending behavior and its related con-cepts of reflection and summarization of feeling may be described in be-havioral terms meaningful to beginning counselors. If this is so, it may be feasible to use a microcounseling framework to teach counselor trainees the basic skills of counseling quickly and effectively.

STUDY 1

Attending Behavior: A Basic Skill of Counseling

An important aspect of establishing a relationship with the client is being aware of, and responsive to, the communications of that individual, and communicating this attentiveness. The communication of attentiveness is seen as a potent reinforcer in counselor-client interaction, as well as playing an important role in the initial establishment of a relationship. Kennedy and Thompson (1967) and Krumboltz, Varenhorst, and Thoresen (1967) have explored this concept in a preliminary manner.

The skill focused on in the first study in this series is one in which the counselor attempts to be attentive, and communicate his attentiveness to the client. Skinner (1953) has noted that the "observer attends to the stimulus and thereby controls it (p. 122)." It is possible to describe attention as controlling the interaction between counselor and client. The counselor could be con-sidered to be conditioned to pay attention to the client because he is rein-forced by the supervisor (and the client) for such behavior. The counselor, by attending to the client, controls the client's behavior in the interview. In effect, this study was intended to teach counselors how to reinforce their clients by paying attention.

Three central aspects of attending behavior have been identified which include both nonverbal and verbal components. The first of these is defined as eye contact, in which the counselor simply looks at the client. Secondly, postural position, movements, and gestures communicate attentiveness. Verbal following behavior represents the counselor's responding to the last comment or some preceding comment of the client without introducing new data. Most would agree that one of the basic tasks of any counselor super-visor is to help the neophyte counselor to relax, pay attention to the client, and refrain from jumping from topic to topic.

This first study applied the techniques of microcounseling to the training in an elementary skill of counseling—attending behavior—of a group of beginning counselors. The prediction was that the training procedure would increase counselor attentiveness and would produce more client satisfaction.

Method

Subjects. The *Ss* of this study were 38 dormitory counselors divided randomly into an experimental and a control group. The "clients" were 38 paid volunteer students who were randomly assigned to counselors.

Microcounseling model. The experimental group went through the following training procedure: (*a*) A 5-minute diagnostic interview was video taped in which counselors-in-training were told to, "Go in and talk with this student; get to know him." (*b*) Trainees next read the "Attending Behavior Manual" which described the basic components of attending behavior. (*c*) Video models of attending behavior as exhibited by effective and less effective counselors were presented, coupled with discussion of the model by the training supervisor. (*d*) The trainee was shown his initial interview and was asked to identify specific instances of attending and nonattending. The supervisor discussed attending behavior concepts with the trainee during the viewing of the first interview. (*e*) The trainee and supervisor reviewed the procedures of attending behavior together. It may be observed that the training procedures involved cue discrimination in the form of video models (Bandura & Walters, 1963), written materials, supervisor's comments, and operant techniques whereby appropriate counselor behavior was rewarded by the supervisor. It was observed that an important part of the training procedure involved the quality of the training relationship with the supervisor. (*f*) As a test, the trainee then returned to the video-taping room and recounseled the same client for 5 minutes. The entire microcounseling teaching unit took approximately 1 hour.

The control group experienced only Steps *a* and *f* of the preceding model. They waited alone in the video-taping room until their second microcounseling session, and occupied themselves by reading textbooks which they had with them or by drinking a coke supplied by *Es*.

It should be observed that the 5-minute sessions on video tape presented rather dramatic evidence of the similarity between this experience and regular counselor practice. Microcounseling breaks counseling into small units and makes possible immediate direct feedback to the trainee, thus maximally facilitating behavior change. Via video tape, a picture of counseling and interpersonal style readily appears and is highly subject to direct observation and analysis.

Instrumentation and scoring of dependent variables. Three methods of evaluating this study were utilized. A scale to assess attending behavior was developed from observation of the video-taped interview and found to have an average interrater reliability over seven raters of .843. The tapes from the interviews were randomly arranged and presented to two raters who rated the television tape on eye contact, posture, and movements and gestures.

A typescript of all interviews was completed and rated for verbal attending behavior by two trained raters. If a counselor comment followed the verbal comments of the client, it was scored "plus." If it did not follow, it was scored "minus." If disagreement between the two raters occurred, the statement was not used. Of 1,904 ratings, the two raters disagreed on only 114, thus illustrating consistent agreement as to verbal attending behavior. Each counselor was scored for the percentage of verbal attending behavior in each session held with a client.

The clients completed a semantic differential form, the Counselor Effectiveness scale (Ivey, Miller, Morrill, & Normington, 1967), following each interview with their counselor. This 25 item form was developed by having two graduate classes in counseling rate video-taped samples of effective and ineffective counseling on 93 pairs of adjectives presented in a semantic differential format. Means were computed on each of the items and those which best separated effective from ineffective counseling were selected for use. Adequate reliability and validity were demonstrated. Analysis of covariance was employed to test for the significance of treatment differences between each of the groups.

Results

Eye contact was the only area where significant differences were noted between experimental and control groups on direct ratings of the video tapes. Table 1 reveals that nonsignificant differences were found between the two groups on posture and counselor movements and gestures.

Judges rated the experimental group significantly higher on their percentage of following behavior. An increase of more than 10% in verbal following may be noted for the experimental group in their ability to attend to the client.

Clients in both experimental and control groups tended to rate their counselors higher following the second microcounseling session than following the first session. However, the experimental group showed a significantly larger improvement than did controls.

Discussion

From the first study, it appears clear that the microcounseling paradigm is a workable framework for teaching basic skills of counseling. It has been possible to identify attending behavior as a relevant counseling skill and to demonstrate that it can be taught to beginning counselors. The training paradigm appears to be economical of staff time and to involve the beginning counselor fully in his own training. Further, attending behavior would appear

TABLE 1

Analysis of Covariance of Judges' Ratings of Attending Behavior and Clients' Ratings of Counselor Effectiveness

Rating	M Interview 1	M Interview 2	Adjusted	Fa
Eye contact				
Experimental	4.16	4.66	4.70	5.30*
Control	4.40	4.34	4.30	
Posture				
Experimental	4.00	4.16	4.15	0.26
Control	3.92	4.10	4.11	
Movement and gestures				
Experimental	3.84	3.87	3.83	0.25
Control	3.61	3.69	3.72	
% of following behavior				
Experimental	85.44	96.31	96.68	6.17*
Control	87.25	89.62	89.25	
Counselor Effectiveness scale				
Experimental	135.11	147.42	147.94	4.43*
Control	136.68	140.37	139.85	

Note: The loss of one S resulted in a total of 36 degrees of freedom.
df $= 1/35$ $p < .05$

to be a helpful skill to the neophyte counselor facing his first practicum interviews.

Basic to the concept of attending behavior appear to be two dimensions, that of maintaining eye contact with the client and that of verbally following what the client has said without introducing new or irrelevant material. While measures of counselor posture and movements and gestures did not achieve statistical significance, it is believed that these are still relevant components of attending behavior. Reviewing the first interview tapes revealed that all but one or two of the counselors-in-training were reasonably relaxed initially. This might well account for the lack of significant change in these areas. However, many trainees found it difficult in their first interview to look at their clients, and kept trying to think of "what should I say next" instead of simply attending to the client.

Client responses on the Counselor Effectiveness scale indicated that the counselors trained in attending behavior were rated as being more effective. It does seem a truism that we tend to favor those who pay attention to us. Much of the beginning counselor supervision in practicum is centered around getting the counselor to listen to his client. The microcounseling framework appears to be a technique by which the supervising counselor can more rapidly introduce his trainee into the basic developmental skills of counseling.

Trainee and client word counts were computed for the first and second interviews. It was found that the experimental group trainees talked 46.85%

of the time in the first interview and 33.03% of the time in the second. Comparable figures for the control group were 42.66% and 37.64%. While reducing verbal participation in the trainee was not a goal of this study, these figures seem to support the validity of the attending-behavior concepts in this study. Matarazzo, Wiens, and Saslow (1966) have suggested that it should be possible to teach counselors an optimum amount of participation in the counseling session.

Skinner (1953) considers attention a generalized reinforcer. He points out:

> The attention of people is reinforcing because it is a necessary condition for other reinforcements from them. In general, only people who are attending to us reinforce our behavior. The attention of someone who is particularly likely to supply reinforcement—a parent, a teacher, or a loved one—is an especially good generalized reinforcer and sets up especially strong attention-getting behavior (p. 78).

It would seem that this study has demonstrated that it is possible to teach beginning counselors to use the reinforcer of attention. Further, it appears that the clients who have been "attended to" tend to rate their counselors higher.

The training of the counselors in this skill of reinforcement, however, represented a more complex process than reward of desired counselor behavior. Cue discrimination through the presentation of video models, training materials, and counselor supervisor comments were also important. In short, the training process was designed to model the behavior and then reinforce the behavior once it had occurred.

It should be mentioned that trainees found the experience a vital and meaningful one for them. They felt they had learned a great deal which they would immediately apply in their counseling setting in the dormitories. Several mentioned that the concepts of attending behavior would help them in their interpersonal relationships. "I spend too much time thinking about what I should say instead of simply listening to the other person," several trainees commented. Another stated, "I could have been giving so much more to the students I work with . . . I had been worrying about myself too much!" These and other related comments lead one to hypothesize that attending behavior has, perhaps, implications beyond the immediate counseling situation.

Some specific limitations to this study should be considered. While paid clients appeared to operate very similarly to regular clients in the 5-minute interviews, it should be noted that this situation is not typical of counseling interviews. Further study to determine the generalizability of learning in the microcounseling setting to actual counseling is required. Attending behavior as a generalized reinforcer in counseling is a relatively new concept, and the utility of this concept needs more demonstration.

STUDY 2

Training Counselors in Reflection of Feeling

Beginning counselors must learn the techniques of effective interpersonal relationships in the counseling interview. Especially important are skills such as empathic understanding and communication of nonpossessive warmth and genuineness.

The purpose of this investigation was to study further the effects of a microcounseling training program upon beginning, prepracticum counselors. One specific counselor skill, that of accurate reflection of feelings, was the focus of this training program. This skill was chosen because of the important part it can play in communicating to the client that "I am with you . . . I can accurately sense the world as you are feeling and perceiving it." This communication is a communication of empathic understanding, a key aspect of an effective interpersonal relationship.

Skinner (1953) suggests that attention is not sufficient in itself as a reinforcer of human beings. He indicates that approval is another generalized reinforcer which may be used to shape the behavior of others. "Another person is likely to reinforce only that part of one's behavior of which he approves, and any sign of his approval becomes reinforcing in its own right (p. 78)." It seems possible that approval of a client's behavior represents selectively attending to only certain aspects of that behavior. The more complex skill of reflection of feeling may represent a focused attending in which the counselor selectively attends to one certain aspect or aspects of the counseling interaction. Truax (1966) also has considered nondirective counseling techniques within a reinforcement framework.

The training paradigm used, microcounseling, involved training of beginning counselors through cue discrimination and the application of reinforcement by supervisors to emitted counselor behavior. An increase in accurate reflection of feeling responses by counselors over trials was predicted.

Method

Subjects. Eleven beginning counselors from the department of psychology, counseling, and guidance at Colorado State College, Greeley, served as *Ss* in this experiment. These *Ss* had no previous counseling experience, and could be considered naïve *Ss*. The "clients" were 11 paid volunteer students from Colorado State University, Fort Collins, who were randomly assigned to counselors.

Microcounseling model. The beginning counselors participated in the following training program: (*a*) A 5-minute initial interview was video taped in which the counselor-in-training was instructed as follows: "The volunteer student whom you will counsel has been instructed to talk about anything that is meaningful to him. During the first brief session, proceed in any way that you would like." Instruction to the "client" was: "You will have three short sessions with a counselor. During these sessions, talk about anything that is meaningful to you, such as your interests, your choice of major, some aspect of yourself, etc." The initial session served to establish a base line of interview performance for each trainee, and allowed the beginning counselor time to become accustomed to the video-tape equipment and recording room. (*b*) Trainees next read the "Reflection of Feeling Manual," and discussed the nature of the skill with a supervisor. (*c*) Video models of reflection of feeling, as portrayed by effective and less-effective counselors were presented, coupled with discussion of the models by the supervisor. (*d*) The trainee was shown his initial interview and was asked to identify instances of reflection of feeling, or instances where the skill might have been utilized. Use of the skill was reinforced by the supervisor, through such comments as, "Yes, that's it!" "Good," etc. (*e*) A 3-minute role-play practice session was video taped, in which an experienced counselor, as client, communicated feeling freely, thus providing ample opportunity for the trainee to practice reflection of feeling. (*f*) Trainee, supervisor, and role player (experienced counselor) viewed the role-playing tape, noting instances of accurate reflection of feeling, and instances where accuracy might be improved. Again, use of the skill was reinforced by the supervisor through verbal comment. (*g*) The trainee conducted a second interview (5 minutes) with the original client,

TABLE 2

Trend Analysis of Mean External Judges' Rating of Counselor's Ability to Accurately Reflect Feeling

Source	df	MS	F	1	Role play$_a$	Trial M 2	3
Trials (A)	2	31.12	23.58**	1.00	2.90	4.00	3.82
Subjects (counselors) (B)	10	3.32	2.52*				
A X B	20	1.32					
Total	32						
Linear components	1	43.68	33.09**				

$_a$Not included in analysis.
*p < .05   **p < .001

with instructions to practice reflecting the feelings being communicated by the client. (*h*) Trainee and supervisor viewed the tape and engaged in further analysis of the trainee's use of the skill. Reinforcement for the trainee's use of the skill was provided by the supervisor. (*i*) The trainee conducted a final 5-minute video-taped interview, again with the original client, and again with instructions to reflect the feelings being communicated. (*j*) The final tape was viewed and discussed by trainee and supervisor. The entire procedure for each trainee was completed within a 2-hour time block.

Instrumentation and scoring of dependent variables. Three techniques of evaluation were utilized in this study. The *Ss'* video-taped interviews were arranged in random order, and then were rated by two external judges on a rating scale (adapted from Truax & Carkhuff, 1967) for accurate reflection of feeling. The two judges were advanced egraduate students in counseling psychology, one with 3 years of experience in counseling and the second with 2 years of experience. Interjudge reliability for these judges was computed and yielded a Pearson product-moment coefficient of .64. Test-retest reliability for the scale, over a 2-week period, was computed (N = 27) and yielded a Pearson product-moment coefficient of .92.

Secondly, at the conclusion of each of the 5-minute sessions, the client rated his counselor trainee on a semantic differential scale, the Counselor Effectiveness scale (Ivey, Miller, Morrill, & Normington, 1967), and also rated the counselor trainee on a relationship questionnaire adapted from Truax and Carkhuff (1967). The counselor completed the semantic differential scale, labeled the Self-Concept scale and the rating scale for accurate reflection of feelings at the conclusion of each of the 5-minute sessions.

A trend analysis design was used to analyze data gathered in this study. The role-playing session was not included in the analysis, since the interview was identifiable to the external judges as they rated the tapes. Trends over three trials were analyzed for each of the criterion measures included in this study.

Results

Table 2 reveals an increase in ratings of accurate reflection of feeling by external judges from first to later interviews. We find a .001 level of significance for the three trials and for linearity.

Tables 3 and 4 illustrate that client ratings of counselor effectiveness and

TABLE 3

Trend Analysis of Counselor Effectiveness as Rated by the Client

Source	df	MS	F	Trial M		
				1	2	3
Trials (A)	2	1716.77	12.76**	125.73	140.64	150.55
Subjects (student volunteers) (B)	10	697.20	5.18*			
A X B	20	134.57				
Total	32					
Linear components	1	3387.68	25.17**			

*p < .01   **p < .001

counselor ability to establish and maintain relationship increased significantly over trials. The linear trends across trials are highly significant.

Tables 5 and 6 portray the counselors' evaluation of their own performance. Again, findings of linear increase over trials may be noted.

Discussion

Support for the hypothesis of this study has been indicated. The trend analysis design reveals that the counselor trainees significantly improved in their ability to reflect feeling over trials in a positive linear fashion. This would lead one to suggest that accurate reflection of feeling is a discreet, identifiable skill, which can be taught to beginning counselors quickly and effectively, via the microcounseling paradigm.

It appears that it is possible to teach the skill of accurate reflection of feeling within a short 2-hour period. Clinical evidence of the validity of the study comes from viewing the tapes of individual counselor trainees over the training period. One notes dramatic changes in trainee behavior. As Mc-

TABLE 4

Trend Analysis of Counselor's Ability to Establish and Maintain Relationship as Rated by the Client

Source	df	MS	F	Trial M		
				1	2	3
Trials (A)	2	85.49	4.00*	22.36	24.09	27.82
Subjects (student volunteers) (B)	10	108.81	5.10**			
A X B	20	21.35				
Total	32					
Linear components	1	163.64	7.66**			

*p < .05   **p < .01

TABLE 5

Trend Analysis of Counselor Self-Concept

Source	df	MS	F	Trial M		
				1	2	3
Trials (A)	2	782.02	8.50*	124.45	130.90	141.18
Subjects (counselors) (B)	10	646.82	7.02**			
A X B	20	92.15				
Total	32					
Linear components	1	1538.91	16.70**			

*p < .01   **p < .001

Luhan (1964) has observed, "The media is the message." In the case of this study, direct viewing of video tapes might well provide the strongest message as to the value of the microcounseling framework. Additional supporting clinical data come from discussion of the study with trainees after they had completed the 2-hour time block. They seemed highly enthusiastic about the changes they had observed in themselves and expressed considerably more faith in themselves as future counselors.

Evidence of the usefulness of the skill of accurate reflection of feeling appears in the client's ratings of the counselor following each session.

TABLE 6

Trend Analysis of Counselor's Own Rating of Ability to Accurately Reflect Feeling

Source	df	MS	F	Trial M		
				1	2	3
Trials (A)	2	21.94	13.63**	3.09	5.09	5.82
Subjects (counselors) (B)	10	7.93	4.93*			
A X B	20	1.61				
Total	32					
Linear components	1	40.91	25.41**			

*p < .01   **p < .001

Counselors were rated as more effective and more understanding after each succeeding session. Similarly, the counselor trainee rated himself more highly after each session. These data, of course are highly susceptible to halo effect and improved ratings could be simply the result of two individuals knowing one another better and feeling more comfortable. In this regard, this study could be criticized for lack of a control group. In Study 1, on attending behavior, it was found that control group clients tended to rate their counselors slightly higher after a second session, but this trend was not statistically significant. Data from this previous study may lend credence to the present significant findings.

Major support of the study lies in the evaluations of the external judges, who rated the randomly presented tapes of all counselors on accurate reflection of feeling. There is consistency in findings, in that independent judges, as well as clients and counselors, saw significant improvement in counselor behavior from first to later trials. This study can be viewed as providing further support to hypotheses of Truax and Carkhuff (1967) as to the feasibility of brief counselor training focused upon interpersonal skills, and the usefulness of skills such as accurate reflection of feeling.

STUDY 3

Training Counselors in Summarization of Feeling

This study, the third in the microcounseling series, is concerned with the skill of accurate summarization of feelings. This skill involves attending to the client, accurately sensing the feelings which are being expressed, and integrating meaningfully the many responses of the person. Through periodic summarizations, one communicates to the person that "I understand what you have been saying, and can sense the world as you are feeling and perceiving it." Accurate summarization of feeling is seen as an extension of attending behavior and reflection of feeling. However, in this case, the counselor is attending to a broader class of client response and must have the skill to bring together seemingly diverse elements into a meaningful Gestalt.

The training paradigm used, microcounseling, once again involved training of beginning counselors through cue discrimination, modeling techniques, video feedback, and the application of reinforcement by supervisors to emitted counselor behavior. An increase in accurate summarization of feeling responses by counselors over trials was predicted.

Method

Subjects. Ten beginning counselors from the department of psychology, counseling, and guidance at Colorado State College, Greeley, served as *Ss* in this experiment. These *Ss* had no previous counseling experience, and no previous experience in earlier research studies. The "clients" were 10 paid volunteer students from Colorado State University, Fort Collins, who were randomly assigned to counselors.

Microcounseling model. The beginning counselors participated in a training model similar to that of the reflection of feeling study. A "Summarization of Feeling Manual" was substituted for the one on the reflection of feeling and video models provided centered around concepts of summarization.

Instrumentation and scoring of dependent variables. Three techniques of evaluation were utilized in this study. The *Ss'* video-taped interviews were arranged in random order, and then were rated by two external judges on a rating scale (adapted from Truax and Carkhuff, 1967, and the previous study on the reflection of feeling) for accurate summarization of feeling. The two judges were advanced graduate students in counseling psychology, both of whom had had at least 1 year of experience as a counselor in a university counseling center. Neither of the judges had participated in the rating of earlier studies. Interjudge reliability for these judges was computed and yielded a Pearson product-moment coefficient of .75.

Secondly, at the conclusion of each interview, the client rated his counselor trainee on a semantic differential scale, the Counselor Effectiveness scale (Ivey, Miller, Morrill, & Normington, 1967), and also rated the counselor trainee on a relationship questionnaire adapted from Truax and Carkhuff (1967). Finally, the counselor completed the semantic differential scale, labeled the Self-Concept scale and the rating scale for accurate summarization of feeling.

A trend analysis design was used to analyze data gathered in this study. The role-playing session was not included in the analysis, since the interview was identifiable to the external judges as they rated the tapes. Trends over three trials were analyzed for each of the criterion measures included in this study.

TABLE 7

Trend Analysis of Mean External Judges' Rating of Counselor's Ability to Accurately Summarize Feeling

Source	df	MS	F		Trial M		
				1	Role play[a]	*2*	*3*
Trials (A)	2	38.44	16.86**	2.00	5.60	4.30	5.30
Subjects (B)	9	8.11	3.56*				
A X B	18	2.28					
Total	29						
Linear component	1	76.05	33.36**				

[a]Not included in analysis.
*p < .05 **p < .001

Results

Table 7 reveals an increase in ratings of accurate summarization of feeling by external judges from first to later interviews. We find a .001 level of significance for the three trials and for linearity.

TABLE 8

Trend Analysis of Counselor Effectiveness as Rated by the Client

Source	df	MS	F	Trial M		
				1	*2*	*3*
Trials (A)	2	1226.30	4.88*	110.64	120.27	131.73
Subjects (B)	10	250.28	.995			
A X B	20	251.51				
Total	32					
Linear component	1	2446.55	9.73**			

*p < .05 **p < .01

Tables 8 and 9 illustrate that client ratings of counselor effectiveness and counselor ability to establish and maintain relationship increased significantly over trials. The linear trends across trials are highly significant.

Tables 10 and 11 portray the counselors' evaluation of their own performance. Again, findings of linear increases over trials may be noted.

TABLE 9

Trend Analysis of Counselor's Ability to Establish and Maintain Relationship as Rated by the Client

Source	df	MS	F	Trial M		
				1	2	3
Trials (A)	2	116.76	22.76*	17.09	18.56	23.36
Subjects (B)	10	87.19	16.99*			
A X B	20	5.126				
Total	32					
Linear component	1	229.14	44.67			

*p < .001

Discussion

The consistent pattern of statistical significance suggests confirmation of the hypotheses of this study. Counselor trainees significantly improved their ability to summarize feeling over trials in a positive linear fashion. Summarization of feeling appears to be a discreet, identifiable skill, which can be taught beginning counselors quickly and effectively, via the microcounseling paradigm.

Again, the ratings of judges who viewed the randomly presented tapes provides the major support of this study. Client ratings of counselor effectiveness were also significantly improved, but these findings are confounded by the possible effects of the client simply "knowing" the counselor better at the time of the later ratings.

TABLE 10

Trend Analysis of Counselor Self-Concept

Source	df	MS	F	Trial M		
				1	2	3
Trials (A)	2	1997.85	19.54*	116.36	135.00	142.56
Subjects (B)	10	1542.03	15.08*			
A X B	20	102.25				
Total	32					
Linear component	1	3770.18	36.87*			

*p < .001

TABLE 11

Trend Analysis of Counselor's Own Rating of Ability to Accurately Summarize Feeling

Source	df	MS	F	Trial M		
				1	2	3
Trials (A)	2	24.58	22.76*	4.27	6.56	7.09
Subjects (B)	10	7.23	6.69*			
A X B	20	1.08				
Total	32					
Linear component	1	43.68	40.44*			

*p < .001

As might be expected, the counselors' ratings of their ability to accurately summarize feeling, and their self-concept ratings improved significantly. Again, these ratings are highly subject to individual bias and halo effect, but they do indicate that the counselors felt they had improved, and few would deny that counselor confidence is an important variable in counseling success. Direct viewing of the video tapes of the counselors provides dramatic and convincing evidence of the validity and power of the microcounseling procedure. The counselors were pleased and impressed with the changes they saw in themselves and this may in part explain the markedly improved self-ratings.

INTEGRATED DISCUSSION OF THE THREE STUDIES

Attending behavior, reflection of feeling, and summarization of feeling are viewed by the authors as different classes of reinforcers. Attending behavior is simply "being with" the client both physically and verbally and thus reinforcing the client for "being himself." Reflection of feeling is seen as selectively attending to the feeling or emotional aspects of an individual's comments during an interview, thus reinforcing only certain aspects of the client's productions. Summarization of feeling involves the first two dimensions, but also requires the counselor to integrate and find common elements in diverse client responses. As such, it probably represents one of the more complex and important skills of the counselor.

The training of the counselors in these reinforcement skills, however, represented a more complex process than reward of desired counselor behavior. It involved cue discrimination through the presentation of models, training materials, and counselor supervisor comments. It involved the positive reinforcement of operants by the supervisor through rewarding appropriate attending behavior. In short, the training process was designed to model the behavior and then reinforce the behavior once it had occurred.

The social learning model of Bandura and Walters (1963) provides an especially relevant discussion of some of the techniques employed in this study. Allen (1967) provides a detailed discussion of the microteaching framework.

Attending behavior offers a new approach to many problems. It can be taught as a technique, but unlike pure technique ("say the client's name at least three times"), attending implies real interaction. In order to engage in the attending behavior of following content by relevant statements, the person must listen to content. To follow communication of feeling by appropriate changes in voice timbre and quality and by appropriate statements, one must attend to the feeling that is being communicated. It is likely that the person who is incongruent will be unable to attend, but attending seems to be self-reinforcing once it is initiated, and may even provide an approach that can be used with those groups that Rogers sees as requiring other than the Rogerian relationship to initiate movement.

This type of training (attending behavior training model) was utilized, outside of any of the actual experiments, with a naïve secretary. Following the first session, her lack of attention was pointed out and she was given instructions on how to pay attention. She returned to reinterview the student, and, after a brief moment of artificiality, began to respond in highly impactful ways. In fact, she looked like an experienced counselor. As a side effect, she entered the office the following Monday anxious to tell about attending to people over the weekend. She felt excited and involved with people in new ways and the impact was even apparent on her husband. This experience may suggest the utility of the concepts in this study for pretraining of clients for counseling, as an adjunct to counseling and therapy itself, and as a research paradigm to examine counseling process.

If attention is the important factor that this suggests, it might provide an explanation for the success and validation of certain varieties of counseling and therapeutic procedures. For example, it has been suggested that an analytic client dreams in Freudian symbols, a Jungian client in mythological symbolism, and a Gestalt client in a wholistic fashion. Could it perhaps be that the therapist simply has selectively attended to the client's verbalizations and consciously or unconsciously reinforced material of a certain nature? It seems reasonable that the counselor attends to the client in a fashion that fits into his own theoretical framework. Furthermore, the inability of some beginning counselors to provide attention in the interview may explain the short interviews they frequently have. In this case, counseling is not a reinforcement process, but actually an extinction series!

It might be helpful to consider if the training model utilized is most appropriate for teaching attending behavior. Is television the key factor in microcounseling, or is it simply clear and accurate supervision? McDonald, Allen, and Orme (1966) varied the methods of treatment in training teachers in a reinforcement skill. They found that maximum feedback conditions similar to those in this study produced most effective training. They noted that this procedure is "the most 'costly' in that it requires the active involvement of the experimenter to describe salient cues and to suggest ways of reinforcing participating behavior that the subject could use (p. 13)." However, informal observation indicated that some individual trainees responded better in different training situations than others. Further research on the method of instruction and the impact of the media seems warranted. Stoller (1965) and Farson (1966) have observed that television equipment did not modify group interaction.

Another important consideration is the most useful type of counsel-recounsel cycle. Clinical observation over these studies suggests that the ideal teaching format is represented by a 5-minute base line session followed by instruction and feedback and then a second 5-minute session. This is followed by more instruction and feedback and a final 5-minute session again followed by feedback. Similar observations have been made by Allen and his associates in connection with microteaching. Experimental evidence is lacking on this point, however.

Some general limitations to these studies should be considered. While paid clients appeared to operate very similarly to regular clients in the 5-minute interviews, it should be noted that this situation is not typical of counseling interviews. Further study to determine the generalizability of learning in the microcounseling setting to actual counseling is required. Attending behavior as a generalized reinforcer in counseling is a relatively new concept, and the utility of this concept needs more demonstration.

A question which might be raised is, "How well will the counselor trainees of this study remember what they have learned?" It is believed that the materials learned in these studies will probably follow usual learning principles. It has been suggested by McDonald, Allen, and Orme (1966) that learning from microteaching training procedures tends to follow usual learning curves. Thus, we would tend to predict extinction of learning in this massed-practice study, but intermittent practice and reinforcement administered during counseling training should again bring about a rapid rise in emitted behavior.

Most counselor educators have spent long hours training beginning and practicum counselors in the skills of counseling, and most would agree that training neophyte counselors in these skills is a difficult and taxing task. Microcounseling training would seem to provide a viable framework to make professional counselor training and the training of lay counselors more meaningful and effective. If it is possible to teach a counselor complex skills of counseling within a 2-hour block of time, it should be feasible to develop an integrated counselor education program based on microcounseling principles. Similarly, the concepts of attending, selective attending, and summarization may have broader implications than counseling practice. These may be skills which are equally important to the teacher, the administrator, and the student. The microteaching and microcounseling framework may be a vehicle by which the developmental skills of living may be taught.

Further new directions for research seem called for within the micro-counseling and attending behavior framework. One of the most promising of these involves identifying the skills of test interpretation. Others might center around the imparting of information in the counseling interview, how to give an interpretation of client behavior, or how to handle silence in the interview. Particularly important will be examination of the degree to which training via microcounseling generalizes to actual counseling practice.

REFERENCES

Allen, D. W. (Ed.) *Micro-teaching: A description*. Stanford, California: Stanford Teacher Education Program, 1967.

Bandura, A., and Walters, R. H. *Social learning and personality development*. New York: Holt, Rinehart and Winston, 1963.

Beck, J. C., Kantor, D., and Gelineau, V. A. Follow-up study of chronic psychotic patients "treated" by college case-aide volunteers. *American Journal of Psychiatry*, 1963, *120*, 269-271.

Carkhuff, R. R., and Truax, C. B. Lay mental health counseling. The effects of lay group counseling. *Journal of Consulting Psychology*, 1965, *29*, 426-431. (a)

Carkhuff, R. R., and Truax, C. B. Training in counseling and psychotherapy: An evaluation of an integrated didactic and experiential approach. *Journal of Consulting Psychology*, 1965, *29*, 333-336. (b)

Farson, R. E. The use of audio-visual input in small groups. Paper presented at the Vocational Rehabilitation Conference "The Use of Small Groups in Rehabilitation," San Diego, 1966.

Ivey, A. E., Miller, C. D., Morrill, W. H., and Normington, C. J. The Counselor Effectiveness scale. Unpublished report, Colorado State University, 1967. (Mimeo)

Kagan, N., Krathwohl, D. R., and Farquhar, W. W. IPR-interpersonal process recall: Stimulated recall by videotape. Research Report No. 24, 1965, Bureau of Educational Research Services, Michigan State University.

Kennedy, D. A., and Thompson, I. Use of reinforcement technique with a first grade boy. *Personnel and Guidance Journal*, 1967, *46*, 366-370.

Krumboltz, J. D. Changing the behavior of behavior changers. *Counselor Education and Supervision*, 1967, *6*, 222-229.

Krumboltz, J. D., Varenhorst, B. B., & Thoresen, C. E. Nonverbal factors in the effectiveness of models in counseling. *Journal of Counseling Psychology*, 1967, *14*, 412-418.

Matarazzo, R. G., Wiens, A. N., & Saslow, G. Experimentation in the teaching and learning of psychotherapy skills. In L. A. Gottschalk & A. Auerbach (Eds.), *Methods of research in psychotherapy*. New York: Appleton-Century-Crofts, 1966.

McLuhan, M. *Understanding media*. New York: McGraw-Hill, 1964.

McDonald, F. J., Allen, D. W., & Orme, M. E. Effect of self-evaluation and social reinforcement on the acquisition of a teaching behavior. Paper presented at the American Educational Research Association Convention, February 1966.

Poser, E. G. The effect of therapists' training on group therapeutic outcome. *Journal of Consulting Psychology*, 1966, *30*, 283-289.

Rioch, M. J., Elkes, C., Flint, A. A., Usdansky, B. S., Newman, R. G., & Silber, E. National Institute of Mental Health pilot study in training mental health counselors. *American Journal of Orthopsychiatry*, 1963, *33*, 678-689.

Skinner, B. F. *Science and human behavior*. New York: Macmillan, 1953.

Stoller, F. H. TV and the patient's self-image. *Frontiers of Hospital Psychiatry*, 1965, *2*, 1-2.

Truax, C. B. Reinforcement and non-reinforcement in Rogerian psychotherapy. *Journal of Abnormal Psychiatry*, 1966, *71*, 1-9.

Truax, C. B., & Carkhuff, R. R. *Toward effective counseling and psychotherapy: training and practice*. Chicago: Aldine, 1967.

Wrenn, C. G. *The counselor in the changing world*. Washington, D.C.: American Personnel and Guidance Association, 1962.

Insight Versus Desensitization in Psychotherapy Two Years after Termination[1]

Gordon L. Paul

After a review of the difficulties of follow-up studies on psychotherapy Sargent (1960) concluded that, "the importance of follow-up is equalled only by the magnitude of the methodological problems it presents." In the absence of a carefully designed outcome study on which to base follow-up investigations, the follow-up may be doomed from the start. Thus, in many studies, the methods of assessment at follow-up differ from those at pretreatment and posttreatment (e.g., Berle, Pinsky, Wolf, & Wolf, 1953; Cowen & Combs, 1950; Sinett, Stimput, & Straight, 1965). Other studies, especially of a retrospective nature, have used assessment procedures of questionable reliability and validity (e.g., Cooper, Gelder, & Marks, 1965; Sager, Riess, & Gundlach, 1964; Schmidt, Castell, & Brown, 1965). Still others have neglected to include appropriate no-treatment control groups for assessing change in the absence of treatment (e.g., Bookbinder, 1962; Fiske & Goodman, 1965; Rogers & Dymond, 1954). The follow-up also suffers, inherently, from the uncontrolled nature of client experiences during the posttreatment period. This is especially important when the time between treatment termination and follow-up is considerably longer than the duration of treatment; environmental experiences during the posttreatment period may have more influence on Ss' status at follow-up than a brief program of treatment some months or years in the past. The greatest confounding comes from the fact that many Ss receive additional treatment of unknown nature during the posttreatment period, thus invalidating the design for determining cause-effect relationships for specific treatment under investigation. This practical problem has limited the value of many follow-up studies (e.g., Braceland, 1966; McNair, Lorr, Young, Roth, & Boyd, 1964; Stone, Frank, Nash, & Imber, 1961).

Overshadowing all other problems of follow-up research is the practical

[1]Reprinted from the *Journal of Consulting Psychology*, 1967, *31*, 333-348, with the permission of the American Psychological Association and the author.

difficulty of sample maintainance and attrition. Even adequately designed studies may not be able to obtain consistent follow-up data on treated *Ss*, let alone controls (e.g., Fairweather & Simon, 1963; Kogan, Hunt & Bartelme, 1953; Lang & Lazovik, 1963). The problem of differential dropout and selective biasing of the sample cannot be ignored, since differences have been found between follow-up returnees and nonreturnees (Fiske & Goodman, 1965), and further, as May, Tuma, and Kraude (1965) point out, even if differences are not found, nonreturnees are clearly different in cooperation, mobility, or both. To highlight the magnitude of this problem, a thorough search of the literature failed to reveal a single study on individual treatment of noninstitutionalized adults which obtained data on all treated *Ss* 2 years or more after treatment termination, nor one which included an attempt to obtain such data on an appropriate group of control *Ss*.

The present study is a 2-year follow-up of an earlier investigation which was presented as a model design for the controlled evaluation of comparative therapeutic outcome (Paul, 1966). In the earlier study, a modified form of Wolpe's (1961) systematic desensitization was found to be significantly more effective in reducing maladaptive anxiety than insight-oriented psychotherapy or an attention-placebo treatment. Additionally, all three treated groups were found to show significant improvement over untreated controls. Although these effects were found at termination of treatment, under stress-condition assessment, and were maintained at a 6-week follow-up, the differing theoretical models from which the treatment techniques are derived make a long-term follow-up even more desirable than is usually the case.

Specifically, the disease-analogy model underlying the insight-oriented approach to psychotherapy would interpret the results obtained by systematic desensitization and attention-placebo treatments as suggestion or positive transference—in either case, results which would be regarded as merely symptomatic and temporary (e.g., Hendrick, 1958). According to this model, not only would *Ss* treated by either systematic desensitization or attention placebo be expected to show "relapse" after the "supporting contact with the therapist fades (Sargent, 1960)," but possibly harmful results would also be expected because of the necessary occurrence of symptom substitution (see Ullmann & Krasner, 1965). In fact, the minimal symptom-substitution effect expected would be an increase in anxiety, introversion, rigidity, or dependency (Fenichel, 1945). Additionally, some unsuccessful cases treated by insight-oriented psychotherapy might be expected to realize benefits at some time after treatment termination when their "insights" have had time to "consolidate" (Sargent, 1960). On the other hand, the learning model underlying systematic desensitization would predict no greater relapse for one group than another after treatment termination, since relapse would be expected to occur only on the occasion of unusual stress or if conditions favoring the relearning of anxiety were encountered. Further, this model would expect to find no change in behaviors that were not the specific focus of treatment, except through generalization or an increase in behavior previously inhibited by target behaviors. Thus, from the learning framework, if any change in anxiety, introversion, rigidity, or dependency were to occur at all after treatment termination, it would be in the opposite direction of that expected from the symptom-substitution hypothesis (Paul, 1966). Although the findings at 6-week follow-up strongly favored the interpretation of the learning model, with none of the results expected on the basis of the disease model forthcoming, it is possible that the first follow-up period was too short to allow the expected processes to show their effects.

In the present study an attempt has been made to overcome the methodological and practical difficulties of follow-up research more adequately than previous attempts. By starting with a well-controlled outcome study, the same measures of assessment could be obtained from *Ss* at a consistent interval for long-term follow-up as were previously obtained at pretreatment and short-term follow-up. Persistent effort resulted in a greater return of data than has been reported before, not only for treated *Ss*, but for untreated controls as well. Additionally, specific frequency data were obtained to allow both the exclusion of *Ss* receiving additional treatment and the assessment of life stresses and possible symptom substitution during the post-treatment period. The major purpose of the present study was: (a) to determine the overall comparative effects of the different treatments from pretreatment to 2-year follow-up and (b) to examine the relative stability of improvement from the 6-week follow-up to the 2-year follow-up, particularly with regard to the questions of differential relapse and symptom substitution versus generalization, as predicted from the conflicting theories on which the treatments were based.

Method

Subjects. The *Ss* included in the present investigation consisted of three groups of 15 *Ss* each (10 males, 5 females) who received individual systematic desensitization, insight-oriented psychotherapy, or attention-placebo treatment and 44 *Ss* (32 males, 12 females) who composed an untreated control group. This included all *Ss* from the previous outcome study (Paul, 1966), except for a group of untreated controls who participated in a different therapy program in another context (Paul & Shannon, 1966). At pretreatment assessment all *Ss* were undergraduates (Mdn = sophomore) enrolled in a required public speaking course at the University of Illinois, ranging in age from 17 to 24 years (Mdn=19). Each *S* was selected on the basis of indicated motivation for treatment, high scores on performance anxiety scales, and low falsification from a population of 380 students who requested treatment for interpersonal performance anxiety, as described in detail in the earlier report (Paul, 1966). Although the public speaking situation was reported to be the most stressful condition imaginable, anxiety was also reported in almost any social, interpersonal, or evaluative situation. As a group, the *Ss* also differed from the normal student population by obtaining higher general anxiety and emotionality scores and lower extroversion scores. The *Ss'* degree of anxiety in performance situations was strong to severe, and was reported to be of 2-20 years duration.

Procedure. Pretreatment assessment consisted of the administration of a battery of personality and anxiety scales to the students enrolled in the speech course the week following their first classroom speech. The battery was constructed specifically to assess focal treatment effects and to show symptom substitution or generalization if such processes were operating. The battery thus included forms of (a) IPAT Anxiety Scale (Cattell, 1957); (b) Pittsburgh Social Extroversion-Introversion and Emotionality Scales (Bendig, 1962); (c) Interpersonal Anxiety Scales (speech before a large group, competitive contest, job interview, final course examination) of the S-R Inventory of Anxiousness (S-R; Endler, Hunt, & Rosenstein, 1962); (d) a scale of specific anxiety in a referenced speech performance (PRCS; Paul, 1966). Following initial selection and prior to treatment assignment, *Ss* underwent stress-condition assessment in which they were required to give a 4-minute speech before an unfamiliar audience which included four psychologists recording the presence or absence of 20 observable manifestations of anxiety during each 30-second period on a timed behavioral checklist. In addition, the palmar sweat index and pulse rate were obtained immediately before the stress speech, as was the Anxiety Differential (see Footnote[2]). All *Ss* underwent stress evaluation except for an equated subgroup of controls initially used to evaluate the effects of the stress-condition assessment itself.

Following stress-condition evaluation the groups were formed, equating all groups on observable anxiety, with *Ss* randomly assigned to therapists. After a short screening intrview, during which standard expectations were established, the treatments began—4 weeks after pretreatment assessment. Five experienced psychotherapists (of Rogerian and Neofreudian persuasion) worked individually with three *Ss* (two males, one female) in each of the three treatment groups for five sessions over a 6-week period. All three treatments were conducted concurrently, with missed sessions rescheduled during the same week. Within the week following treatment termination, a posttreatment stress-condition assessment was obtained on treated *Ss* and no-treatment controls, including the same measures used in the pretreatment stress condition. The first follow-up (FU_1) data were then obtained by a second administration of the test battery to all *Ss* 6 weeks after treatment termination. Attitudinal and improvement ratings were also obtained from

---

[2]The original battery also included a form of the Anxiety Differential (Husek & Alexander, 1963). This form was excluded from follow-up analysis since an additional stress administration was not obtained.

treated *Ss* and therapists. The details of all aspects of procedure and results through FU_1 are reported in the earlier study (Paul, 1966).

The 2-year follow-up (FU_2) procedure required tracking down the *Ss* for a third administration of the test battery which had been administered at pretreatment and FU_1. For FU_2 the test battery was augmented to obtain specific frequency data regarding the occurrence of stress during the post-treatment period; the frequency of external behaviors which might reflect predicted symptom-substitution effects of increased dependency, anxiety, or introversion; and information concerning additional psychological treatment or use of drugs which might affect *S's* behavior or response to the anxiety scales.

Information on external stress was obtained by requesting *Ss* to indicate the number of times each of a number of events occurred since the last contact (FU_1). These events covered five major areas of stress: (a) illness or death of loved ones; (b) conflict (with fiancé or spouse, with persons in authority); (c) change in family structure (engagement, marriage, separation, divorce, pregnancy, or birth); (d) personal illness or accident; (e) change in work or living arrangements (move to a different residence, move to a different city, take a new job, change vocational goals, leave college).

Behavioral frequencies regarding possible "symptom-substitution" consisted of the following 13 items:

1. In the past two weeks, how many times did you seek advice, guidance or counsel from: friends?   ; spouse/fiancé?   ; instructor/supervisor?   ; parents?   ; physician?   ; others (please specify)?   .

2. In the past two weeks, how many times was advice, guidance, or counsel offered which you did not seek from: (same as #1).

3. In the past two weeks, how many times did you accept advice, guidance, or counsel when it was provided from: (same as #1).

4. Of your close friends and relatives, with how many different people would you currently feel that you could discuss personal problems should the need arise?

5. To how many clubs or organizations do you currently belong?

6. How many dances, parties, or similar social events have you attended in the past month?

7. In the past month, how many events have you attended as a "spectator" (such as concerts, meetings, sporting events, etc.)?

8. How many times in the past month have other persons been to your home (or room) to visit you?

9. In the past month, how many times have you visited or "gone-out" with another person?

10. Of the different people you have visited, gone-out with socially, or who have visited you in the past month, how many were: males?   ; females?

11. How many times have you participated in group discussions in the past month?

12. In the past three months, how many times have you spoken or appeared before a group?

13. How many different groups have you appeared before in the past three months?

Additional information was requested regarding the date and audience size of public appearances in order to appropriately analyze the PRCS and S-R speech scales. The same self-ratings of specific and general improvement which were obtained from treated Ss at FU_1 were also included at FU_2.

The procedure for FU_2 contact ran as follows: 24 months from the date of treatment termination a packet containing the test battery, behavioral questionnaires, and rating scales was mailed to the last known address of each S. The packet was accompanied by a cover letter explaining the importance of participation for one last time and was otherwise designed to enlist cooperation, including an offer to furnish the results of the investigation. This letter set a date 3 weeks in the future by which the completed forms were to be returned in a stamped, self-addressed envelope which was provided. Those Ss not returning forms by the first due date were sent a personal letter which further stated the importance of their specific participation, and a new due date was set 2 weeks hence. The Ss not responding to the second letter were then sent a complete new packet by registered mail, as were those Ss for whom new addresses were necessary. Those Ss not responding to the third letter were personally contacted by telephone and reminded of the importance of returning the data, and a promise was elicited to do so immediately. An arbitrary cut-off date was set exactly 27 months after treatment termination, for determining "non-returnee" status of contacted Ss. Thus, although FU_2 was designated as a 2-year follow-up, the actual time from termination was 25-27 months, closer to 2 years from FU_1 than from treatment termination.

Results

Return Rate. Of first concern was the adequacy of the follow-up procedure for locating Ss and eliciting their cooperation. Even though the sample was highly mobile (64% no longer in the local area, and 27% out of state or out of the country) all treated Ss and all but three control Ss were located. Complete data were returned by 100% of the treated Ss (N =45), and 70% of the controls (N=31). Of the 13 nonreturning controls (10 males, 3 females), 1 was deceased, 1 was in a mental hospital, 1 flatly refused, 7 failed to return after multiple contact, and 3 could not be located. Thus, the return rate was 79% for contacted controls who could return data, still significantly lower than the return rate for treated Ss (p less than .001, Fisher exact probabilities test).

Since the purpose of the long-term follow-up was to determine the effects of the specific treatments included in the previous outcome study, Ss who received three or more sessions of psychological treatment during the posttreatment period were excluded from further analyses. On this basis, 3 *Ss* were excluded from the insight-oriented group, as were 1 each from systematic-desensitization and attention-placebo groups, and 12 returning controls; the difference between the proportion of treated *Ss* and controls receiving treatment during the follow-up period being highly significant ($\chi^2=9.87$, df$=1$, p greater than .01). Additionally, one desensitization *S* was excluded because she was undergoing chemotherapy for a thyroid deficiency at FU_2, and one control was excluded on the basis of an extreme falsification score. While argument could be made either for including *Ss* who received additional treatment or for counting all *Ss* as relapses, the data available on such additional treatment is unclear. It appears that most of the treated controls, two of the treated insight *Ss*, and the attention-placebo *S* did seek treatment for anxiety-related difficulties, while the desensitization *S* and one insight *S* sought primarily vocational counseling.

Although data obtained at pretreatment and FU_1 revealed no significant differences between the treated *Ss* who obtained additional treatment and those who did not, there is no question that the retained controls constituted a biased subsample of the original control group. The nonreturning controls were found to differ from the retained controls in showing significantly greater increases from pretreatment to FU_1 (Pre-FU_1) on the general and examination anxiety scales, and a higher rate of academic failure over the follow-up period (78% versus 32%). Those controls excluded because they received treatment during the follow-up period also differed from retained controls by showing a greater Pre-FU_1 decrease in general anxiety, lower extroversion scores, and significantly greater increases on all specific anxiety scales. Even though there were no differences in demographic variables between retained controls and those lost or excluded, the retained controls appear to have improved more from pretreatment to FU_1, therefore raising the possibility that differences between treatment groups and controls at FU_2 may underestimate treatment effects. Likewise, if *Ss* excluded on the basis of additional treatment really were cases of relapse, the differential exclusion of these *Ss* would operate most in favor of the control group and, secondly, in favor of the insight-oriented group, while biasing results against systematic desensitization and attention-placebo treatments.

Comparative Treatment Effects from Pretreatment to FU_2 (Pre-FU_2).

The overall evaluation of treatment effectiveness is most reasonably made by a comparison of Pre-FU_2 changes between groups, since Pre-FU_1 changes had been subjected to detailed analysis earlier. Two scales of the battery (PRCS and S-R speech) focus specifically on performance anxiety in the speech situation, the specific treatment target. Unlike pretreatment and FU_1 assessments, however, there was no common reference speech for PRCS, and the size of audiences to which *Ss* had been exposed varied so widely that the separate consideration of S-R speech was no longer meaningful.

Therefore, these two scales were converted to T scores and combined to form a Speech Composite score before analyses were undertaken. While the Speech Composite provides evaluation of specific treatment effects, the additional S-R scales report on performance anxiety in three different inter-personal-evaluative situations, none of which was the specific focus of treatment. These latter scales, along with the general scales on Social Extroversion, Emotionality, and General Anxiety, provide information on generalization or, conversely, symptom substitution. Before carrying out the main analyses on the data, the possibility of systematic differences attributable to the five participating therapists was investigated. As was previously found on pretreatment and posttreatment stress-condition data and Pre-FU$_1$ analyses, in no instance for any measure were significant or suggestive Pre-FU$_2$ differences found among the overall (main) effects achieved by the five therapists or among the effects achieved by different therapists with the three different treatment procedures (interactions). Consequently, the Ss within treatment groups have been pooled in the following analyses.

The Speech Composite and each of the additional scales from the test battery were subjected to three-way analyses of variance (Treatments, Pre-FU$_2$, Subjects) on the scores of Ss retained at FU$_2$. Means and standard deviations for all assessment periods are presented in Table 1 for specific scales and in Table 2 for general scales.

These analyses indicate highly significant Pre-FU$_2$ changes (p less than .01; df=1/53), not only for the Speech Composite (F=82.70), but also for all other specific anxiety scales (F = 35.94, 26.93, 10.39 for S-R Interview, Examination, and Contest, respectively) and general scales (F = 12.69 and 15.21, respectively, for Extroversion and IPAT Anxiety Scale) except Emotionality, which only approached significance (F = 3.05, p less than .10). More important, significant Treatment X Pre-FU$_2$ interactions (df = 3/53) were obtained for the Speech Composite (F = 3.68, p less than .05) and for S-R Interview (F = 5.14, p less than .01), S-R Examination (F = 6.96, p less than .01), and IPAT Anxiety Scale (F = 3.46, p less than .05), indicating differential changes among groups from pretreatment to the 2-year follow-up. The nature of these changes may be seen in Figure 1, which represents the mean change for each group from pretreatment to FU$_1$ and FU$_2$ for all scales of the test battery. Unlike Pre-FU$_1$ changes, where significant overall effects were found only for speech anxiety and extroversion, the significant Pre-FU$_2$ main effects reported above reflect general trends in the improved direction for all scales at FU$_2$.

Of the significant Pre-FU$_2$ interactions, of most interest is the Speech Composite, which reflects change in the focal area of treatment. Inspection of Figure 1 reveals that all four groups maintained their relative positions from FU$_1$ to FU$_2$, with slight additional shifts in the direction of lower mean anxiety scores for all groups. As was the case with Pre-FU$_1$ comparisons, all three treatment groups were found to show significant improvement over controls ($t = 3.70, 2.04$, and 2.38 for desensitization, insight, and attention-placebo groups, respectively; p less than .05), with no significant difference between the mean anxiety reduction achieved by the attention-placebo group and the insight group (t less than 1). Also, like Pre-FU_1 comparisons, *Ss* treated by systematic desensitization showed significantly greater mean Pre-FU_2 reductions in anxiety on the Speech Composite than *Ss* who were treated by insight-oriented psychotherapy ($t = 2.09$, p less than .05). However, even though the magnitude of the difference between mean anxiety-reduction scores of the desensitization group and the attention-placebo group for Pre-FU_2 comparisons was the same as that of Pre-FU_1 comparisons, these differences were no longer found to be significant at FU_2 (t less than 1). This was the result of greater variability in the Pre-FU_2 change scores of the attention-placebo group, primarily due to a drop of 71 points for one attention-placebo *S*. The overall effects between these two groups may be seen better in the individual data presented below.

Having found essentially the same results to obtain for focal treatment effects at the 2-year follow-up as at the 6-week follow-up, the significant interactions between groups and Pre-FU_2 change scores on the other scales of the test battery become of interest. Of the additional specific anxiety scales and general scales, a significant interaction effect was found only for IPAT Anxiety in the earlier analysis of Pre-FU_1 data. The source of that interaction was found in significantly greater anxiety reduction for desensitization and attention-placebo groups than for controls. A significant overall increase in extroversion was also found on Pre-FU_1 analysis, but no significant interaction was obtained over that time period. As indicated above, significant Pre-FU_2 interactions were again found for IPAT Anxiety and, in addition, for S-R Interview and Examination anxiety scales. Inspection of the nature of these changes (Figure 1) showed continued improvement over the follow-up period for the desensitization group on the S-R Interview Scale, such that the Pre-FU_2 reduction for the desensitization group was significantly greater than that for controls ($t = 1.75$, p $<$ .05) and approached significance when compared with insight and attention-placebo groups (respectively, $t = 1.39$, 1.61; p $<$ .10). The source of the significant Pre-FU_2 interaction for S-R Examination was found in significantly greater reductions for both desensitization and attention-placebo *Ss* over controls ($t = 2.44, 1.75$; p $<$ .05) and for desensitization over insight ($t = 1.72$, p $<$ .05). Figure 1 shows that the significant interaction obtained on IPAT Anxiety at FU_2 is a result of the combined FU_2 reduction obtained by the desensitization and attention-placebo groups as compared to insight and control groups, although the latter two groups improved sufficiently from FU_1 to FU_2 that individual between-group comparisons alone were no longer significant. By the 2-year follow-up, the desensitization group had continued to show increased Social Extroversion scores to the point that the Pre-FU_2 increase in extroversion was significantly greater than that of the other three groups ($t = 2.06$, df =

53, p < .05). No other mean group comparisons approached significance from pretreatment to FU_2.

TABLE 1

Mean Scores on Specific Anxiety Scales at Pretreatment, 6-Week Follow-Up (FU₁), and 2-Year Follow-Up (FU₂) for Subjects Retained at FU₂

Treatment	Testing	Speech Composite		S-R Interview		S-R Examination		S-R Contest	
		M	*SD*	*M*	*SD*	*M*	*SD*	*M*	*SD*
Desensitization	Pretreatment	115.5	9.74	43.2	11.01	46.8	10.32	35.6	7.92
(N = 13)	FU₁	85.0	16.10	37.4	8.82	43.2	10.81	35.5	7.28
	FU₂	82.5	16.07	31.5	8.79	36.5	9.28	30.5	6.68
Insight	Pretreatment	117.7	7.15	37.6	9.67	42.5	10.79	40.8	8.73
(N = 12)	FU₁	103.4	14.18	35.6	11.94	42.2	12.01	39.1	10.24
	FU₂	95.2	18.70	31.3	9.42	39.0	8.99	36.3	10.77
Attention-	Pretreatment	110.7	11.98	34.8	7.34	40.6	9.79	36.9	9.69
Placebo	FU₁	86.4	12.47	32.1	7.22	35.9	12.23	34.0	9.75
(N = 14)	FU₂	82.9	20.85	28.7	8.03	32.1	7.74	28.9	10.40
Control	Pretreatment	110.9	12.20	37.2	12.98	40.7	10.62	33.9	11.51
(N = 18)	FU₁	104.3	14.21	34.7	10.16	41.9	11.29	36.3	8.19
	FU₂	99.2	21.66	32.2	10.98	38.4	11.07	33.2	8.11

TABLE 2

Mean Scores on General Scales at Pretreatment, 6-Week Follow-Up (FU₁), and 2-Year Follow-Up (FU₂) for Subjects Retained at FU₂

Treatment	Testing	Extroversion-Introversion		Emotionality		IPAT Anxiety	
		M	*SD*	*M*	*SD*	*M*	*SD*
Desensitization	Pretreatment	14.1	7.58	19.8	6.03	40.7	10.69
(N = 13)	FU₁	17.9	8.45	18.9	6.16	38.2	11.18
	FU₂	19.9	6.18	17.5	7.08	32.0	10.01
Insight	Pretreatment	16.4	6.57	17.2	5.59	33.7	10.09
(N = 12)	FU₁	18.9	4.70	18.3	6.12	35.0	11.72
	FU₂	18.9	4.64	15.6	6.56	30.5	12.29
Attention-Placebo	Pretreatment	14.1	8.15	18.1	6.02	35.4	9.77
(N = 14)	FU₁	17.1	7.68	16.8	7.01	30.7	11.74
	FU₂	16.1	7.01	17.1	6.75	28.2	12.12
Control	Pretreatment	17.9	5.53	17.9	5.92	37.7	16.91
(N = 18)	FU₁	20.2	6.30	18.4	6.31	37.7	11.48
	FU₂	19.4	6.56	17.2	7.97	33.6	14.34

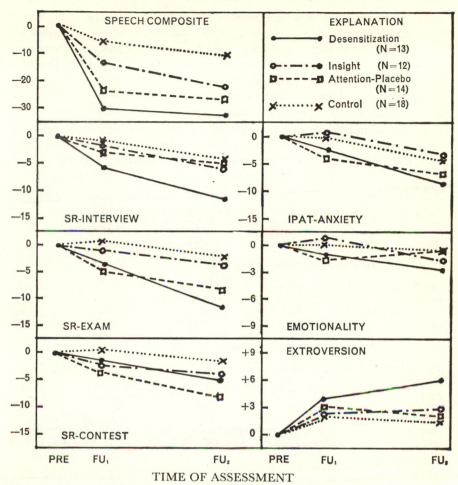

FIG. 1. Mean change from pretreatment to 6-week follow-up (FU₁) and 2-year follow-up (FU₂) for *Ss* retained at FU₂.

Although self-ratings of improvement by treated *Ss* had previously failed to discriminate between groups, direct ratings of perceived improvement were still included at FU₂ because of widespread usage in other follow-up studies. As before, in sharp contrast to the specific measures of anxiety reduction, no significant differences were found among groups on mean self-ratings of improvement. The *Ss* in all three treatment groups gave mean ratings ranging from "somewhat improved" to "much improved" for both specific reduction of performance anxiety and improvement in other areas.

Individual *S* Improvement from Pretreatment to FU₂

Since clinical workers are more often concerned with percentage improvement in individual cases than with mean group differences, and since negative treatment effects or symptom substitution would be more easily identified from data on individuals, all test data were further evaluated on the basis of individually significant Pre-FU$_2$ change scores. An individual case was classified as "significantly improved" on each side if the Pre-FU$_2$ reduction in anxiety score or increase in extroversion score exceeded 1.96 times the standard error of measurement for the instrument (two-tailed .05 level, as previously determined from a population of 523, Paul, 1966). Likewise, an individual case was classified as "significantly worse" on each scale if a Pre-FU$_2$ increase in anxiety score or decrease in extroversion score exceeded 1.96 times the standard error of measurement for the instrument.

TABLE 3

Percentage of Cases Showing Significant Change From Pretreatment to 2-Year Follow-Up

Treatment	Significantly improved	No change	Significantly worse
Focal treatment (Speech Composite)[a]			
Desensitization	85%	15%	—
Insight	50%	50%	—
Attention-Placebo	50%	50%	—
Control	22%	78%	—
All other comparisons (six scales)[b]			
Desensitization	36%	64%	—
Insight	25%	71%	4%
Attention-Placebo	25%	70%	5%
Control	18%	74%	8%

Note:—N = 13, 12, 14, and 18, respectively, for desensitization, insight, attention-placebo and control. Classifications derived by two-tailed .05 cut-offs on each individual change score (see text).
[a]$X^b = 11.64, p < .01$ [b]$X^2 = 8.11, p < .05$

Overall Pre-FU$_2$ improvement rates presented in Table 3 again disclosed significant differences between groups not only for focal treatment effects from the Speech Composite, but for all other comparisons as well. Particularly striking was the finding that not a single case retained a FU$_2$ in any group showed a significant increase in performance anxiety. Additionally, the percentage improvement of groups was remarkably consistent with a similar classification made earlier on the basis of pre- to posttreatment change from stress-condition data. By comparing the percentage of improved *Ss* in the attention-placebo group with untreated controls, it was possible to estimate the percentage of *Ss* responding favorably to merely undergoing treatment, over and above the base-rate improvement from extra treatment experiences throughout the 2.5-year period—28%. Similarly, by comparing the percentage of *Ss* improved under attention-placebo with those improved under insight-oriented psychotherapy and systematic desensitization, it was possible to estimate the percentage of additional *Ss* receiving lasting benefit from either the achievement of "insight" or "emotional re-education," over and above the non-specific effects of undergoing treatment. For *Ss* receiving systematic desensitization, these comparisons revealed an additional lasting improvement of 35% for focal effects and 11% for generalized effects over that improvement expected from attention placebo. Again, no differences were found between the effects achieved by insight-oriented psycho therapy and attention-placebo treatment, although both produced better improvement rates than untreated controls. The "other comparisons" in Table 3 also favored a generalization interpretation of the effects of desensitization for changes found in areas which were not the specific focus of treatment, without the slightest suggestion of symptom substitution. Symptom substitution would be reflected in higher percentages in the "significantly worse" category for both attention-placebo and desensitization groups.

COMPARATIVE RELAPSE AND SYMPTOM SUBSTITUTION OVER THE FOLLOW-UP PERIOD

While overall Pre-FU_2 evaluations gave no suggestive evidence to support the symptom-substitution hypothesis, nor any evidence that more *Ss* treated by desensitization and attention-placebo programs became significantly worse in any area, no information on relapse can be obtained from Pre-FU_2 comparisons. Rather, cases of relapse must be identified as those cases showing a significant increase in anxiety as reflected on the Speech Composite from FU_1 to FU_2. Similarly, if a symptom-substitution process were operating, a higher percentage of change in the "worse" direction should be obtained from FU_1 to FU_2 on nonfocal scales for desensitization and attention-placebo *Ss* who maintained improvement on the Speech Composite. As noted above, the data presented in Figure 1 show no evidence of relapse or symptom substitution for the groups as a whole from FU_1 to FU_2.

Before concluding that the symptom-substitution effects and differential relapse predicted by the disease model had not occurred, a more sensitive analysis was made of the individual data from FU_1 to FU_2. A case was classified as significantly worse on each scale if from FU_1 to FU_2 an increase in anxiety on the Speech Composite (relapse) or other anxiety score (symptom substitution) or a decrease in extroversion score (symptom substitution) exceeded 1.65 times the standard error of measurement for the instrument (one-tailed .05 level cut-offs). The percentage of *Ss* maintaining status versus the percentage "getting worse" from FU_1 to FU_2 for each group is presented in Table 4. No significant differences between groups were found on any measure. In fact, as the figures for the Speech Composite demonstrate, there was not a single case which could be considered a relapse in any of the retained *Ss* from the three treatment groups. Additionally, the percentage of scores in the significantly worse direction, which would reveal symptom substitution, did not differ from the .05 level for any group. If Ss who received additional treatment during the follow-up period were to be included as cases of relapse, the figures would be even less in favor of the predictions based on the disease model, with 93% maintaining status for both desensitization and attention-placebo groups, as compared to 80% for insight and less than 40% for controls.

TABLE 4

Percentage of Cases Showing Relapse or Symptom Substitution From 6-Week Follow-Up To 2-Year Follow-Up

Treatment	Maintained FU_1 status	Significantly worse
Focal treatment (Speech Composite)		
Desensitization	100%	—
Insight	100%	—
Attention-Placebo	100%	—
Control	89%	11%[a]
All other comparisons (six scales)		
Desensitization	97%	3%[b]
Insight	96%	4%[b]
Attention-Placebo	94%	6%[b]
Control	93%	7%[b]

Note:—N = 13, 12, 14, and 18, respectively, for desensitization, insight, attention-placebo, and controls. Classifications derived by one-tailed .05 cut-offs on each individual change score (see text).
[a] "Relapse." [b] "Symptom substitution."

The frequency data obtained from the 13-item behavioral questionnaire specifically constructed to reveal hypothesized symptom-substitution effects also failed to provide any support for the symptom-substitution hypothesis. Kruskal-Wallis one-way analyses of variance by ranks over the four groups on each item produced an $H < 3.66$ ($p > .30$) on all items but one. On that item—No. 9, frequency of social exchange—the value of H approached the .10 level of significance and was in favor of the desensitization group. In fact, a significant coefficient of concordance ($W = .47$, $p < .01$) over all items was obtained, with the desensitization Ss receiving an equal mean rank with the insight Ss, both in the direction opposite to symptom-substitution effects. Similarly, Kruskal-Wallis analyses over the four groups for frequencies of each of the five areas of stress reported over the follow-up period failed to reveal significant differences between groups (all $H < 3.66$, $p > .30$; except C, "Change in family structure," where $H = 5.08$, $p < .20$). Thus, while the occurrence of stress might be considered as evidence of symptom substitution or an external influence on relapse (Stone, *et al.* 1961,) these questions need not be of concern in the present study, since no differences in the reported occurrence of stress approached significance between groups.

Interrelationships among Variables

Since the earlier study assessed specific improvement through several different instruments, persons, and situations in addition to the instruments on which FU_2 data were obtained, information relating to both predictive and construct validity of improvement may be gained through the correlation of previous improvement scores with those obtained at FU_2. For systematic agreement across different instruments, positive correlations would be expected between all change scores for each measure of performance anxiety. FU_1 improvement ratings of *Ss* and therapists should be positively correlated with *Ss'* ratings at FU_2. Further FU_1 ratings of improvement should

TABLE 5

Correlation of Prior Improvement Scores with All Change Scores from Pretreatment to 2-Year Follow-Up

Prior improvement data	Subject FU_2 rating of improvement Specific	Other	Speech Composite	S-R Interview	S-R Exam	S-R Content	IPAT Anxiety	Emotionality	Extroversion
Pre- to post treatment stress-condition change									
Physiological composite	−.33*	−.31*	.11	.13	.32*	.22	.46**	.38**	−.09
Behavioral checklist	−.34*	−.13	.61**	.07	.20	.17	.20	.15	−.25*
Anxiety differential	−.33*	−.27*	.44**	.28*	.22	.26*	.46**	.23	−.34*
Standardized therapist post treatment rating									
Specific improvement	.30*	.15	−.51**	−.18	−.24	−.31*	−.38**	.04	.12
Other improvement	.02	.03	.01	.07	.00	.02	.08	−.10	−.24
Specific prognosis	−.35*	−.31*	.50**	.13	.30*	.11	.24	.02	−.17
Other prognosis	−.19	−.19	.25	.05	.01	−.11	.16	−.09	−.32
Subject FU_1 rating									
Specific improvement	.68**	.47**	−.56**	−.04	−.30*	−.19	−.18	.03	.34*
Other improvement	.56**	.65**	−.24	−.15	−.03	−.19	−.11	.08	.20

Note:—N = 44 for stress condition; N = 39 for ratings.
*p < .05   **p < .01

be negatively correlated with Pre-FU$_2$ performance-anxiety change scores. Opposite relationships would be expected for therapist posttreatment ratings of prognosis, since these scales were reversed.

Table 5 presents the correlations of pre to posttreatment stress-condition change scores, therapist posttreatment ratings, and FU$_1$ ratings of treated *Ss* with FU$_2$ ratings of treated *Ss* and Pre-FU$_2$ change on the Speech Composite and all other scales of the test battery. Specific FU$_2$ improvement data (*Ss'* ratings, Pre-FU$_2$ Speech Composite) were significantly correlated in the expected direction, with all indicants of specific improvement at posttreatment and FU$_1$, except for the relationship between the Physiological Composite and the Speech Composite. Previous analyses had also failed to find significant relationships between physiological and self-report data, although physiological change was significantly correlated with observable manifestations of anxiety under stress conditions as assessed by the behavioral checklist.

Of the correlations presented in Table 5, the relationship of the behavioral checklist with Pre-FU$_2$ assessments is of a special importance. The behavioral checklist was the most objective measure of all instruments used and was highly reliable (interrater reliability $= .96$). Additionally, checklist data were obtained in a situation where target behaviors were most likely to occur, and pre- to posttreatment checklist change was consistently related to all other prior indicants of specific anxiety reduction. The correlation of .61 between pre- to posttreatment change on the behavior checklist with Pre-FU$_2$ change on the Speech Composite is strong evidence for both the construct validity of focal improvement at FU$_2$ and for the predictive validity of observable posttreatment improvement.

Table 5 also reveals discriminative relationships in the correlations of therapist and subject ratings with Pre-FU$_2$ improvement. Therapist ratings of specific improvement and prognosis were significantly correlated with Pre-FU$_2$ Speech Composite change and with FU$_2$ ratings of improvement by treated *Ss*. Conversely, therapists' ratings of general improvement and prognosis were not significantly related to specific improvement, although "other prognosis" was related to Pre-FU$_2$ change in extroversion. Likewise, *Ss'* ratings at FU$_1$ were significantly related to Pre-FU$_2$ change in a discriminative way, although "method factors" predominate in improvement ratings of *Ss* as they had earlier.

The correlation of specific improvement data from the earlier time periods with Pre-FU$_2$ change on the scales of the test battery which were not directed towards focal treatment effects also showed several significant relationships. Inspection of the prime correlations among all variables presented in Table 5 found the source of covariation in every instance to result primarily from increased relationships at posttreatment and FU$_2$, with several of the prime correlations also reaching the .01 level of significance. The significant correlations presented in Table 5 may be interpreted as evidence for the stability of improvement and generalization effects, rather than as a result of relationships existing before treatment began. Further, when the specific posttreatment and FU_1 improvement variables from Table 5 were correlated with FU_1—FU_2 change for test battery scales, several low, but significant, coefficients were obtained ($Mdn/r/ = .31$), all of which indicated that those *Ss* who showed greatest reduction in performance anxiety at posttreatment and FU_1 also showed greatest specific and generalized additional improvement over the period between FU_1 and FU_2. Since no significant correlations were obtained between pretreatment scores on the three general scales and change on the specific anxiety scales from Pre-FU_1, FU_1—FU_2, or Pre-FU_2, the slight additional improvement from FU_1 to FU_2 may be interpreted as the continuing effects of changes taking place during the treatment period, rather than as a function of pretreatment personality dimensions.

TABLE 6

Intercorrelations of Each Test Battery Scale over the Three Testing Periods for Subjects Retained at FU_2

Scale	Stability coefficient[a]		
	Pre-FU_1	Pre-FU_2	FU_1-FU_2
Speech Composite	.27	.29	.68
S-R Interview	.57	.53	.63
S-R Examination	.50	.52	.51
S-R Contest	.47	.43	.64
IPAT Anxiety	.76	.44	.63
Emotionality	.80	.64	.72
Extroversion	.82	.59	.71

Note:—$N = 57$; $p = .05$, $r = .22$; $p = .01$, $r = .31$
[a]Pearson r's.

Further information concerning the stability of scores for each scale of the test battery over treatment and follow-up periods, may be seen in the test-retest correlations from Pre-FU_1, Pre-FU_2, and FU_1—FU_2 (Table 6). The greater stability of Speech Composite scores from FU_1 to FU_2 as compared to Pre-FU_1 and Pre-FU_2 relationships, again indicated the influence of treatment effects obtaining after pretreatment assessment, with *Ss* holding relative positions in a reliable manner over the 2 years following FU_1. However, it appears that relatively greater position changes in Extroversion and IPAT Anxiety occurred over the follow-up period than over the treatment period.

Intercorrelations of FU_2 scores for all scales of the test battery revealed essentially the same relationships as those reported earlier for FU_1 scores. Significant intercorrelations were obtained among all scales (Mdn r = .51), except Extroversion which was significantly related only to the Speech Composite ($r = -.27$, $p < .05$). While the combined relationships reported above and in the earlier study support the assumption that FU_2 measures were internally consistent, the reliability of the Pre-FU_2 change for the primary measure can be directly estimated. The Pre-FU_2 changes for PRCS and S-R Speech (the scales which were converted to T scores and summed to obtain the Speech Composite) correlated .64, from which the reliability of the Speech Composite change can be estimated (by Spearman-Brown formula) at .78.

Although no differences between groups were found for the 13 items of the behavioral questionnaire, indirect support for the validity of the items was obtained through correlational analyses. Moderate but significant correlations were found among the items, which clustered in the following way: Nos. 1, 2, and 3 (Mdn r = .53); Nos. 6, 9, and 10 (Mdn r = .43); Nos. 3, 5, 8, 11, 12, 13 (Mdn r = .35). Only No. 7 was unrelated to other items. Numerous significant correlations (Mdn/r/ = .32) were found between the items of the second and third clusters and all scales of the FU_2 test battery, indicating that *Ss* obtaining lower anxiety scores and higher extroversion scores also tended to report having more close friends, belonging to more organizations, attending more social events, entertaining more, "going out" more, and more frequent group discussions and public appearances. Similarly, of the five areas of stress on which frequency data were obtained, all but one (change in family structure) were significantly intercorrelated (Mdn r = .35). With one exception, no significant correlations were found between reported stress frequencies and items of the behavioral questionnaire, nor between either FU_1—FU_2 or Pre-FU_2 change for any scale of the test battery and stress frequencies. The exception was a significant relationship between the reported frequency of occurrence of change in family structure and FU_1—FU_2 change in extroversion ($r = -.42$, $p < .01$); that is, those *Ss* increasing in extroversion from FU_1 to FU_2 tended to report less change in family structure over the same time period.

One last check on the symptom-substitution hypothesis was carried out by correlating Pre-FU_2 change on the Speech Composite with all other data. Several significant correlations were obtained between Pre-FU_2 Speech Composite change and items from the behavioral questionnaire, but all were in the opposite direction predicted by the disease model and favored a generalization interpretation. Intercorrelations of Pre-FU_2 change scores among all seven scales of the test battery revealed positive correlations between change on the Speech Composite and change on all other anxiety scales (Mdn r = .34) and a negative correlation with change in Extroversion ($r = -.30$). Similar relationships were found among the other scales, with positive correlations among all anxiety and emotionality change scores and negative correlations between the latter and change in Extroversion. Of the 15 correlations, 10 achieved statistical significance (Mdn/r/ = .29).

Discussion

In general, the combined findings from individual and group data as well as correlational analyses showed the relative gains in focal treatment effects found earlier to be maintained over the 2-year follow-up period. Some additional relative improvement in related areas was found for *Ss* treated by systematic desensitization and, to a lesser extent, for those treated by attention placebo. Like the findings at 6-week follow-up, in no instance were the long-term effects achieved through insight-oriented psychotherapy significantly different from the effects achieved with attention-placebo treatment, although both groups showed significantly greater treatment effects than untreated controls. As a group, the systematic desensitization *Ss* continued to show greater positive treatment effects than any other group, with evidence of additional generalization, and no evidence even suggestive of symptom substitution. In fact, the comparative findings at 2-year follow-up are so similar to the findings at post-treatment and 6-week follow-up that the detailed discussion of results in relation to previous research, theoretical hypotheses concerning factors and effects within treatments, and methodological implications for research and clinical practice which were presented earlier (Paul, 1966, pp. 71–99) require no modification and need not be reiterated here.

The finding that effects of systematic desensitization are maintained over the follow-up period with evidence of additional improvement through generalization is consistent with the results of the only other controlled follow-up of systematic desensitization therapy (Lang & Lazovik, 1963) and with the suggestive findings from follow-up reports of accumulated case studies (Lazarus, 1963; Wolpe, 1961). Although all previous long-term follow-up studies have suffered considerably from the methodological problems described at the beginning of this report, the general trend of results for psychological treatment of noninstitutionalized adults has been for treatment effects to be maintained or slightly improved over the follow-up period (Stone *et al.* 1961). Consistent with this trend, the present investigation found no relapse for any of the retained treated *Ss*, no matter what treatment they had received.

While these findings were somewhat surprising for systematic desensitization and insight-oriented psychotherapy, the stability of improvement resulting only from the nonspecific effects of attention-placebo treatment was almost completely unexpected. This was especially true since previous studies of placebo responsiveness had not only found relapse on 3-6 month follow-up (Gliedman, Nash, Imber, Stone & Frank, 1958), but further, that *Ss* who improved most at the time of their initial placebo experience were more likely to relapse than those who improved least (Frank, Nash, Stone & Imber, 1963). The difference between the latter effects of pure placebo (inert medication) and lasting effects of the attention-placebo treatment of the present investigation may lie in changes in attitudes and expectancies resulting from the interpersonal relationship with the therapist functioning as a "generalized reinforcer" (Krasner, 1955). Stone *et al.* (1961) point out that the long-term success of any form of treatment depends in large part on the extent to which changes that are accomplished are supported by the client's subsequent life experiences. This fact might be extended to suggest that no matter how change is brought about, it is likely to be maintained in a supportive environment which reinforces resulting behavior, and it is not likely to be maintained if the resulting behavior is not reinforced or if new aversive consequences or extreme stress reinstitute negative emotional responses. While systematic desensitization produced a more direct modification of the emotional reactions associated with interpersonal performance situations, resulting in significantly higher improvement rates, the emergent behaviors of *Ss* experiencing anxiety reduction from all three treatments were likely to be regarded as socially appropriate and were likely to be rewarded, independently of the manner in which change initially came about.

The usual concern with "spontaneous remission" rates from other populations need not be considered in this investigation, since an untreated control group from the same population was assessed on the same instruments as were the treatment groups. Even though results were favorably biased towards the controls, due to differential loss of *Ss*, superior long-term effects for all treatment groups were still obtained. Additionally, the 22% "improved" without treatment at the 2-year follow-up for a favorably biased untreated subgroup seriously questions the "two-thirds spontaneous remission" rate so frequently quoted (e.g., Eysenck, 1966). Of course, Lesse (1964) notes:

> The concept of anything that is labeled as "spontaneous" must be considered in the light of the fact that it is spontaneous only because we do not understand the causes for the change or are at the present time unable to measure various factors that influence it. In all probability, therefore, so-called spontaneous remissions are probably not spontaneous at all (p. 111).

There is no reason to believe that factors other than the same environmental influences which maintained improvement for treated *Ss* were involved in the improvement and stability of untreated controls. In fact, processes similar to desensitization may take place through environmental interaction in the absence of formal treatment (Stevenson, 1961), and considerable nonspecific therapy may be expected without contacting a socially designated psychological helper (Goldstein, 1960).

While this investigation was able to overcome methodological difficulties more adequately than previous attempts, it still suffered from difficulties inherent in the nature of follow-up studies. The tight control procedures maintained during the earlier outcome study were not possible once *Ss* were "turned loose" after the 6-week follow-up. When control is not possible, attempts at assessment are a second-best choice. Although *Ss* were asked to indicate whether or not treatment had been received during the follow-up period, only 5 indicated that they had, when a total of 17 were actually identified as having received treatment through a survey of clinics and therapists. Considering the high return rate for this investigation, the problem of *Ss* not reporting additional treatment in other studies could be astronomical. Even though a higher return rate was obtained than in previous follow-up studies, total assessment of cause-effect relationships for treatment groups was not possible owing to the necessity of *S* exclusion. Additionally, the untreated controls were known to be a favorably biased subgroup which may have under-estimated treatment effects and over-estimated (un)spontaneous remission. Although the assessment instruments used possessed adequate reliability and validity for determining effects, the mobility of the sample precluded use of the instrument which was known to provide the most objective evaluation (i.e., the behavioral checklist).

These inherent difficulties have led some investigators to question the value of long-term follow-ups. May *et al.* (1965) point out:

> formal, controlled studies are doomed to depreciate progressively with the passage of time from the end of the controlled treatment period with much of their discriminating power being eroded by contamination . . . it is inevitable that the longer the follow-up, the more all treatments approximate the same end result (p. 762).

On the basis of their own research, Stone *et al.* (1961) state further that, "evaluation of different forms of psychotherapy should be primarily in terms of their immediate results (p. 420)." In essential agreement, the stability of treatment effects over the 2-year follow-up period in the present study, combined with the failure to find a single case which could be considered evidence of relapse or symptom substitution for any treated *S*, suggests that the short-term follow-up provided adequate evaluation of comparative treatment effects. Thus, for the evaluation of psychological treatment with non-institutionalized adults, more scientifically useful information is likely to be obtained if future efforts are directed towards short-term follow-ups, in which total sample assessment of treated *Ss* may be obtained, rather than longer follow-ups, which suffer from differential attrition and the effects of uncontrolled environmental influences. The number and timing of follow-ups should be determined by the nature of the population and problem, rather than preconceived theoretical notions (Paul, in press).

However, the methodological difficulties of follow-up studies should not overshadow the major findings of the present investigation. Namely, that modified systematic desensitization produced significant and lasting reductions in maladaptive anxiety, not only on an absolute level, but also in comparison with other treatment and control groups. None of the effects predicted on the basis of the traditional disease-analogy model was forthcoming, while considerable evidence was found for a learning model. Results as consistent as these are rare in the psychotherapy literature and require not only replication, but also an extension of evaluations across differing populations of clients, therapists, and problems, as well as parametric investigations of the mechanics involved.

REFERENCES

Bendig, A. W. Pittsburgh scale of social extroversion-introversion and emotionality. *Journal of Psychology*, 1962, *53*, 199-210.

Berle, B. B., Pinsky, R. H., Wolf, S., & Wolff, H. E. Appraisal of the results of treatment of stress disorders. *Research Publications Association for Research in Nervous and Mental Disease*, 1953, *31*, 167-177.

Bookbinder, L. J. Follow-up versus discharge status of psychiatric inpatients. *Journal of Clinical Psychology*, 1962, *18*, 501-503.

Braceland, F. J. (Ed.) Special section: Follow-up studies. *American Journal of Psychiatry* 1966, *122*, 1088-1124.

Cattell, R. B. *The IPAT Anxiety Scale*. Champaign, Ill.: Institute for Personality and Ability Testing, 1957.

Cooper, J. E., Gelder, M. G., & Marks, I. M. Results of behavior therapy in 77 psychiatric patients. *British Medical Journal*, 1965, *1*, 1222-1225.

Cowen, E. L., & Combs, A. W. Follow-up study of 32 cases treated by nondirective psychotherapy. *Journal of Abnormal and Social Psychology*, 1950, *45*, 232-258.

Endler, N. S., Hunt, J. McV., & Rosenstein, A. J. An S-R inventory of anxiousness. *Psychological Monographs*, 1962, 76 (17, Whole No. 536).

Eysenck, H. J. The effects of psychotherapy. New York: International Science Press, 1966.

Fairweather, G. W., & Simon, R. A further follow-up of psychotherapeutic programs, *Journal of Consulting Psychology*, 1963, *27*, 186.

Fenichel, O. *The psychoanalytic theory of neuroses*. New York: Norton, 1945.

Fiske, D. W., & Goodman, G. The posttherapy period. *Journal of Abnormal Psychology*, 1965, *70*, 169-179.

Frank, J. D., Nash, E. H., Stone, A. R., & Imber, S. D. Immediate and long-term symptomatic course of psychiatric outpatients. *American Journal of Psychiatry*, 1963, 120, 429-439.

Gliedman, L. H., Nash, E. H., Imber, S. D., Stone, A. R., & Frank, J. D. Reduction of symptoms by pharmacologically inert substances and short-term psychotherapy. *A.M.A. Archives of Neurology and Psychiatry*, 1958, *79*, 345-351.

Goldstein, A. P. Patient's expectancies and nonspecific therapy as a basis for (un)spontaneous remission. *Journal of Clinical Psychology*, 1960, *16*, 399-403.

Hendrick, I. *Facts and theories of psychoanalysis*. New York: Knopf, 1958.

Husek, T. R., & Alexander, S. The effectiveness of the Anxiety Differential in examination situations. *Educational and Psychological Measurement*, 1963, *23*, 309-318.

Kogan, L. S., Hunt, J. McV., & Bartelme, P. *A follow-up study of the results of social case-work*. New York: Family Service Association of America, 1953.

125

Krasner, L. The use of generalized reinforcers in psychotherapy research. *Psychological Reports*, 1955, *1*, 10-25.

Lang, P. J., & Lazovik, A. D. Experimental desensitization of a phobia. *Journal of Abnormal and Social Psychology*, 1963, *66*, 519-525.

Lazarus, A. A. The results of behaviour therapy in 126 cases of severe neuroses. *Behaviour Research and Therapy*, 1963, *1*, 69-79.

Lesse, S. Placebo reactions and spontaneous rhythms: Their effects on the results of psychotherapy. *American Journal of Psychotherapy*, 1964, 18 (Monogr. Suppl. No. 1), 99-115.

May, P. R. A., Tuma, A. H., & Kraude, W. Community follow-up of treatment of schizophrenia—issues and problems. *American Journal of Ortho-psychiatry*, 1965, *35*, 754-763.

McNair, D. M., Lorr, M., Young, H. H., Roth, L., & Boyd, R. W. A three-year follow-up of psychotherapy patients. *Journal of Clinical Psychology*, 1964, *20*, 258-263.

Paul, G. L. *Insight vs. desensitization in psychotherapy: An experiment in anxiety reduction.* Stanford: Stanford University Press, 1966.

Paul, G. L. Behavior modification research: Design and tactics. In C. M. Franks (Ed.), *Assessment and status of the behavioral therapies and related developments.* New York: McGraw-Hill, in press.

Paul, G. L., & Shannon, D. T. Treatment of anxiety through systematic desensitization in therapy groups. *Journal of Abnormal Psychology*, 1966, *71*, 124-135.

Rogers, C. R., & Dymond, R. F. (Eds.) *Psychotherapy and personality change.* Chicago: University of Chicago Press, 1954.

Sager, C. J., Riess, B. F., & Gundlach, R. Follow-up study of the results of extramural analytic psychotherapy. *American Journal of Psychotherapy*, 1964, *18* (Monogr. Suppl. No. 1), 161-173.

Sargent, H. D. Methodological problems of follow-up studies in psychotherapy research. *American Journal of Psychotherapy*, 1960, *30*, 495-506.

Schmidt, E., Castell, D., & Brown, P. A retrospective study of 42 cases of behavior therapy. *Behaviour Research and Therapy*, 1965, 3, 9-19.

Sinett, E. R., Stimput, W. E. & Straight, E. A five-year follow-up study of psychiatric patients. *American Journal of Orthopsychiatry*, 1965, *35*, 573-580.

Stevenson, I. Processes of "spontaneous" recovery from the psychoneuroses. *American Journal of Psychiatry*, 1961, *117*, 1057-1064.

Stone, A. R., Frank, J. D., Nash, E. H., & Imber, S. D. An intensive five-year follow-up study of treated psychiatric outpatients. *Journal of Nervous and Mental Disease*, 1961, *133*, 410-422.

Ullmann, L. P., & Krasner, L. (Eds.) *Case studies in behavior modification.* New York: Holt, 1965.

Wolpe, J. The systematic desensitization treatment of neuroses. *Journal of Nervous and Mental Disease*, 1961, *132*, 189-203.

Behaviour Rehearsal vs Non-Directive Therapy vs Advice in Effecting Behavior Change[1]

Arnold A. Lazarus

Introduction and Procedure

To date, the only behaviour therapy techniques to have been experimentally tested are systematic desensitization and aversion therapy (Lazovik and Lang, 1960; Lang and Lazovik, 1963; Lazarus, 1961; Paul, 1966; Feldman and McCulloch, 1965). The present paper offers the first objective clinical appraisal of *behaviour rehearsal* (Lazarus, 1963, 1964, 1965), which has also been called "behaviouristic psychodrama" (Wolpe, 1958; Sturm, 1965) role-playing, and play-acting. The appellation "behaviour rehearsal" seems preferable because it indicates both the content and intent of the actual procedure. Behaviour rehearsal is a specific procedure which aims to replace deficient or inadequate social or interpersonal responses by efficient and effective behaviour patterns. The patient achieves this by practicing the desired forms of behaviour under the direction and supervision of the therapist.

Behaviour rehearsal is most commonly employed with patients lacking in assertive behaviour. The therapist plays the role of someone to whom the patient usually reacts with excessive anxiety, while the patient is directed to respond in an uninhibited, forthright and even aggressive manner. Repeated rehearsals usually diminish the patient's anxieties so that he is eventually able to extend his gains beyond the confines of the consulting room. Role reversal (where the therapist plays the patient's role and models the desirable responses) is often employed and affords a useful means of learning by imitation (Bandura, 1961, 1965).

The following is a characteristic account of a training procedure designed for the development of assertive responses by means of behaviour rehearsal (Lazarus, 1965): "In this method patient and therapist role-played various scenes which posed assertive problems for the patient. . . expressing disagreement with a friend's social arrangements, asking a favour,

[1]Reprinted from *Behavior Research and Therapy*, 1966, *4*, 209-212 with permission of the author and Pergamon Press.

upbraiding a subordinate at work, contradicting a fellow employee, refusing to accede to an unreasonable request, complaining to his employer about the inferior office fixtures, requesting an increment in salary, criticizing his father's attire, questioning his father's values, and so forth. Commencing with the less demanding situations, each scene was systematically rehearsed until the most troublesome encounters had been enacted to the satisfaction of patient and therapist. The therapist usually role-played the significant persons in the patient's life according to descriptions provided by the latter. The patient's behaviour was shaped by means of constructive criticism as well as modelling procedures in which the therapist assumed the patient's role and demonstrated the desirable responses. A situation was regarded as "satisfactorily covered" when (1) the patient was able to enact it without feeling anxious (if he became tense or anxious while rehearsing a scene, deep relaxation was applied until he felt calm again); (2) when his general demeanor, posture, facial expression, inflection in tone, and the like, lent substance to his words (repeated play-backs from a tape recorder helped to remove a querulous pitch from his voice) and (3) when agreement was reached that his words and actions would seem fair and fitting to an objective onlooker. In order to expedite the transfer from consulting room to actual life, the patient was initially encouraged to apply his newly acquired assertive skills only when negative consequences were highly improbably. . . He soon grew proficient at handling most situations that called for uninhibited and forthright behavior. . ."

In addition to their use in the acquisition of assertive responses, behaviour rehearsal procedures can be applied to a variety of behaviour patterns. Here are some typical complaints to which their application would be relevant:

(a) "I'm being interviewed for a job next week and I just don't know how to get across the fact that I really know my work although my qualifications are not as high as they should be."

(b) "I keep putting off 'phoning Mary for a date because I don't know what to say to her."

(c) "I'm completely useless at starting conversations with strangers."

(d) "How can I get my husband to realize that if I take a morning job, the house and the children will not be neglected?"

(e) "In two weeks' time I'm having an oral test on counselling techniques. I wonder what sort of questions they can put to me?"

(f) "I never know what to say when people ask me questions about my daughter who is in a mental hospital."

People seldom enter therapy solely for help with isolated problems of this kind, but they frequently raise them during therapy. Traditional psychotherapists usually handle these individual difficulties by reflection or interpretation; and some of those who are more directive may offer advice. It is obviously important to compare the relative effectiveness of reflection-interpretation, advice, and behaviour rehearsal in meeting these situations.

The present study was stimulated about a year ago when a 19-year-old girl consulted the writer primarily for the alleviation of tension headaches and dysmenorrhea. She felt that her symptoms were largely a reaction to the stresses at home (her widowed mother had remarried some 2 years previously and the patient had become progressively more antagonistic to the fact that her stepfather was inclined to over-assert his authority over her). She considered it necessary to live away from home but hesitated to make the move as she felt that this would hurt her mother. A previous therapist, after exploring the dynamics of the situation, was in agreement that a break from home was indicated. The patient had derived comfort and reassurance from this therapy but she lacked the instrumental responses for putting her insights into action. "I don't know how to put it to my Mom. . . My stepfather is very good to her and I don't want to breed any ill-will between them." The writer advised her to stop procrastinating and to discuss the matter with her parents, deflecting the emphasis away from her negative attitude towards her step father, but stressing instead that two therapists considered it necessary for her to live away from home so as to develop self-sufficiency and independence (which was in fact a subsidiary goal). A week later, she stated that she had still not "plucked up enough courage" to confront her parents, and bolstered her passive attitude with elaborate rationalizations. Behaviour rehearsal was then employed. The therapist commenced the procedure by playing the patient's role while she in turn played the part of her mother. The roles were then reversed and the patient finally succeeded in acting her own part in a rational, persuasive and tactful manner. She telephoned the following day to inform the therapist that she had discussed the matter with her parents and that, after minor objections, they had agreed to accede to her wishes. It might be mentioned in passing that her tension headaches soon disappeared and her bouts of dysmenorrhea, although still troublesome, became less debilitating.

Cases like the one above have repeatedly suggested the superior effectiveness of behaviour rehearsal in teaching people to meet and cope with specific interpersonal problems, but as in the foregoing instance, there was no clear indication that behaviour rehearsal alone deserved credit for the final execution of the desired response. To what extent had the previous therapist's dynamic exploration and reassurance paved the way? What role was played by the writer's explicit advice which he proffered before employing behaviour rehearsal? In order to assess the value of behaviour rehearsal *per se* the following plan was adopted.

Each patient who had received no previous treatment and who brought specific social and/or interpersonal difficulties to the attention of the therapist (regardless of their overall problems and primary reasons for seeking therapy) was treated for these specific problems by reflection-interpretation, by direct advice, or by behaviour rehearsal. Patients were arbitrarily assigned to one of the three procedures. When patients presented more than one specific problem area, the most pressing difficulty was selected for treatment. (It might be noted that at the completion of the experiment, two patients who each raised three specific interpersonal problems, received a reflective-interpretative treatment for one of their difficulties; advice was dispensed in the hope of overcoming a second problem; and behaviour rehearsal was employed with the remaining problem. In each instance, the problem area which received behaviour rehearsal was soon resolved, but the difficulties which were treated by advice and by means of interpretation remained unresolved until they too received behaviour rehearsal.)

A maximum of four 30-min sessions was devoted to each treatment condition. If there was no evidence of change or learning within one month the treatment was regarded as having failed. The criterion of change or learning was objective evidence that the patient was indeed behaving adaptively in the area which had previously constituted a problem—the reticent and socially awkward young girl was going out on regular "dates"; the company executive was effecting a promising merger with a rival concern; the secretary had received her much desired salary increment; the timid suitor had successfully proposed marriage to his girlfriend; the considerate husband had persuaded his wife that it would be to their ultimate advantage to move out of her parents' house into a home of their own; and so forth. The experiment was terminated when seventy-five patients had been evenly covered by the three treatment procedures. The therapeutic results are shown in Table 1. Of the thirty-one patients who did not benefit either from reflection-interpretation or from advice, twenty-seven were then treated by means of behaviour rehearsal. There was evidence of learning in twenty-two (81 per cent). Thus, the overall effectiveness of behaviour rehearsal in fifty-two cases was 86.5 per cent.

TABLE 1

Outcome of Treatment

Treatment procedure	No.	Evidence of learning	Percentage
Reflection-interpretation	25	8	32
Advice	25	11	44
Behavior rehearsal	25	23	92

Discussion

These results suggest that behaviour rehearsal is significantly more effective in resolving specific social and interpersonal problems than direct advice or non-directive therapy. Since all three therapeutic procedures were administered by the writer, however, the possibility of experimenter bias has not been excluded. Nevertheless on theoretical grounds one may predict the superior effectiveness of behaviour rehearsal. This technique is a crucial and versatile learning device which places exclusive emphasis on *active partici- pation*. Sturm (1965) has indicated that techniques like behaviour rehearsal would reveal an advantage over traditional psychotherapy in that they have "a far greater potential to (1) generate vivid, life-like behaviour and cues, thereby maximizing the utility of response and stimulus generalization; (2) condition a *total* behavioural response—physiological, motoric, and ideational —rather than one merely verbal, and (3) dispense the powerful reinforce- ments of enacted models and other characters, who in real life or in fantasy have already dispensed reinforcements." Sturm also notes that the skillful application of flexible techniques like behaviour rehearsal helps to create near-veridical behaviour while focusing on the problem at hand, thereby facilitating the patient's ease and efficiency in participating and learning. In short, it may be argued that behaviour rehearsal deserves a more pro- minent place in the repertoire of therapists of diverse theoretical persuasions.

REFERENCES

Bandura, A. Psychotherapy as a learning process. *Psychological Bulletin*, 1961, *58*, 143-157

Bandura, A. Behavioral modification through modelling procedures. In (Eds. Krasner, L. and Ullmann, L. P.) *Research in Behavior Modification*, 1965, pp. 310-340. New York: Holt, Rinehart and Winston.

Feldman, P. and McCulloch, M. The application of avoidance learning to the treatment of homosexuality. *Behav. Res. & Therapy*, 1965, *2*, 165-172.

Lang, P. J. and Lazovik, A. D. The experimental desensitization of a phobia. *J. abnorm. soc. Psychol.*, 1963, *66*, 519-525.

Lazarus, A. A. Group therapy of phobic disorders by systematic desensitization. *J. abnorm. soc. Psychol.*, 1961, *63*, 504-510.

Lazarus, A. A. The results of behavior therapy in 126 cases of severe neurosis. *Behav. Res. & Therapy*, 1963, *1*, 69-79.

Lazarus, A. A. Behavior therapy with identical twins. *Behav. Res. & Therapy*, 1964, *1*, 313-319.

Lazarus, A. A. Behavior therapy, incomplete treatment, and symptom substitution. *J. nerv. ment. Dis.*, 1965, *140*, 80-86.

Lazovik, A. D. and Lang, P. J. A laboratory demonstration of systematic desensitization psychotherapy. *J. of Psychol. Stud.*, 1960, *11*, 238-247.

Paul, G. L. *Insight Vs. Desensitization in Psychotherapy: An Experiment in Anxiety Reduction*, 1966. Stanford: Stanford University Press.

Sturm, I. E. The behavioristic aspect of psychodrama. *Group Psychother.*, 1965, *18*, 50-64.

Wolpe, J. *Psychotherapy by Reciprocal Inhibition*, 1958, Stanford: Stanford University Press.

Wolpe, J. and Lazarus, A. A. *Behavior Therapy Techniques*, 1966, Oxford: Pergamon Press.

Effect of Planned Reinforcement Counseling on Client Decision-Making Behavior[1]

T. Antoinette Ryan and John D. Krumboltz

One of the major goals of guidance is the development of clients' decision-making behavior (Gelatt, 1962; Rothney, 1958). For many clients the counseling process is aimed at helping them achieve more realistic choice-making based on consideration of relevant information, weighing of alternatives and selection of their final goal in terms of the greatest probability of success for attaining values held by the individual client.

As clients engage in their decision-making process there are at least two kinds of statements that can be distinguished: (1) *deliberation statements* which involve a tentative weighing of alternatives, and (2) *decision statements* which involve conclusions that have been reached in the past, alternatives that have been rejected or decisions that have been reached during the counseling interview. Some clients perpetually are undecided, weighing the alternatives indefinitely, and never arriving at any decision. One of their problems is the inability to make a decision even after weighing the evidence relating to each possible alternative. On the other hand, some clients jump to decisions quickly without giving consideration to alternative courses of action or even to relevant facts which may affect the decision they have reached.

While it might take more than the wisdom of Solomon to know when a client has deliberated sufficiently about the relevant facts and alternatives to justify making a decision, it would be valuable to know whether or not the counselor had the power to influence the client's efforts to make either deliberation-type statements or decision-type statements. The purpose of the present study was to determine whether or not a counselor can influence the relative frequency of deliberation and decision responses and whether or not such an influence generalizes outside the counseling interview.

Verbal reinforcement already has been shown to be effective in influencing behaviors ranging from the frequency of plural nouns (Green-

[1]Reprinted from the *Journal of Counseling Psychology*, 1964, *11*, 315-323, with the permission of the American Psychological Association and the authors.

spoon, 1955) to the length of time an interviewee speaks before stopping (Matarazzo, 1963). Verbal reinforcement was the primary means used in the present study to influence the relative number of deliberation versus decision responses made by each client.

METHOD

Sample

Sixty college students comprised the sample for this study. Subjects were drawn from the male population of students enrolled in a lower division psychology course at Sacramento City College during the Fall Semester, 1962.

Treatment

The psychology course in which *Ss* were enrolled provided for student-counselor conferences. These counseling sessions were used for the planned reinforcement counseling. The counseling interviews were held in the counseling center, in the offices to which students regularly reported for counseling interviews. One semi-structured interview approximately 20 minutes in length was held with each client. Three types of interviewing procedure were defined and *Ss* were assigned randomly to the three treatment conditions: (1) decision group, in which *Ss* were reinforced for decision responses relating to educational and vocational planning; (2) deliberation group, in which *Ss* were reinforced for deliberation responses relating to educational and vocational planning; and (3) control group, in which *Ss* were not reinforced for either deliberation or decision responses. *Ss* in each treatment were assigned randomly to two counselors.

A *decision response* was defined as a verbal statement by the client which indicated that he had decided on a course of action, had selected a goal, or had eliminated an alternative with regard to his educational or vocational plans. Decision responses included expressions of verbal intention to act at a future date as well as reports of decisions made or actions taken at a prior time. Some examples of decision responses are as follows: "I joined the service." "I am spending more time studying now." "I decided to get math out of the way."

A *deliberation response* was defined as a verbal statement by the client in which he weighed alternatives, considered possibilities or deliberated about outcomes in terms of his probability of success with reference to educational or vocational planning. Examples of deliberation responses are as follows: "I want to look over the general overall requirements before I plan my course." "I don't know if two years in service will work against me or not." "If I don't major in accounting, maybe I can get into a course in automation."

Many responses could not be classified as either decision responses or deliberation responses and, hence, were designated as *other responses*. Another response was one which lacked a stated or implied reference to deliberating or deciding about educational or vocational plans, lacked clarity or precise-ness in referring to goal selecting behavior, or referred to topics which were unrelated to educational or vocational plans. Examples of other responses are as follows: "Adolescence is just something you go through." "Those men were really scholars and gentlemen." "I like to watch TV."

Prior to the experiment each of two counselors classified responses from 12 tape recorded interviews into the three categories. By correlating the number of responses of each type as judged by each of two independent raters, a coding reliability of .90 was obtained for decision responses, .88 for deliberation responses, and .81 for other responses.

The interview was divided into five periods. The opening and closing periods were not timed exactly. The operant, treatment and extinction periods were timed precisely, by use of an automatic timer with bell attachment. At the close of the opening period, counselor turned a switch which started the pre-set timer. A muted bell sounded at the end of operant, treatment and extinction periods. It is suggested that the use of the timer did not have the effect of making the interview unrealistic, since students were accustomed to timers and the sound of bells in the counseling setting. None of the clients commented about the bell. Neither counselor observed any apparent effect on clients as a result of the timer.

The five periods of the interview were as follows: (1) *Opening*. About two minutes. Counselors made introductory remarks, concluding with the following statement of instructions. "You are enrolled in Psychology 51, aren't you? (Yes) As you probably know, this course was planned to include individual conferences. The course outline provides that each student in the class may have some time devoted to individual counseling. We've arranged to have your counseling interview this morning (afternoon). The session will take about 20 minutes. OK?

"The counseling interviews are for two purposes. First, we want to give some attention to you to help you in defining your future plans. Second, we want to get a general idea of the problems and ideas that follows like you are considering, so that we may improve the counseling services for our students. We want to get a general idea of the educational and vocational plans and decisions that fellows like you have made and are considering. In order to help us get the general picture, we will use a tape recorder, but don't worry about your thoughts being made public. We won't use your name at all. What we are interested in is the general picture of the way fellows think about school, the kinds of ideas that they are considering and the decisions they have made.

"During the interview I would like to have you do most of the talking. If you will express your ideas and your thoughts, then, at the end of the interview I will try to answer any questions you may have.

"Will you please talk to me quite freely for the next 15 minutes? Tell me about the educational and vocational ides you may be considering and the decisions you may have made. OK?"

(2) *Operant*. Three minutes. Counselors gave cues in the form of questions designed to encourage both decision and deliberation responses. Examples of cue questions are as follows: "What ideas have you been considering and what decisions have you made with regard to your vocational goal?" "Since you first started thinking about developing an educational plan, what sort of things have you considered and what kind of educational planning have you done?" "What have you done in the way of thinking or acting that would lead you toward your goals?" Clients made responses. No reinforcement was given for decision or deliberation responses.

(3) *Treatment*. Six minutes. Counselors gave cues. Clients made responses. Counselors reinforced appropriate decision and deliberation responses, according to the treatment group to which *Ss* were assigned.

The verbal reinforcement was given by the counselor immediately following the selected response for the client. It was expected that the reinforcement would follow an intermittent schedule because of the nature of the counseling interview setting (Krasner, 1962). In previous studies it as been found that about 70 to 80 per cent of reinforceable responses actually would be reinforced by the counselor. Reinforcers consisted of such verbal expressions as "Good," "Fine," "That's a good idea," or any other verbal or nonverbal sign of approval by the counselor.

(4) *Extinction*. Six minutes. Counselor gave cues. Clients made responses. No reinforcement was given for decision or deliberation responses.

(5) *Closing*. About three minutes. Verbal awareness test and interview closing.

Awareness Test

In closing the interview, each counselor asked the following three questions:
1. "Did the tape recorder influence your responses?"
2. "Did any of my activities directly influence your responses? If so, which activities?"
3. "Did you notice that you were acting any differently after the start of the interview than at the beginning? If so, how?"

The first question was considered a buffer question and was not scored. The awareness score was based on *S's* responses to questions 2 and 3. An example of partial awareness would have been as follows: "It seems as if you said something like 'good' or 'fine' every now and then when I said certain things." A response indicating complete awareness would be, for example, "Every time I stated a decision, you indicated that you approved."

Generalization Test

To test the extent to which behavior modification in the counseling setting as a result of counselor reinforcement would generalize to a non-counseling setting, a projective-type story completion task was given to all *Ss* following completion of reinforcement interviews as a regular classroom assignment. The story completion assignment consisted of four incomplete stories describing conflict situations. One of the four stories, for example, began as follows:

It was Ken's second year in college. A committee of student leaders had asked to meet with Ken, and at the meeting one of the students made the following proposal: "Ken, we are asking you to run for student body president. We think you would make a great president. We know that most of the students will support you." Ken replied, " [space for 100 words].

Analysis of story completions was accomplished by rating individually each of the completions in each protocol. Two independent scores were derived for each story completion. One score indicated on a five-point scale the strength and frequency of decision responses and the other score indicated strength and frequency of deliberation responses.

Inter-rater reliability for ratings on decision and deliberation responses for the four story completions was established by performing analyses of variance using two-way classification without replication and using these data to compute intraclass correlation coefficients. The intraclass correlation was used to establish reliability, because there were two sets of ratings on one variable with ratings within the sets unordered. Inter-rater reliability for decision response ratings on story completions 1, 2, 3 and 4 were found to be .86, .87, .89 and .74, respectively. Inter-rater reliability for deliberation response ratings on story completions 1, 2, 3 and 4 were found to be .66, .71, .71 and .63, respectively. All correlations were significant beyond the .05 level.

RESULTS

Deliberation Responses, Counseling Interview

Means and standard deviations of deliberations responses in the counseling interview are shown in Table 1.

An analysis of variance was performed using a Lindquist Type III design to allow for one within-*Ss* variable (interview periods) and two between-*Ss* variables (counselors and treatments). Table 2 summarizes the analysis of variance of deliberation responses for two counselors and three treatment conditions across operant, treatment and extinction periods.

Two error terms were used for tests of significance, one for testing within subjects (error w), and one for testing between subjects (error b). The main effects of counselor and treatment and counselor by treatment interaction were tested against error (b). The main effect of interview period and all interactions involving interview period were tested against error (w).

The significant F for counselor by period by treatment interaction suggests that change in mean number of deliberation responses across periods was not consistent among treatment conditions and counselors. Inspection of means (Table 1) indicates that the deliberation group increased in mean number of deliberation responses from operant to treatment period and de-

creased from treatment to extinction. At the same time the decision group-
decreased from operant to treatment, and held a constant rate throughout
extinction. The deliberation response rate for the control group remained
relatively constant throughout the interview. The deliberation response
rate which was plotted by counselor across operant, treatment and extinction periods for three treatment groups did not display parallel behavior.

The significant treatment by period and counselor by period interactions qualifies interpretation of the main effects for treatment and interview periods. The change in mean number of deliberation responses across

TABLE 1

Means and Standard Deviations of Deliberation Responses by Counselor, Treatment Group and Period of Interview (N = 10 in each cell)

| | | Counselor | | | | | |
| | | 1 | | 2 | | Total | |
Treatment	Period	Mean	SD	Mean	SD	Mean	SD
Experimental Group A:	2 Operant	3.6	2.50	3.6	2.07	3.60	2.80
Decision Responses	3 Treatment	3.8	2.27	3.0	2.75	3.40	2.56
Reinforced	4 Extinction	2.6	1.43	4.2	1.99	3.40	1.91
Experimental Group B:	2 Operant	7.6	4.18	5.6	3.98	6.60	4.20
Deliberation Responses	3 Treatment	5.0	2.93	13.3	4.96	9.15	5.82
Reinforced	4 Extinction	2.5	1.86	5.8	3.09	4.15	3.04
Control Group C:	2 Operant	3.8	3.52	5.0	2.24	4.40	3.01
Decision and Deliberation	3 Treatment	3.9	4.23	3.1	1.87	3.50	3.29
Responses Non-Rein- forced	4 Extinction	4.0	2.60	4.7	3.26	4.35	2.97

TABLE 2

Analysis of Variance of Deliberation Responses by Treatment Group, Counselor and Period of Interview

	df	SS	MS	F
Between-Subjects	59	1,512.99		
Counselor	1	73.47	73.47	3.90
Treatment	2	338.21	169.10	9.97**
Counselor X Treatment	2	83.21	41.60	2.21
Error (b)	54	1,018.10	18.85	
Within-Subjects	120	1,234.62		
Period of Interview	2	59.14	29.57	4.68*
Period X Counselor	2	54.68	27.34	4.33*
Period X Treatment	4	201.66	50.42	7.98**
Period X Counselor X Treatment	4	236.39	59.10	9.35**
Error (w)	108	682.75	6.32	
Total	179	1,747.61		

**$p < .01$ *$p < .05$

periods essentially was due to the increased deliberation response rate during treatment period for the deliberation group under one counselor.

Simple effects of treatment and counselor, and treatment by counselor interaction for one level only of interview period (treatment) were tested using a simple factorial design. The error term was computed from results for the treatment level of interview period. Analysis of variance for these data is presented in Table 3.

The significant counselor by treatment interaction reported in Table 3 and shown in table of means (Table 1) suggests that during treatment the mean number of deliberation responses for the three treatment groups differed between the two counselors.

The counselor by treatment interaction has qualified the significant main effect for treatment, suggesting that the differences among treatment groups were reflected mainly in the deliberation responses of the deliberation group

TABLE 3

Analysis of Variance of Deliberation Responses by Treatment and Counselor During Treatment Period

	SS	df	MS	F
Counselor	74.81	1	74.81	5.99*
Treatment	433.30	2	216.65	17.29***
Counselor X				
Treatment	276.04	2	138.02	11.06***
Error	673.50	54	12.47	
Total	1,457.65	59		

***p < .001   *p < .05

TABLE 4

Means and Standard Deviations of Decision Responses by Counselor, Treatment Group and Period of Interview ($N = 10$ in each cell)

		1		2		Counselor Total	
Treatment	Period	Mean	SD	Mean	SD	Mean	SD
Experimental Group A:	2 Operant	14.4	4.72	11.8	4.14	13.10	4.62
Decision Responses	3 Treatment	12.8	3.82	18.1	5.41	15.45	5.38
Reinforced	4 Extinction	9.3	3.13	9.5	4.94	9.40	4.14
Experimental Group B:	2 Operant	8.6	5.94	16.2	4.85	12.40	6.62
Deliberation Responses	3 Treatment	8.8	2.40	8.9	2.95	8.85	2.69
Reinforced	4 Extinction	7.1	3.14	14.0	4.69	10.55	5.28
Control Group C: Decision	2 Operant	14.4	6.44	15.2	5.95	14.80	6.21
and Deliberation Res-	3 Treatment	9.8	3.57	11.0	3.00	10.40	3.35
ponses Non-Reinforced	4 Extinction	8.1	2.47	10.8	3.89	9.45	3.53

under Counselor 2. The main effect for counselors was due almost entirely to differences between the deliberation groups assigned to the two counselors. The deliberation response rate for other treatment groups varied only slightly between counselors.

Decision Responses, Counseling Interview

Means and standard deviations of decision responses in the counseling interview are shown in Table 4. An analysis of variance of decision responses for two counselors and three treatment conditions across operant, treatment and extinction periods appears in Table 5.

Two error terms were used for tests of significance, one for testing within effects (error w), and one for testing between effects (error b). The counselor and treatment main effects and counselor by treatment interaction were tested against error (b). The main effect of interview period and all interactions involving interview period were tested against error (w).

TABLE 5

Analysis of Variance of Decision Responses by Treatment Group, Counselor and Period of Interview

	df	SS	MS	F
Between-Subjects	59	2,397.95		
Counselor	1	273.80	273.80	7.92
Treatment	2	126.30	63.15	1.83
Counselor X Treatment	2	132.30	66.15	1.91
Error (b)	54	1,865.55	34.55	
Within-Subjects	120	2,636.25		
Period of Interview	2	396.13	198.06	13.72**
Period X Counselor	2	14.94	7.47	.52
Period X Treatment	4	427.97	106.99	7.41**
Period X Counselor X Treatment	4	327.16	81.79	5.66**
Error (w)	108	1,560.05	14.44	
Total	179	5,124.20		

**p < .01

The significant period by treatment by counselor interaction reported in the variance analysis suggests that the change in mean number of decision responses between period was not consistent among the three treatment groups and was not the same for the two counselors.

Inspection of Table 4 indicates that the decision group increased in decision response rate from operant to treatment and decreased from treatment to extinction. The other two treatment groups, in which decision responses were not reinforced, decreased in decision response rate from operant to treatment, and held relatively constant throughout extinction. Comparison of decision responses between counselors indicated that the increase of decision responses during treatment was due mainly to decision responses for the decision group under one counselor.

Simple effects of treatment and counselor, and treatment by counselor interaction for one level of interview period were tested using a simple factorial design. The error term was computed from results for the treatment level only of interview period. Analysis of variance for these data is presented in Table 6.

TABLE 6

Analysis of Variance of Decision Responses by Treatment and Counselor During Treatment Period

Source	SS	df	MS	F
Counselor	72.60	1	72.60	4.95*
Treatment	476.43	2	238.22	16.07**
Counselor X				
Treatment	75.10	2	37.55	2.53
Error	800.60	54	14.82	
Total	1,424.73	59		

**p < .01   *p < .05

The significant treatment effect indicates that the mean decision response rate differed among treatment groups. Means reported in Table 4 reveal that the decision group, in which decision responses were reinforced, had a higher decision response rate than either of the other treatment groups. A significant difference between counselors in mean number of decision responses during treatment period was found.

Generalization of Decision-Making Behavior

In order to test generalizability of decision-making behavior from the reinforcement counseling interview to a non-counseling setting, a projective-type story completion task was given as a classroom assignment. Table 7 shows means and standard deviations for decision response ratings for the four story completions for the three treatment groups.

An analysis of variance produced an F value of 11.11 between treatments which with 2 and 57 degrees of freedom was significant at the .01 level. Individual comparisons between the decision groups and the deliberation group on number of decision responses revealed a difference of 1.80, with t value of 2.30, significant at the .05 level. Comparison between decision group and control group on decision rating revealed a difference of 1.77 with t value of 2.26, significant beyond the .05 level. No significant differences were found between the deliberation group and the control group.

These findings suggest that reinforcement for decision responses during counseling interviews served to strengthen the decision habit, so that *Ss* who had been reinforced in counseling for decision responses made more decision responses when given conflict situations in the story completion task, than *Ss* who had not been reinforced for decision responses in counseling.

TABLE 7

Means and Standard Deviations of Decision Responses Ratings on Story Completions

	Story Completion							
	1		2		3		4	
Treatment	*Mean*	*SD*	*Mean*	*SD*	*Mean*	*SD*	*Mean*	*SD*
Experimental Group A: Decision Responses Reinforced	1.13	.57	1.07	.89	1.26	.79	.73	1.21
Experimental Group B: Deliberation Responses Reinforced	.43	.56	.89	.93	.76	.83	.38	.65
Control Group C: Decision and Deliberation Responses Non-reinforced	.80	.59	.60	.52	.79	.63	.40	.44

Table 8 reports means and standard deviations for deliberation response ratings on story completions under the three conditions. An analysis of variance was performed on the data, but the main effects for treatment for deliberation responses were not significant at conventional levels ($F = 2.28$, $df = 2.57$). In three of the four stories the deliberation group did produce the highest number of deliberation responses even though the differences were not large enough to reach statistical significance.

The tendency to make decision responses, which was produced during a 20-minute counseling interview, clearly generalized to a non-counseling setting. Evidence for the generalizability of deliberation responses is not as strong.

Awareness

A structured verbal questionnaire given during the closing period of the interview was used to ascertain if experimental *Ss* were aware of an explicit relationship between response and reinforcement. The results of the awareness test indicated that none of the *Ss* was able to verbalize the response-reinforcement contingency. It seems clear that the counselor can influence the relative frequency of decision and deliberation responses without the client being aware of the process. It also is possible that under operational conditions many counselors may not be aware of the types of responses they are reinforcing.

Counselors might enhance their effectiveness if they become aware of the types of response they are reinforcing, and if they inform their clients of their intent to use planned reinforcement counseling.

TABLE 8

Means and Standard Deviations of Deliberation Response Ratings on Story Completions

| | Story Completion | | | | | | | |
| | 1 | | 2 | | 3 | | 4 | |
Treatment	Mean	SD	Mean	SD	Mean	SD	Mean	SD
Experimental Group A: Decision Responses Reinforced	1.22	.80	1.14	.79	1.22	.79	1.43	.98
Experimental Group B: Deliberation Responses Reinforced	2.17	.83	1.44	.68	1.93	.95	1.27	1.00
Control Group C: Decision and Deliberation Responses Nonreinforced	1.24	.86	1.40	.62	1.29	.92	1.57	.91

SUMMARY

The purpose of this study was to investigate the effectiveness of planned reinforcement counseling in increasing client decision and deliberation responses. The sample consisted of 60 male college students, assigned randomly to three treatment groups: (1) decision group, in which clients' decision responses were reinforced; (2) deliberation group, in which clients' deliberation responses were reinforced; and (3) control group, in which neither decision nor deliberation responses were reinforced.

A semi-structured counseling interview was held with each client. During the treatment period of the interview, counselors reinforced appropriate decision and deliberation responses. Following the interview a projective-type story completion task was given as a classroom assignment to to test generalizability of behavior modification.

Analyses of data revealed the following: (1) Under reinforcement for deliberation responses *Ss* increased deliberation response rate significantly and when reinforcement was withdrawn, *Ss* decreased deliberation response rate. (2) Under reinforcement for decision responses, *Ss* increased decision response rate significantly, and when reinforcement was withdrawn *Ss* decreased decision responses. (3) Counselors varied in reinforcing effectiveness. Differences between counselors may have been related to personality differences or to differences in cueing or reinforcing procedures. In this study no attempt was made to control for personality differences. Future experiments may profitably explore reinforcing effectiveness of various personality

types for various types of *Ss* and tasks. (4) Decision-making behavior generalized to a non-counseling setting. (5) None of the *Ss* indicated awareness of
the response-reinforcement contingency.

This study demonstrates that counselors have the power to influence
the clients' tendency to make either decision or deliberation responses; and
that behavior modification in a counseling setting generalized to a non-
counseling environment.

REFERENCES

Gelatt, H. B. Decision-making: a conceptual frame of reference for guidance and counseling. *J. counsel. Psychol.*, 1962, *9*, 240-245.

Greenspoon, J. The reinforcing effect of two spoken sounds on the frequency of two responses. *Amer. J. Psychol.*, 1955, *68*, 409-416.

Krasner, L. The therapist as a social reinforcement machine. In H. H. Strupp and L. Luborsky, (Eds.) *Research in Psychotherapy*, Vol. II, Washington, D.C.: Amer. Psychological Assoc., 1962.

Matarazzo, J. D., Weitman, M., Saslow, G., & Wiens, A. N. Interviewer influence on durations of interviewee speech. *J. verb. Learn. verb. Behav.*, 1963, *1*, 451-458.

Rothney, J. W. M. *Guidance practices and results*. New York: Harper, 1958.

Ryan, T. Antoinette. Effect of planned reinforcement counseling on client decision-making behavior. Unpublished doctoral dissertation, Stanford University, 1963.

The Effect of Behavioral Counseling in Group and Individual Settings on Information-Seeking Behavior[1]

John D. Krumboltz and Carl E. Thoresen

One interpretation of the counselor's role is that it is his job to help students learn how to make wise decisions (Gelatt, 1962). Students may learn sound decision-making procedures by engaging in these procedures in connection with their own plans.

While it is not possible to specify what the final decision should be for any particular individual, the process in which an individual should engage if he is to maximize the probability of eventually arriving at a wise decision can be specified. Such a process would include considering several alternative courses of action, exploring relevant information about the possible outcomes of each alternative, and weighing the information obtained with more subjective value judgments in an attempt to achieve the outcomes considered most worthwhile.

The present study was designed to investigate ways of increasing the information-seeking behavior of students about their own educational and vocational decisions. The basic problem was to determine which of several behavior change techniques, when applied in either individual or small group settings, would best promote the independent information-seeking behavior of students.

One technique was termed "reinforcement counseling" and has been derived from work in verbal operant learning (Krumboltz, 1963; Schroeder, 1964). Studies in verbal operant learning have clearly demonstrated that the probable frequency of an operant can be increased when it is followed by a positive reinforcer (Greenspoon, 1962; Krasner, 1962). Most of these studies have used a discrete response class, such as personal pronouns or animal responses, with college students in a laboratory setting or with abnormal subjects. Reinforcement effects have usually been assessed immediately without determining whether there is generalization to behavior outside the labora-

[1]Reprinted from the *Journal of Counseling Psychology*, 1964, *11*, 324-333, with permission of the American Psychological Association and the authors.

tory. Certain types of verbal and non-verbal stimuli have been identified as positive reinforcers since they increased the frequency of the response class which preceded them.

The second general technique, termed "model-reinforcement counseling," has involved the presentation of a social model who demonstrates the desired behavior. Research evidence has attested to the effectiveness of social models in promoting certain types of learning (Bandura & Walters, 1963). Reinforcement, while not essential to the acquisition of responses, does affect the rate and magnitude of learning from models as well as the subsequent performance of learned responses. Some evidence suggests that more prestigeful and socially powerful models contribute to a greater matching of the models' behavior by observers (Bandura, 1962; Maccoby, 1954; Mussen & Distler, 1959). Studies have indicated that physically present models are not significantly more effective than audio or video presented models (Bandura, Ross & Ross, 1962; Walters, Llewellyn-Thomas & Acker, 1962). Providing a prestigeful social model and positively reinforcing indications of matching responses has been shown to be highly effective in changing the behavior of observers (Krumboltz, 1963; Schroeder, 1964).

The present study, based on prior research in operant learning and social modeling, has certain unique features relevant to counseling:

1. A specific behavioral outcome, information-seeking behavior, was defined in advance, and alternative experimental treatments were designed to promote that particular behavior.

2. The present study was designed to promote a socially meaningful and socially desirable response class rather than a discrete but socially meaningless response class.

3. Treatments were assessed by reports of behavior which occurred outside the counseling interview, not by behavior which occurred during the interview.

4. To promote generalizability of results the experiment was replicated with six different counselors in six different schools.

5. Subjects were normal 11th-grade high school students who had requested special counseling about future plans rather than college students who volunteered for a psychological experiment or abnormal subjects.

6. To control for the "Hawthorne Effect," an additional control group received special attention and contact with the counselor but did not receive the experimental treatments.

7. Each technique was applied in both individual and group counseling sessions to ascertain the effect of the group setting.

8. No attempt was made to disguise the response class that was being reinforced. On the contrary, students were made well aware of the counselor's interest in their vocational and educational explorations.

PROCEDURE

This study was replicated in each of six suburban high schools in the vicinity of Stanford University. All 11th-grade students were asked to indicate if they would be interested in receiving special counseling about their future educational and vocational plans. Between 48 and 63 percent of the students in each high school volunteered to participate. All students were informed that it might not be possible to provide the special counseling for everyone who requested it. In each high school 20 boys and 20 girls were selected at random from those who volunteered. Two boys and two girls in each high school were assigned at random to each treatment group; four boys and four girls were assigned at random to the inactive control and to the reserve groups. Reserve group subjects were not included in the analysis, so the total N was 192.

Treatments

Subjects were assigned to the two principal treatments, reinforcement counseling and model-reinforcement counseling, applied in both individual and group settings, and to two kinds of control groups plus a group of reserve subjects.

Individual Reinforcement Counseling. The counselor introduced himself, stressed that the students had volunteered to receive special counseling and said in effect, "The purpose of our getting together is to discuss your ideas about post high school plans. I usually tape record counseling sessions because it helps me remember what was said. If there are no objections, I'll tape record our session. (Pause) A very important part of making future plans is the getting of information—information that is relevant and accurate. Perhaps you have already taken steps to get information about future plans, such as talking to someone who is in the field of work in which you are interested. Well, why don't you tell me about what you have been thinking about in terms of your future plans?"

The counselor carefully listened during the session for any response which he judged to be of an information-seeking type. The counselor reinforced verbally any indication that the subject had sought, was presently seeking or intended to seek information relevant to his own educational or vocational plan. The following are examples of verbal information-seeking responses:

    a. "I suppose I ought to find out how much college costs."
    b. "Could I talk to an electrician about apprentice training?"

The counselor attempted to reinforce information-seeking responses with some kind of verbal reinforcer. While a stimulus cannot be termed reinforcing until observation establishes that it strengthens the frequency of the preceding operant, it was assumed from past experience that certain counselor responses such as the following were positively reinforcing stimuli:

    a. "Yes, that would be a good thing to know."

b. "Excellent idea."

c. "Mm-hmm."

Non-verbal cues such as smiling, forward body posture and head nodding, were also used.

To increase the occurrence of verbal information-seeking responses, the counselors periodically used "cues" (Ryan & Krumboltz, 1964; Rickard, 1961). Such cues were questions designed to increase verbal information-seeking responses. Examples include the following:

a. "How would you handle this question of what college to attend?"

b. "There are several ways of getting information about a particular job. Where would you begin?"

The counselor closed the interview by asking each subject to summarize the specific steps which he might take to seek information about his future plans. The counselor verbally reinforced each summary statement and added any specific steps not mentioned by the subject. The counselor asked subjects if they might begin acting on some of the specific steps before the second interview.

The second counseling interview occurred approximately one week after the first interview. The second session began with the counselor saying in effect, "Hello. I'm happy that we could get together again. At the close of our last interview we mentioned several things which you might do in getting information about your future plans. I'm wondering if you remember what some of these things were? Have you done anything this last week or thought about some ways in which you could get information?" The counselor reinforced any verbal information-seeking behavior on the part of the subject and terminated in a manner similar to that of the first interview.

Group Reinforcement Counseling. The group reinforcement counseling was virtually identical to the above except that the counselor worked with a group of two boys and two girls. The counselor's introductory remarks included the following addition: "I thought that since you all have expressed similar concerns about making future plans and decisions that perhaps together we might be able to help each other. As you all know students often face similar problems and may be able to suggest to one another possible steps in making decisions and choosing alternatives."

The counselor sometimes refrained from interrupting the verbal interaction to reinforce an information-seeking response. Instead the counselor often waited for a pause and then reiterated and reinforced the subject's information-seeking response. The second group counseling session was held one week after the first, and the same reinforcement counseling procedures were utilized.

Individual Model-Reinforcement Counseling. The counselor's introduction to the model-reinforcement counseling was similar to that of the individual reinforcement counseling session with this addition: "But before we start discussing this I thought you might be interested in hearing a tape recording of a boy who faced a problem similar to yours. This student was a very good athlete, active in school clubs and was quite popular. He was concerned about how best to make some decisions about what he was going to do after he graduated from high school. He has been really pleased with his decision and he gave us permission to let other high school students listen to this recorded interview. Let's listen to it. You might have some questions to ask about it when it is over."

A 15-minute edited tape recording of a counseling interview which had been used previously (Krumboltz, 1963; Schroeder, 1964) was then played. In this interview the model student verbalized many information-seeking responses, asking questions about possible outcomes and alternatives and suggesting ways in which he might find answers. The model counselor reinforced his question-asking and information-seeking responses and occasionally provided additional suggestions of ways in which he could find the information he sought.

After playing the model tape the counselor said, "Well, why don't you tell me what you've been thinking about in terms of your future plans?" The counseling session continued with the counselor reinforcing any information-seeking response of the subject in the same manner as in the individual reinforcement counseling treatment.

The second counseling session one week later was conducted in the same way as the individual reinforcement counseling second session. No model tape was played in the second session.

Group Model-Reinforcement Counseling. Group model-reinforcement counseling was similar to group reinforcement counseling except that the same model tape recording described above was played during the first session. The counselor then reinforced members of the group for information-seeking responses in the same manner as indicated previously. The second session one week later was the same as described above.

Individual Control Film Discussion. In order to control for the "Hawthorne Effect," an active control group was included in which the counselor provided nonspecific attention to subjects. The counselor acknowledged their request for special counseling and then introduced a film or filmstrip with a comment that viewing and discussing the film might prove helpful. Following the viewing of the film, or filmstrip, the counselor asked subjects for their reactions to the film or filmstrip. The counselor discussed the general problem of future planning, but no systematic attempt was made to reinforce verbally the subject's information-seeking responses. No second session was held.

Group Control Film Discussion. The group session was similar to the above individual session in procedures. Questions from subjects were referred to other subjects to stimulate a general discussion. Again, no systematic attempt was made to reinforce information-seeking behavior. No second session was held.

Inactive Control. Subjects were assigned to the inactive control group from the same pool of volunteers from which the other treatments received subjects. The control group subjects were not contacted by the special counselor in any way. These subjects as well as all others were eligible to participate in their school's regular guidance program.

Reserve Pool. In each high school four boys and four girls were assigned to a reserve category in case any member of the other treatment groups was absent or dropped out of school. These subjects were not included in the analysis of the results unless they were drawn to replace some other subject in the experiment.

Training of Special Counselors

The six special counselors were graduate students enrolled in the Counseling Practicum course at Standford University during the 1962–63 academic year. There were five females and one male. Four were experienced teachers while the other two had had one year of practice teaching experience. One of the six had worked as a part-time secondary counselor for two years.

One counselor was assigned to each high school in October of 1962 on the basis of convenience of location and matching of time schedules. The experiment was conducted in February and March of 1963. For purposes of statistical analysis, these six special counselors and the six participating schools are considered a fixed constant factor and will henceforth be referred to as the counselor-school effect.

The special counselors participated in weekly seminars, read various assignments and spent one-half day per week in their respective schools as part of their training. The rationale of behavioral counseling was discussed and role-playing situations were devised during the weekly seminars. Counselors were provided with interview rating sheets on which to categorize verbal information-seeking responses and other responses during the interviews. Each counselor had practice in exercising the rapid judgement needed in deciding whether or not a given statement was to be classified as an information-seeking response.

Counselors selected subjects from the pool of volunteers in their high school to practice interviewing prior to the beginning of the experiment itself. These practice sessions were tape-recorded and were used for discussion and analysis during the seminar. Regularly scheduled individual interviews were also held between each counselor and one of the instructors.

Criteria

The criterion behavior for this investigation consisted of the frequency and variety of student information-seeking behaviors which occurred outside the counseling interview during a three-week period of time after the first counseling interview. Approximately three weeks after the first counseling interview each of the 192 subjects was interviewed by a member of the evaluation team. These interviewers were not the counselors involved in the study and did not know the type of treatment each subject received. During the interview each subject was asked a series of predetermined questions, some of which were designed to elicit self-reports of information-seeking behavior. Buffer questions were used to disguise the purpose of the interview and to vary the interview format. Each affirmative information-seeking report was followed by other questions to find out precisely how much and what kind of information-seeking behavior was performed by each subject during the specified three-week interval. The following are examples of information-seeking behavior covered by the interview questions:

a. Writing to request a college pamphlet, catalog or an occupational pamphlet.
b. Reading books, magazine articles or other material about occupations or educational institutions.
c. Talking to parents, teachers or other relevant persons who have worked or are working in an occupation or school being considered.
d. Visiting or making definite plans to visit schools or places of employment that are being considered.
e. Seeing the regular high school counselor to gain information relevant to future plans.

While subjects had no known reason to falsify or exaggerate the extent of their recent information-seeking behavior, it was considered essential to verify their self-reports. Previous evidence had demonstrated the validity of self-reports of information-seeking behavior (Krumboltz, 1963; Schroeder, 1964). The names of three subjects from each high school were selected at random for verification. Three names were then assigned to each of six research team members who then conducted follow-up procedures of each subject's self-report. The follow-up procedures included such things as interviewing parents, relatives, teachers, students and employed persons to find out whether the subject had discussed some educational or vocational matter with them, checking with librarians to see whether or not a particular book was checked out during the specified period of time and checking with the regular counselor in the school to see whether appointments had been scheduled by each subject. Of 85 information-seeking behaviors reported by these 18 subjects, 79 were verified and 6 were unconfirmable. None of the reported behaviors was invalidated. Thus, no evidence of falsification of self-reports was obtained, a finding consistent with that of the earlier study.

For each subject two scores were derived from the interview protocol, the *frequency* of information-seeking behavior and the *variety* of information-seeking behavior. The frequency refers to the total number of information-seeking behaviors, e.g., writing to four different colleges for catalogs would give a frequency of four. The *variety* refers to the number of different *types* of such behaviors, e.g., writing for four different catalogs and talking to three students from Harvard would constitute only two different varieties of information-seeking behavior, though the frequency would be seven.

Results

A 4 × 2 × 6 × 2 analysis of variance was computed using treatments, sex of subjects, counselor-schools and treatment setting as the independent variables. Separate analyses were computed for the frequency and the variety of information-seeking behavior. Both analyses are summarized in Table 1. Three of the four main effects reached at least the .05 level of significance for both criterion variables. The four treatments produced highly significant differences. There were also significant differences between the sexes and among the six counselor-schools. The main effect for treatment setting was not significant for either variable. The interpretation of these main effects is complicated by the presence of several significant interactions. For both variables the interaction between the treatment and sex of subject was significant. In addition, three other interaction effects reached at least the .05 level for the frequency criterion.

TABLE 1

Analyses of Variance of Frequency and Variety of External Information-Seeking Behavior

	Source	df	Frequency MS	Frequency F	Variety MS	Variety F
A.	Treatment	3	151.48	53.56***	105.52	56.13***
B.	Sex of Subject	1	13.55	4.79*	10.55	5.61*
C.	Counselor-School	5	15.47	5.47***	5.13	2.72*
D.	Setting (Indiv. vs. Group)	1	0.05	0.00	1.88	1.00
AB		3	10.55	3.73*	5.09	2.70*
AC		15	6.21	2.20*	2.99	1.59
AD		3	4.88	1.73	2.14	1.14
BC		5	5.15	1.82	2.00	1.06
BD		1	1.51	.53	2.75	1.47
CD		5	7.47	2.64*	2.01	1.07
ABC		15	3.03	1.07	1.01	0.54
ABD		3	4.23	1.49	1.80	0.96
ACD		15	3.96	1.40	2.07	1.10
BCD		5	8.23	2.91*	3.41	1.81
ABCD		15	3.57	1.26	2.31	1.23
Within Cells		96	2.83		1.88	
Total		191				

*p < .05   ***p < .001

The nature of the sex by treatment interaction and the main effects attributable to the four treatments and the two sexes can be seen in Table 2. The original hypotheses in this study stated that the model-reinforcement treatment would be more effective than the reinforcement treatment and that the reinforcement treatment in turn would be more effective than the

TABLE 2

Mean Frequency and Variety of External Information-Seeking Behaviors by Treatment and Sex of Subject

| | Frequency | | | Variety | | |
	Male	Female	Total	Male	Female	Total
Model-Rein- forcement	5.04	5.04	5.04	4.29	4.33	4.31
Reinforcement	3.42	5.33	4.38	3.25	4.66	3.96
Control Film Discussion	2.04	1.96	2.00	1.83	1.87	1.85
Control	1.25	1.54	1.40	1.16	1.54	1.35
Total	2.94	3.47	3.20	2.63	3.10	2.87

control procedures. No differences were hypothesized between the control film discussion group and the inactive control group. On the average the results were as predicted on both the frequency and the variety variables. The model-reinforcement treatment proved most effective, followed by the reinforcement treatment. The inactive control group was least active. It will also be seen that on the average the females engaged in both a greater frequency and a greater variety of information-seeking behavior than did the

TABLE 3

t–Values for Hypothesized Differences between Treatments on Frequency and Variety of External Information-Seeking Behavior

Treatment Comparisons	Frequency Males	Females	Total	Variety Males	Females	Total
Model-Reinforce- ment vs. Rein- forcement	3.33***	–0.57	1.94*	2.63**	–0.84	1.25
Reinforcement vs. Control Film Discussion	2.84**	6.94***	6.92***	3.59***	7.06***	7.54***
Control Film Discussion vs. Inactive Control	1.63	0.86	1.74	1.70	0.84	1.79

$*p < .05$ $**p < .01$ $***p < .001$

males. The reason for the significant interaction appears to be attributable to the differential effectiveness of the model-reinforcement and the reinforcement treatments for males and females. The hypothesized differences between treatments were tested separately for statistical significance as reported in Table 3. For males the difference between the model-reinforcement and the reinforcement treatments was highly significant with the model-reinforcement treatment proving most effective. For females the differences were slight but in the opposite direction from that predicted. Thus model-reinforcement counseling was more effective than reinforcement counseling for the males but not for the females.

The differences between the reinforcement treatment and the control film discussion group were highly significant for both sexes on both variables in the predicted direction. The control film discussion procedure produced uniformly more information-seeking behavior in all of the groups than did the inactive control procedure, but none of the differences reached the .05 level using a two-tail *t-test*.

The nature of the interaction between treatment and counselor-schools can be seen in Table 4. In four of the six schools the direction of the differences

TABLE 4

Mean Frequency of External Information-Seeking Behavior by Treatment and Counselor-Schools

Counselor-School	Model-Reinforcement	Reinforcement	Control Film	Control	Total
A	5.12	3.12	2.00	0.63	2.72
B	4.38	4.38	3.38	2.00	3.53
C	4.25	3.62	1.50	1.37	2.69
D	7.62	5.12	2.25	2.12	4.28
E	5.50	6.12	1.25	1.25	3.53
F	3.37	3.87	1.62	1.00	2.47
Total	5.04	4.38	2.00	1.40	3.20

was exactly as predicted, but with counselor-schools E and F the reinforcement treatment produced slightly higher frequencies of information-seeking behavior than did the model-reinforcement treatment. Table 4 also permits inspection of the means associated with each of the six counselor-schools.

TABLE 5

Mean Frequency of External Information-Seeking Behavior by Sex of Subject, Counselor-School and Setting

Counselor-School	Individual Setting			Group Setting		
	Male	Female	Total	Male	Female	Total
A	2.62	2.25	2.44	1.75	4.25	3.00
B	3.75	3.25	3.50	2.63	4.50	3.56
C	2.25	3.12	2.68	2.50	2.88	2.69
D	3.50	3.88	3.69	5.75	4.00	4.87
E	3.25	5.50	4.37	2.25	3.12	2.68
F	2.88	2.38	2.63	2.13	2.00	2.06
Total	3.04	3.40	3.22	2.83	3.46	3.14

The differences between these means proved to be significant, as reported in Table 1, but the exact cause for this difference cannot be isolated since subjects were not assigned at random to the six counselor-schools.

The nature of the remaining two significant interaction effects can be seen in Table 5. With four of the six counselor-schools the group setting produced slightly higher mean frequencies than did the individual setting. However, with counselor-schools E and F the individual setting produced higher frequencies of information-seeking behavior than the group setting. On the average there was no significant difference between individual and group settings, but within certain of the counselor-schools differences between these two settings were large enough to produce the significant interaction effect.

The significant second order interaction involving sex of subject, counselor-school and setting can also be observed in Table 5. The relative effectiveness of group and individual counseling appears to depend not only on factors associated with the different counselors and schools but also upon the sex of the subjects involved.

TABLE 6

Significance of the Differences between Mean Frequencies and Varieties of External Information-Seeking Behavior in Individual and Group Settings

| | | | Setting | | |
Sex of Subject	Criterion	Treatment	Indiv.	Group	t
M	Freq.	M-R	4.33	5.75	2.07*
M	Freq.	R	4.08	2.75	1.94
M	Var.	M-R	4.08	4.50	.75
M	Var.	R	3.83	2.66	2.09*
F	Freq.	M-R	5.00	5.08	.12
F	Freq.	R	5.33	5.33	.00
F	Var.	M-R	4.41	4.25	.29
F	Var.	R	4.67	4.67	.00

*$p < .05$ (two-tail test)

The interaction between treatment and setting did not reach conventional levels of significance. However, since the distinction between individual and group settings had most meaning for subjects in the model-reinforcement and reinforcement treatments, a separate breakdown and analysis for these two treatments by setting is summarized in Table 6. The results indicated that for males model-reinforcement counseling was more effective in group settings than it was in individual settings. Reinforcement counseling with males, however, was more effective in an individual setting than it was in a group setting. For females, the settings and treatments produced virtually identical frequencies and varieties of information-seeking behavior. A complete report of all means and standard deviations for all combinations of independent variables is available elsewhere (Thoresen, 1964).

Discussion

On the basis of these results the following conclusions seem warranted:

1. When model-reinforcement counseling and reinforcement counseling were specifically designed to increase the occupational and educational information-seeking behavior of students, each counseling technique produced more specific information-seeking behavior than that performed by equivalent control groups.
2. The model-reinforcement treatment was more effective for the male students than was reinforcement counseling, but a similar difference for females was not found.
3. Although individual and group counseling settings were equally effective on the average, male subjects receiving model-reinforcement counseling were stimulated more by the group than the individual setting. Reinforcement counseling for males was more effective in the individual than in the group setting.
4. The significant main and interaction effects for counselor-schools indicate that different counselors and/or school settings have differential effects with males and females in group and individual counseling.

One reason why model-reinforcement counseling was more effective for males might be that the model student was a high school male who discussed the field of law, college athletics and ROTC. Such concerns had little direct interest for most females. The model-reinforcement counseling procedure might have been more effective than reinforcement counseling for the females if a female model had been used. A study is currently underway to investigate this possibility. In addition, five of the six counselors were females. The addition of a male model might have lent more authority to the female counselors in the eyes of the male subjects.

In the group settings there were two males and two females. The combination of the tape-recorded male model plus another male counselee might have made the group setting seem particularly relevant to the males. This might explain the superority of group model reinforcement for males. In the reinforcement counseling treatment, however, most of the males were counseled by a female, a situation which might have been easily tolerable in an individual setting but which might have proved more embarrassing in a group situation with only one other male and two females. Such after-the-fact speculating can only be verified by future experimentation.

The fact that individual and group counseling were not equally effective with each of the counselor-schools cannot be fully explained. It seems quite likely that some of the counselors were more effective in group settings than others, but it could also be that some schools had provided more group work experience for their students than other schools. Most of the special counselors felt more threatened by the group counseling than the individual counseling, and some of them undoubtedly responded to this stress more effectively than others. However, the specific factors which caused group counseling to be more or less effective in some situations than in others need further exploration.

Many questions remain unanswered. What effect would different kinds of models have on the information-seeking behavior of various types of students? Are certain kinds of verbal reinforcers more effective when used by certain counselors than by others? Would a greater or lesser number of counseling interviews have produced greater differences? Would a live model or a model presented by means of both audio and video media have been more or less effective? How does the timing of the counselor's reinforcement affect the amount of information-seeking behavior produced? Would techniques similar to these be equally effective in producing other kinds of behavior change desired by counselees?

This study has deomonstrated that counselors can design specific procedures that will result in measurable behavior change on the part of students. In this particular study it was information-seeking behavior that provided the criteria, but counseling itself involves much more than merely promoting information-seeking behavior. In vocational and educational counseling, students need help in formulating reasonable alternatives, discovering the likelihood that they will be successful in each alternative, finding relevant information about where each alternative would lead, considering the relative values associated with each outcome and weighing all these factors carefully in arriving at a tentative decision. Carefully designed procedures for helping students accomplish each of these types of behavior have not yet been devised, but future experimentation may clarify the techniques that will prove most beneficial.

Similarly, a behavioral approach to counseling may prove equally effective with "personal" and "emotional" types of problems. The difficulty for the counselor is one of penetrating the abstract labels which customarily characterize maladaptive behavior to specify the particular change in behavior that the client wishes to make (Krumboltz, 1964). Once the behavior has been defined, a strategy can be developed to increase the likelihood that such a behavior will occur in the future. Work in these directions is just beginning.

REFERENCES

Bandura, A., & Walters, R. H. *Social learning and personality development*. New York: Holt, Rinehart and Winston, 1963.

Bandura, A., & McDonald, F. J. The influence of social reinforcement and the behavior of models in shaping children's moral judgments. *J. abnorm. soc. Psychol.*, 1963, *67*, 274-281.

Bandura, A. J., Ross, D., & Ross, S. A. Imitation of film-mediated aggressive models. *J. abnorm. soc. Psychol.*, 1963, *66*, 3-11.

Bandura, A. J. Social learning through imitation. In M. R. Jones (Ed.), *Nebraska symposium on motivation*. Lincoln, Neb.: Univer. of Nebraska Press, 1962. pp. 211-269.

Gelatt, H. B. Decision-making: a conceptual frame of reference for counseling. *J. counsel. Psychol.*, 1962, *9*. 240-245.

Greenspoon, J. Verbal conditioning and clinical psychology. In A. J. Bachrach (Ed.), *Experimental foundations of clinical psychology*. New York: Basic Books, 1962, pp. 510-553.

Krasner, L. The therapist as a social reinforcement machine. In H. H. Strupp & L. Luborsky (Eds.), *Research in psychotherapy*, Vol. II. Washington, D.C.: Amer. Psychol. Assoc., 1962.

Krumboltz, J. D. Counseling for behavior change. Paper presented at the American Personnel and Guidance Association Convention, Boston, Mass., April, 1963. (Mimeo.).

Krumboltz, J. D. Parable of the good counselor. *Personnel Guid. J.*, 1964, *43*, 118-124.

Maccoby, Eleanor E. Role-taking in childhood and its consequences for social learning. *Child Development*. 1959, *30*, 239-252.

Mussen, P. H., & Distler, L. Masculinity, identification, and father-son relationships. *J. abnorm. soc. Psychol.*, 1959, *59*, 350-356.

Rickard, H. C. Manipulating verbal behavior in groups: a comparison of three intervention techniques. *Psychol. Rep.*, 1961, *9*, 729-736.

Ryan, T. Antoinette, & Krumboltz, J. D. Effect of planned reinforcement counseling on client decision-making behavior. *J. counsel. Psychol.*, 1964, *11*, 315-323.

Schroeder, W. W. The effect of reinforcement counseling and model-reinforcement counseling on information-seeking behavior of high school students. Unpublished Ph.D. dissertation, Stanford Univer., 1964.

Thoresen, C. E. An experimental comparison of counseling techniques for producing information-seeking behavior. Unpublished Ph.D. dissertation, Stanford Univer., 1964.

Walters, R. H., Llewellyn-Thomas, E., & Acker, C. W. Enhancement of punitive behavior by audio-visual displays. *Science*, 1962, *136*, 872-873.

Control of Hyperactivity by Social Reinforcement of Attending Behavior[1]

K. Eileen Allen, Lydia B. Henke, Florence R. Harris, Donald M. Baer, and Nancy J. Reynolds

There exists now a series of experimental field studies applying reinforcement principles to problem behaviors of preschool children. These studies have dealt with crying (Hart, Allen, Buell, Harris, & Wolf, 1964), regressive crawling (Harris, Johnston, Kelley, & Wolf, 1964), isolate play (Allen, Hart, Buell, Harris, & Wolf, 1964), passivity (Johnston, Kelley, Harris, & Wolf 1966), non-cooperative behaviors (Hart, Reynolds, Brawley, Harris, & Baer, 1966), self-mutilative scrathing (Allen & Harris, 1966), autistic behavior (Brawley, Harris, Peterson, Allen, & Fleming, 1966; Wolf, Risley, & Mees, 1964) and classroom disruptiveness (Allen, Reynolds, Harris, & Baer, 1966). In each instance, the behavior under examination was highly responsive to adult social reinforcement. The present study was conducted to ascertain whether similar social reinforcement procedures could alter the hyperactivity of a 4-year-old boy who tended to flit from activity to activity.

Attending behavior, commonly referred to as "attention span," has long been recognized as a crucial and desirable alternative to hyperactivity. What has not always been clear is the extent to which attending is a behavior which teachers can help a child to develop, although Patterson (Patterson, Jones, Whittier, & Wright, 1965) has done work in this area with older children. Thus it is of interest to determine if systematic social reinforcement can increase the duration of a young child's attending to an activity, and also to analyze the successive steps a teacher might take in helping a child to maintain his attention to an activity for increasingly long periods.

One of the ultimate objectives of preschool education is, of course, to develop a child's skills in using materials constructively and creatively. An essential first step toward this objective sometimes must be to increase the time the child spends engaging in each activity. Fortunately, duration of attention can be defined, observed, and reliably recorded in the field situation.

[1]Reprinted from the *Journal of Educational Psychology*, 1967, *58*, 231-237, with the permission of the American Psychological Association and the authors.

Method

Subject

James was one of 16 normal children of middle-socioeconomic status who comprised the 4-year-old group in the Laboratory Pre-school. At the inception of the study, he was 4 years, 6 months old and had been attending school for 3 months.

James was a vigorous, healthy child with a well-developed repertoire of motor, social, and intellectual skills. Although he made a comfortable adjustment to school during the first few weeks, a tendency to move constantly from one play activity to another, thereby spending little time in any one pursuit, was noted early. Since such behavior is common to some young children in a new situation, his teachers merely continued their friendly efforts to engage him in more prolonged and concentrated use of materials.

After 12 weeks James showed no diminution in number of activity changes during play periods. An observer then was assigned to record his behavior, noting his activities and the time spent in each. Records kept over 5 school mornings showed that although occasionally James stayed with an activity for 1, 2, or 3 minutes, the average duration of an activity was less than 1 minute. The parent reported that the same kind of "flightiness" had long caused concern at home. It was agreed that a study be made of ways of helping James to increase his attending behavior.

Procedure

The procedure for increasing the duration of time spent in any activity was to make adult social reinforcement contingent solely on the subject's (*S's*) emitting attending behavior for a specified minimum period of time. Attending behavior was defined as engaged in one activity. This included play activity (a) with a single type of material, such as blocks or paint; (b) in a single location, such as in the sandbox or at a table; or (c) in a single dramatic role, such as sailor or fireman. Adult social reinforcement (Bijou & Baer, 1965) was defined as one or more of the following teacher behaviors: talking to *S* while facing him within a distance of 3 feet, or from a greater distance using his name; touching *S*; and giving him additional materials suitable to the ongoing activity. Withholding or withdrawing social reinforcement consisted of turning away from *S*; not looking or smiling at him; not speaking to him; and directing attention to some other child or activity.

One teacher was assigned major responsibility for maintaining reinforcement contingencies. However, since the two other teachers might at times also deliver or withhold reinforcement, each had to remain constantly aware of the conditions in force.

The design of the study required four successive experimental stages, as delineated by Harris (1964).

Base line. The existing rate, or operant level, of activity changes prior to systematic application of adult social reinforcement was recorded for several play sessions.

Reinforcement. Social reinforcement was presented immediately when attending behavior had been emitted for 1 unbroken minute. Reinforcement was maintained continuously until *S* left the material or the area or verbalized a change in his play role. Immediately consequent upon such a shift in play activity, social reinforcement ceased until 1 minute of attending behavior had again been emitted. The procedure was continued until attending behaviors had materially increased.

Reversal. Then, to ascertain whether social reinforcement was in fact the determining factor in modifying the behavior under study, reinforcement was again delivered on a noncontingent basis such as had been in effect during the base-line period. This reversal of contingencies was carried out long enough to yield a clear assessment of the effects of the changed conditions.

Reinstatement. During this period, the procedures in effect during the second stage, Reinforcement, were reinstituted. After attending behaviors had again increased in duration, the criterion for presenting social reinforcement was raised to 2 minutes.

Recording

The *S's* attending behavior and adult social reinforcement, as previously defined, were coded and recorded in successive 10-second intervals by an observer using a stopwatch and a red flashlight with a magnet attached. The recording system was similar to that described by Allen *et al.*, (1964). Each period of attending to one activity was enclosed in brackets. Since an increase in attending behavior brought a corresponding decrease in the number of activity changes, data on attending behavior were counted and graphed in terms of the number of activity changes occurring within successive 50-minute time units. In general, but not necessarily, two 50-minute periods indicated 1 day of recording of play time exclusive of teacher-structured or teacher-directed activities.

During the two reinforcement stages, the observer used a flashlight to inform teachers when *S* reached criterion for social reinforcement. The cue consisted of placing the flashlight on top of the metal clip of the clipboard as soon as *S* had emitted 1 minute, and later 2 minutes, of attending behavior. When the behavior stopped, the observer removed the flashlight and placed it under the clipboard, where it remained out of sight until criterion attending behavior had again been emitted. Teachers were instructed to maintain awareness of the flashlight position and to check it before giving *S* any social reinforcement.

Periodically throughout the study, observer reliability on attending behaviors, activity changes, and adult social reinforcement was checked by an independent observer. Agreement of records ranged between 97% and 100%. No post checks of attending behavior could be made because the study was terminated by the close of the school year, at which time the family moved to another city.

In addition to the behavior under study, some assessment of whether social aspects of *S*'s behavior were affected by changes in his attending behavior seemed desirable. Therefore, *S*'s verbalizations, proximity to, and cooperation with other children were defined, coded, and recorded. The quality of the child's social behavior was estimated by considering co-operative behavior as high-level social behavior and mere proximity as low-level social behavior, in contrast to isolate behavior, which was considered non-social. Interrater reliability on these parameters ranged between 84% and 92%.

Results

Base-line—Stage 1. The number of activity changes that James made in each of 21 successive 50-minute periods of free-choice play, both indoors and out, is shown in Figure 1. The fewest numbr of activity changes were 33 during Period 12, with an average duration of 1 minute 29 seconds per activity. The greatest number of activity changes occurred in Period 14, with 82 changes and an average duration of 37 seconds per activity. The overall average for the base-line state (the operant level of the behavior under study) was 56 activity changes per 50-minute period, with an average duration of 53 seconds per activity.

The amount of teacher reinforcement presented to James on a random, noncontingent basis averaged 16% of each session. This rate was within the normal range in this pre-school of amount of teacher attention per child.

Reinforcement—Stage 2. This stage comprised seven 50-minute periods, as shown in Figure 1. Activity changes ranged from a high of 41 in Period 22 (the first period of experimental procedures) to a low of 19 in Period 28 (the last period of experimental procedures). The overall average of activity changes for the seven periods was 27, with an average duration of 1 minute 51 seconds per activity, or twice that of the base-line stage. Teacher reinforcement during Stage 2 averaged 38% of each period.

Reversal—Stage 3. During the four-period reversal stage (Figure 1, Stage 3), activity changes rose markedly. An average of 51 activity changes per period occurred, with an average duration of 59 seconds per activity. Both measures (number of changes and average duration) were comparable to the base-line stage. During the reversal teacher attention averaged 14% of each period.

Reinstatement—Stage 4-A and B. Reinforcement contingencies during Stage 4-A, Figure 1, were the same as those in effect during Stage 2. Under these conditions, the rate of activity changes again dropped markedly, with a high of 31 and a low of 12 (Periods 33 and 36, respectively). The overall average of activity changes for the eight periods of Stage 4-A was 20, with an average duration of $2\frac{1}{2}$ minutes per activity. Teacher reinforcement during Stage 4-A averaged 31% of each period.

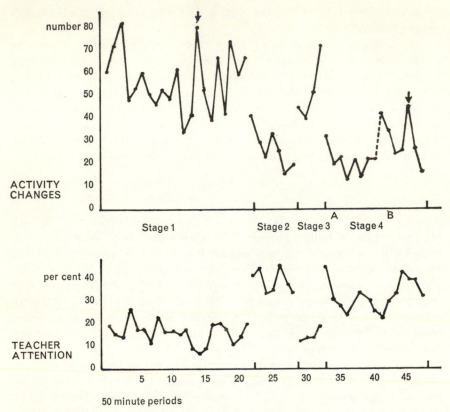

FIG. 1. Number of activity changes of S during 50-minute periods throughout study, compared with concurrent percentage of time S received teacher attention. (Stage 1, base-line of activity change under non-contingent attention. Stage 2, attention contingent on 1 minute of attending. Stage 3, base-line condition. Stage 4, contingent attending as in Stage 2; at dotted line, criterion for attending raised to 2 minutes. Arrows indicate days S's mother visited.)

In Period 41 (Figure 1, Stage 4-B) the criterion for delivery of social reinforcement was raised to 2 minutes of attending behavior. Some increase in number of activity changes occurred during Period 41, with a subsequent leveling off. During this part of Stage 4, the greatest number of activity changes was 45, occurring in Period 45; the fewest number, 16, occurred in Period 47. The average number of activity changes during Stage 4-B was 32 per period, with an average duration of 1 minute 34 seconds per activity. Teacher reinforcement averaged 33% of each period.

The overall average for Period 4 (A and B combined) was 27 changes per session, with an average duration of 1 minute 51 seconds per activity.

Social behavior. The quality of social behavior was defined and measured as high, low, and isolate. Although not under experimental manipulation, it merits remark for its constancy throughout the experimental procedures. The averages per session were as follows:

	High	Low	Isolate
Stage 1	45%	37%	16%
Stage 2	50%	38%	12%
Stage 3	48%	40%	13%
Stage 4-A	49%	39%	13%
Stage 4-B	41%	44%	15%

These figures were well within the range of the pre-school's normative social behavior.

Discussion

The data presented in Figure 1 give strong support to the hypothesis that attending behavior is "teachable" in the sense that it can be shaped and maintained by teachers. Moreover, adult social reinforcement again appears to be a powerful instrument for this purpose. When adult social reinforcement was given in a systematic fashion, solely as an immediate consequence of continuing attending behavior, the number of activity changes diminished to half the number that occurred under the more usual, non-systematic adult procedures of the base-line and reversal stages.

The continuing fluctuation of the data which occurred during each of the experimental periods may merit comment. Behavior does, of course, vary somewhat from day to day. The factors responsible for this variability were not brought under experimental control. Many of them are inherent in the field setting of a preschool, and could hardly be controlled in that setting. It is apparent, though, that systematic control of adult social reinforcement, which is readily achieved, is sufficient to override these factors (Bare & Wolf, 1966).

Two of the high points in activity changes, Periods 14 and 45, suggest possible examples of such uncontrolled factors. During Periods 14 and 45 James's mother was present for the entire morning. She interacted with him freely each time he contacted her and went with him frequently when he requested her to come and look at a particular object or play situation. In addition, she made frequent suggestions that he "settle down" and paint her a picture, build with blocks, or "tend to his own business." The mother appeared to have more reinforcing value than the teachers on these novel occasions, a fact not surprising in itself. The fact that the mother was often reinforcing behaviors incompatible with the behavior that teachers were shaping strengthened the original hypothesis that the child's short attention span was in fact a function of adult social reinforcement.

No formal attempt was made to secure data on the quality of James's attending behaviors. In the judgment of the teachers, however, the quality improved steadily. During Stage 4, James frequently spent 15 to 20 minutes pursuing a single activity such as digging, woodworking, or block building.

Within these activities he made frequent excursions to get additional materials relevant to his project, such as a wheelbarrow or a dirt sifter. By definition, such departures were recorded as activity changes, even though he returned and continued with the same play. Such occasions, clearly delineated in the data, teachers considered evidence of improved quality of attending, for the trips were relevant to a core activity, rather than a series of unrelated activity changes as were typical of Stages 1, 2, and 3. The data thus are probably a conservative estimate of the degree of change produced in James's attention span.

The data on social behavior are of particular interest for they answer in part the often-asked question regarding peripheral effects on overall behavior patterns when one aspect of behavior is under intensive treatment. As was indicated, there was no change in the quality of James's social interaction, already deemed satisfactory by teachers at the start of the study, though the number of separate contacts did decrease, as was predicted. These data add to the evidence that only the behavior specifically being worked on increases or decreases as a function of the reinforcement contingencies.

Throughout the study, the child's mother was informed of procedures and progress in frequent parent conferences. However, no systematic attempts were made to program presentation of social reinforcement from the family. For one thing, the mother worked, and there were frequent changes of babysitters. Nevertheless, the mother reported that James had "settled down" considerably at home. She kept no data to substantiate these statements, but did relate several incidents which indicated that there was some generalization from preschool to home. Both the mother and the teachers judged that James was eminently more ready for kindergarten at the end of the study than he had been prior to it. The importance of intensive attending behavior to future learning is obvious. The ease of socially altering attending behavior in *either* direction, while perhaps less obvious, is no less important to an analysis of children's intellectual, perceptual, and social development.

REFERENCES

Allen, K. E., Hart, B. M., Buell, J. S., Harris, F. R., & Wolf, M. M. Effects of social reinforcement on isolate behavior of a nursery school child. *Child Development*, 1964, *35*, 511-518.

Allen, K. E., & Harris, F. F. Elimination of a child's excessive scratching by training the mother in reinforcement procedures. *Behaviour Research and Therapy*, 1966, *4*, 79-84.

Allen, K. E., Reynolds, N. J., Harris, F. R., & Baer, D. M. Elimination of disruptive classroom behaviors of a pair of preschool boys through systematic control of adult social reinforcement. Unpublished manuscript, University of Washington, 1966.

Baer, D. M., & Wolf, M. M. The reinforcement contingency in preschool and remedial education. Paper presented at the meeting of the Carnegie Foundation Conference on Preschool Education, Chicago, January 1966.

Bijou, S. W., & Baer, D. M. *Child development*. Vol. 2, New York: Appleton-Century-Crofts, 1965.

Brawley, E. R., Harris, F. R., Peterson, R. F., Allen, K. E., & Fleming, R. E. Behavior modification of an autistic child. Unpublished manuscript, University of Washington, 1966.

Harris, F. R., Wolf, M. M., & Baer, D. M. Effects of adult social reinforcement on child behavior. *Young Children*, 1964, *20*, 8-17.

Harris, F. R., Johnston, M. K., Kelley, C. S., & Wolf, M. M. Effects of positive social reinforcement on regressed crawling in a preschool child. *Journal of Educational Psychology*, 1964, *55*, 35-41.

Hart, B. M., Allen, K. E., Buell, J. S., Harris, F. R., & Wolf, M. M. Effects of social reinforcement on operant crying. *Journal of Experimental Child Psychology*, 1964, *1*, 145-153.

Hart, B. M., Reynolds, N. J., Brawley, E. R., Harris, F. R., & Baer, D. M. Effects of contingent and non-contingent social reinforcement of the isolate behavior of a nursery school girl. Unpublished manuscript, University of Washington, 1966.

Johnston, M. K., Kelley, C. S., Harris, F. R., & Wolf, M. M. An application of reinforcement principles to development of motor skill of a young child. *Child Development*, 1966, *37*, 379-387.

Patterson, G. R., Jones, R., Whittier, J., & Wright, M. A. A behavior modification technique for the hyperactive child. *Behaviour Research and Therapy*, 1965, *2*, 217-226.

Wolf, M. M., Risley, T., & Mees, H. Application of operant conditioning procedures to the behavior problems of an autistic child. *Behaviour Research and Therapy*, 1964, *1*, 305-312.

Group Counseling and Behavior Therapy with Test-Anxious College Students[1]

Martin Katahn, Stuart Strenger, and Nancy Cherry

While test anxiety seems to be fairly widespread among college students, the magnitude of the problem together with the lack of clear-cut therapeutic procedures has discouraged the development of regular continuing programs for test-anxious students on most college campuses. Wolpe's (1958) procedures for systematic desensitization seem to be especially well suited to this problem in terms of both their reported effectiveness in reducing anxiety (Eysenck & Rachman, 1965; Grossberg, 1964) and their efficiency in time and personnel. Lazarus (1961) has reported success using desensitization with phobic reactions in a group setting, which further increases the economy of the procedures. While not specifically aimed at the problem of test anxiety, work done by Spielberger and Weitz (1964) indicates that group-counseling procedures may be effective in improving the grades of generally anxious, under-achieving college students. Only a limited number of students, however, benefited from the counseling procedures without desensitization, and a number of other factors interfered with the program's overall effectiveness. Nevertheless, this program of counseling is one of but 2 out of 15 studies mentioned by Chestnut (1965) in which group counseling had any effect on the academic achievement of underachieving college students. Similarly, Chestnut's results, while encouraging, seem ambiguous since changes due to counseling were manifested only in differences in regression coefficients among treatment and control groups. These regression coefficients related pre- and post-counseling grade-point averages (GPAs). Significant pre- and post-counseling changs in GPAs themselves were not obtained.

This paper describes a group-behavior therapy approach to the treatment of test anxiety which combines systematic desensitization and counseling procedures. The aim of these therapy groups was to change directly behaviors which are maladaptive in the academic setting. Systematic

[1]Reprinted from the *Journal of Consulting Psychology*, 1966, *30*, 544-549, with the permission of the American Psychological Association and the authors.

desensitization was used to bring the students' anxiety within manageable limits and counseling (suggestion and advice) was used to help the students develop the necessary skills for improved academic performance.

Method

Participants. The 45 students involved in this study were Vanderbilt University undergraduates enrolled in one or more psychology courses during the fall and spring semesters of the 1964–65 academic year. A group program for test-anxious students was described in four second-year psychology classes during regular class periods by the senior author. Following the program's description, students were given a questionnaire containing 8-point scales on which they rated their tension, excitement, and feelings of unpleasantness before, during, and after examinations. Students wishing to participate in one of the test-anxiety groups so indicated at the end of the questionnaire. Scores on a 16-item true-false version of the Test Anxiety Scale (TAS) (Sarason, 1958) were available for all students from previous testing earlier in the semester.

Forty-five students obtained scores of 10 or more on the TAS (the upper 25% of the distribution). Of these, 22 indicated a desire to participate in the program. Sixteen of these were initially selected for the program simply because their schedules permitted them to attend the meetings. The other six had conflicting schedules and comprised a volunteer control group. All remaining students with TAS scores over 10 comprised a nonvolunteer group. The first group of eight students (four males and four females) began meeting in October 1964, and the second group (four males, four females) began meeting in February 1965. Two of the eight students in the second group, both males, felt that the group might not be suited to their particular problems at the end of the first group meeting and decided not to participate. Data for these two subjects are not included in any of the analyses (their mean GPA decreased by .06 of a point during the period of this investigation).

In addition to changes in TAS scores, results were assessed on the basis of any differences in cumulative GPA before the semester of counseling and (a) for the fall group, the average of the two semesters following counseling, and (b) for the spring group the semester following counseling. GPAs at Vanderbilt are a weighted average in which 3 points are credited for each hour of A, 2 for B, 1 for C, and 0 for D and F. (Differences in hours credited for graduation requirements for D and F grades are irrelevant for GPA computations in this study.) A 1.00 average is required of students in order to remain in good standing, and a 2.00 average (honor roll) is obtained by about 15% of the student body.

Procedure. Space limitations naturally preclude detailed presentation of the procedures and the content of group discussions.[2] In brief, groups met with a leader and coleader (the senior author and one or the other of the junior authors) for a total of eight sessions, each approximately 1 hour in length. The senior author would be considered psychoanalytically oriented by previous training, and the coleaders were advanced graduate students who had participated in other forms of group therapy prior to this study. The meetings were held in a psychology department seminar room, with members seated in lightly padded armchairs around a long table. The first session began with general introductions of the students to each other. The leader stated the purpose of the group, emphasizing that the members shared common reasons for their participation. He explained the theoretical orientation under which he would operate (Wolpe, 1958), with examples of how anxiety may be acquired and how it might be reduced. The group members then discussed their own particular problems, with the leaders themselves contributing examples from their own personal experience. Students found that certain types of experiences were likely to elicit a great deal of anxiety in everyone, for example, waiting for the professor to hand out the test 5 minutes before the examination or taking out their notes to study the night before the test. They also found that their anxiety could be manifested in idiosyncratic ways, for example, becoming anxious as they found that they could not keep up with the professor while taking notes during classes, feeling their hands cramp up while writing answers to the test, or just taking out their books to study the material before a regular class period. Most students felt some degree of anxiety when they were faced with telling their parents about their grades. This discussion lasted approximately 25 minutes. At that point the leader explained the procedure for constructing an anxiety hierarchy (Wolpe, 1958). Students were asked to list 10 experiences which elicited various amounts of anxiety. They then ranked these experiences in the order of increasing anxiety from 1 to 10 so that 1 was the experience which elicited the least anxiety and 10 was the experience which elicited the greatest amount of anxiety. A typical hierarchy is as follows: (1) going into a regularly scheduled class period, (2) going into a regularly scheduled class in which the professor asks the students to participate, (3) sitting down to study before a regularly scheduled class, (4) having a test returned, (5) studying for a class in which I am scared of the professor, (6) seeing a test question and not being sure of the answer, (7) studying for a test the night before, (8) waiting to enter the room where a test is to be given, (9) being called on to answer a question in class by a professor who scares me, and (10) being in the class

[2]A manual used by the counselors in the training of deep muscle relaxation in the groups is available upon request from the first author of the paper, together with transcribed excerpts taken from tape recordings of ongoing groups, which convey something of the mood and nature of the group meetings. Sections of the recorded interviews are now being analyzed according to three content analysis methods (Jaffe, 1961; Laffal, 1960; Lennard & Bernstein, 1960). The authors would like to thank three of the counselors now active in the test-anxiety programs, Norman E. Wheeler, C. Warren Thompson, and Leighton J. Cunningham, for their invaluable assistance in this project. Copies of the sections of the tapes which were analyzed, together with the results are also available upon request.

waiting for the examination to be handed out. After approximately 10 minutes of work on the anxiety hierarchies, the leader interrupted, asking the students to consider their experiences during the coming week, so that they would be able to complete their hierarchies at the next session. The remaining 15 minutes were devoted to the first steps in relaxation training.

The procedures followed in relaxation training were an adaptation of those used by Wolpe (1958). The role of the skeletal muscle system in the feeling of anxiety was explained. As an example, the leader and coleader demonstrated the feeling of tension in the arms by circulating around the room holding the students' wrists and asking them to push and pull as hard as they could against the stabilizing pressure exerted by the leader and coleader. Each student was then asked to pull as hard as he could against the pressure exerted by the leader (or coleader) for about 5 seconds. Then he was instructed to relax slowly and to let his arm fall onto the arm of his chair or into his lap. This procedure was repeated with each arm, with the leader and coleader checking to be sure that each student was able to achieve a satisfactory degree of relaxation. (In this and the following session one student was unable to learn the relaxation procedures in the group setting. Two private meetings were held with the leader in order to train him in the relaxation procedures. He was able to learn them in these two meetings, and his progress in the group was satisfactory.) The first meeting ended with this preliminary demonstration of the relaxation procedures. Students were told that the relaxation procedures would be completed at the next meeting and reminded to keep track of their anxiety experiences during the following week so that they would be able to complete their anxiety hierarchies at the second session.

The second session and the sessions thereafter began with the leaders asking one or the other of the following questions: "How have things been going this week?" or "What kinds of experiences have you been having this past week?" Whenever possible the leaders made definite suggestions for the handling of certain problems. For example, if a student had trouble organizing himself for studying before a test or before a class, he was encouraged to set himself a minimum goal that he coud be quite sure of reaching and then, over time, to increase the requirement he set for himself. Many students seemed to be so anxious about their course work that just the thought of studying before a class elicited enough anxiety to prevent them from sitting down and working. By the third or fourth session, after they had had practice in relaxation, they were instructed in how to use these procedures to reduce their tension before studying, while at the same time setting for themselves a reasonable period of time for working.

Some students reported feeling guilty about not working hard enough, no matter how long they studied. This led to discussions over the role of work and play in their education and of ways of planning each day's work so that reasonable amounts of time were spent in both activities. Since most of the test-anxious students felt that grades were terribly important, some time was spent discussing the aims of education, professors' attitudes toward grades, and what professors themselves might find rewarding about teaching. Ways of studying and of rehearsing the material in lectures and texts were discussed.

Sometime during the second meeting it was suggested that students buy a book entitled *On Becoming an Educated Person* by Virginia Voeks (1964). This book discusses a number of problems faced by students during their college careers and makes certain suggestions for overcoming them. The leaders suggested that students read this book, paying special attention to anything that was personally relevant and perhaps bringing in their thoughts and questions for discussion by the group. No attempt was made by the leaders to refer to anything specific in this book.

After approximately 20 minutes of discussion at the start of this second meeting, another 10 to 15 minutes were spent in completing the anxiety hierarchies. The leaders helped by giving examples of the kinds of experiences students in general might have with respect to academic anxieties. The students were encouraged to make their anxiety hierarchies as specific as possible so that with each item an actual scene could be visualized during the desensitization procedures which were to follow. The remaining 25 minutes were devoted to completing the relaxation training. In contrast to Wolpe's procedure, training proceeded from the toes to the head. Select muscle groups were chosen for tensing and relaxing and the leaders circulated around the room holding ankles, knees, etc., in order to illustrate the difference in feeling between tension and relaxation.

Students were asked to practice their relaxation procedures preferably twice but at least once a day for 15 minutes. In the remaining sessions, approximately 40 minutes were devoted to group discussion and the remaining 20 minutes to systematic desensitization. During systematic desensitization students were asked to pick three items from their hierarchies, starting with the item which elicited the least amount of anxiety. Systematic desensitization began in the third session with each scene envisioned three times for 5 to 10 seconds. While anxiety was occasionally not completely extinguished to a particular scene before going on to the next, it was, in these groups, invariably reduced from the first presentation to the third. During remaining sessions, students were asked to pick up where they left off, beginning with the last scene to which they had been able to completely extinguish anxiety and going on with two more for that particular session. Occasionally a student would report that certain of the items on his list, which he had not yet worked on, were no longer very anxiety producing, but that certain things had happened to him during the week which did cause considerable anxiety. He was encouraged to delete irrelevant items and to substitute these new items at their appropriate place. As early as the fourth session, students began to report signs of improvement, for example, sleeping better before a test than they ever had before and no longer getting writer's cramps while they were taking notes in class or in writing answers to test questions.

Students were encouraged to attempt to generalize the results of their relaxation training to other situations which might cause them to feel some anxiety. Special emphasis was placed on the role of breathing as an aid to relaxation. Students were told that with practice they would soon learn to substitute a relaxation response in every anxiety producing situation by simply "letting go" in the tense part of their bodies after taking a deep breath and exhaling. As the sessions progressed, students reported increasing ability to do this.

Results and Discussion

Mean GPAs before and after the group program are presented in Table 1. For Treatment Group 1 (TG 1) the "after" average is the mean of the first and second semester during and after participation in the program. For Treatment Group 2 (TG 2) the "after" average is for the semester in which the students completed the program. Averages for control subjects obtained from the fall semester are averaged in a way similar to that used for TG 1. Averages for controls obtained during the spring semester are averaged in a way similar to that for TG 2. It can be seen from Table 1 that the mean GPA of the treatment groups increased from 1.28 to 1.63, while the mean of the control groups increased from 1.30 to 1.36. Since results did not appear to differ between treatment groups or between types of controls, for statistical comparison, TGs 1 and 2 are combined into a single treatment group while volunteer and nonvolunteer control groups are combined into a single control group. Comparing GPAs before and after the program, the interaction of groups by grades before and after, was significant, $F = 4.42$, p, $< .05$ [Lindquist (1953) Type I analysis of variance]. A t test directly comparing the grades of the treatment group before and after was significant at the .01 level ($t = 3.46$). The small change in the control group mean was not significant. Thus, the group program had a significant effect on the academic achievement of the students who participated.

TABLE 1

Grade Point Averages Before and After the Group Test-Anxiety Program for Treatment and Control Groups

	Before	After
Treatment Group I (N = 8)	1.42	1.74
Treatment Group II (N = 6)	1.11	1.46
Mean of treatment groups	1.28	1.63
Volunteer controls (N = 6)	1.24	1.24
Nonvolunteer controls (N = 23)	1.31	1.39
Mean of control groups	1.30	1.36

A question might be raised concerning the duration of the program's effects. This can be partly answered by looking at the GPA's for TG 1 alone since this group was started in the fall semester and students completed six of the eight sessions before their final examinations in that semester. Their mean GPA increased from 1.42 to 1.72 during the first semester of their participation. The program ended for this group during the second week of the second semester. Their average for that semester remained higher than that before treatment—1.75.

Results for individuals in the group program indicate that 11 of the 14 students increased their GPA after participation. Of the three who did not, two were failing to maintain satisfactory grades before the program. One of these, a draft-eligible male, decided during the program to go into the Army at the end of that semester. His average fell from .88 to .53. The other, a girl, decided to transfer to another school. Her average fell from .73 to .60. The third, another girl, had a decrease of .02 points in a GPA which was 1.96 to begin with. Among the 11 students who increased their GPA, 3 had unsatisfactory averages before group participation (.81, .97, and .90). These averages increased to 1.00, 1.38, and 1.20, respectively, after group participation. Whereas only one student was on the honor roll before the group program, six made 2.00 averages after participation. In view of the borderline and conditional nature of changes reported by other investigators (Chestnut, 1965; Spielberger & Weitz, 1964) and the general failure of most programs designed to influence academic achievement, these results seem striking indeed. Further evidence of the value of combined behavior therapy and counseling has recently been reported by Paul and Shannon (1966). After participation in a group program similar to that presented here, students suffering from interpersonal performance anxiety in a public speaking course showed significantly higher overall academic achievement. Test anxiety was treated as a subsidiary problem in Paul and Shannon's groups.

The effects of the present group program were not dependent upon the sex of the participants. Males and females showed almost identical increases —females from 1.36 to 1.70, males from 1.18 to 1.53. The higher overall average for females is consistent with a university-wide tendency and is probably due to the fact that admission requirements are much more stringent for females than for males at Vanderbilt.[3]

TAS scores for the treatment groups decreased from an average of 12.4 before treatment to 7.1 after completing the program ($t = 8.60, p < .01$). It was possible to get an "on-the-spot" evaluation of the treatment's effect on TAS scores for the first group at the conclusion of their final psychology

---

[3]Latest GPA including fall 1965 indicate that for seven students still in college, average posttreatment GPAs are 1.56 compared with 1.31 prior to participation. This offers further evidence regarding the permanency of the results. (Of the 14 original students, 2 left as indicated above, 3 graduated, 1 left following her marriage, and 1 transferred to a school closer to home following the death of her father.)

examination and to compare their changes with that of eight control *Ss* who happened to be in one particular course. It will be recalled that students had had six of eight scheduled meetings up to that time. The students involved were given the TAS immediately after finishing the final exam, just before handing in their completed papers. The eight treatment *Ss* had a TAS score of 11.6 prior to treatment. They obtained a score of 9.2 at the time of this exam. Eight control *Ss* in this class decreased from 11.2 to 10.4. While the interaction, Groups X Ratings, just failed to reach significance ($F = 4.17$, with 4.60 needed for $p = .05$), it was felt that a direct *t* test of the difference$_1$ was in order because of the specific predictions made for the treatmens group. For the treated group, a test of the difference in TAS scores resulted in a *t* value of 4.00, $p < .01$, while a test of the difference for the control *Ss* was not significant ($t = 1.08, p > .30$). Thus, after six sessions, it appears that the program was having an ameliorative effect on self-reported test anxiety.

While it is difficult to define the exact nature of the factors producing GPA gains and the changes in TAS scores, the general theoretical orientation of the test-anxiety program is that students with a high degree of anxiety associated with taking tests have somehow learned patterns of behavior which are essentially maladaptive in the academic setting. Therapy took the form of eliminating some of the old responses and of teaching new responses which were more adaptive. Little or no attention was focused on how the old habits were acquired or upon any underlying personality problems. Wolpe's (1958) procedures for systematic desensitization were applied to decondition some of the anxiety experienced by group members. After the conclusion of the group program, all members reported that the relaxation procedures were helpful in alleviating some of the physical symptoms accompanying their anxiety, for example, general tension, difficulty in sleeping the night before an examination, intestinal problems, and in one case a skin rash. In the case of the girl with the skin rash, there was no appearance of this symptom during final-examination week following her participation in the group. While the relaxation procedures and the desensitization process seemed important to the students, they *invariably* felt (in response to a questionnaire item at the conclusion of the program) that the most important aspects of the program were just being able to talk about their problems with other students, finding out that there were others having similar experiences, and learning how to organize their study habits. Several of the students commented that it was very helpful getting to know a professor better and becoming acquainted with a teacher's point of view. Thus, from the students' standpoints, changes in their approaches to studying and in their attitudes toward education were more responsible for their increased academic effectiveness than were the desensitization procedures. While these comments add little to its resolution, they serve to highlight the significance of the recent controversy between Breger and McGaugh (1965, 1966) and Rachman and Eysenck (1966) concerning the exact nature of the changes which take place in behavior-oriented therapy and the factors responsible for such changes. Since the counseling procedures were combined with systematic desensitization in the present study, it is impossible to determine which aspect of the program was, in fact, more important. Working within a behavior therapy conceptualization, Lazarus (1961) has suggested that the medium of verbal interchange within the interviewing situation may itself bring about the incidental or nonspecific reciprocal inhibition of neurotic responses. At the present time a program is under way comparing the effects of the counseling procedure alone, systematic desensitization alone, and the combination as reported in this paper. Prestige of the therapist is also being controlled by using both advanced graduate students and full time faculty as leaders.

It seems worth pointing out that while the groups were unconcerned with any fundamental personality change, many members expressed increased satisfaction with themselves in general as well as greater comfort in the academic environment. The effects of the combination of counseling and behavior therapy seemed to generalize to other situations. For example, one student, a musician, reported feeling much more relaxed when he performed in public and very happy over that development since he did not come into the group with that goal in mind.

While the results of this study strongly indicate that systematic desensitization coupled with behavior-oriented discussion in a group setting is an effective and economical approach to the treatment of test anxiety, a number of other factors may have influenced the outcome of the program. First of all, the participating students were highly motivated volunteers who entered the program with a specific purpose in mind, which contrasts with the orientation of the usual counseling program for underachieving students. Secondly, all participants were in some nonintroductory level psychology course, which reflects an interest in psychological processes. Thirdly, the groups were led by a full-time professor in the department who indicated to the group that he had a research interest in the proceedings. Finally, no controls for placebo effects, prestige of the therapist or therapist differences were contained in the present design. It goes almost without saying that these variables should be examined in future research.

REFERENCES

Breger, L., & McGaugh, J. L. Critique and reformulation of "learning-theory" approaches to psychotherapy and neurosis. *Psychological Bulletin*, 1965, *63*, 338-358.

Breger, L., & McGaugh, J. L. Learning theory and behavior therapy: A reply to Rachman and Eysenck. *Psychological Bulletin*, 1966, *65*, 170-173.

Chestnut, W. J. The effects of structured and unstructured group counseling on male college students' underachievement. *Journal of Counseling Psychology*, 1965, *12*, 388-394.

Eysenck, H. J., & Rachman, S. *The causes and curse of neurosis*. San Diego: Knapp, 1965.

Grossberg, J. M. Behavior therapy: A review. *Psychological Bulletin*, 1964, *62*, 73-88.

Jaffe, J. Dyadic analysis of two psychotherapeutic interviews. In L. A. Gottschalk (Ed.), *Comparative psycholinguistic analysis of two psychotherapeutic interviews*. New York: International Universities Press, 1961.

Laffal, J. The contextual associates of sun and God in Schreber's autobiography. *Journal of Abnormal and Social Psychology*, 1960, *61*, 474-479.

Lazarus, A. A. Group therapy of phobic disorders by systematic desensitization. *Journal of Abnormal and Social Psychology*, 1961, *63*, 504-510.

Lennard, H. J., & Bernstein, A. *The anatomy of psychotherapy*. New York: Columbia University Press, 1960.

Paul, G. L., & Shannon, D. T. Treatment of anxiety through systematic desensitization in therapy groups. *Journal of Abnormal Psychology*, 1966, *71*, 124-135.

Rachman, S., & Eysenck, H. J. Reply to a "Critique and Reformulation" of behavior therapy. *Psychological Bulletin*, 1966, *65*, 165-169.

Sarason, I. G. Interrelationships among individual difference variables, behavior in psychotherapy, and verbal conditioning. *Journal of Abnormal and Social Psychology*, 1958, *56*, 339-351.

Spielberger, C. D. & Weitz, H. Improving the academic performance of anxious college freshmen: A group counseling approach to the prevention of under-achievement. *Psychological Monographs*, 1964, *78*, (13, Whole No. 590).

Voeks, V. *On becoming an educated person*. Philadelphia: Saunders, 1964.

Wolpe, J. *Psychotherapy by reciprocal inhibition*. Stanford: Stanford University Press, 1958.

The Desensitization of Test-Anxiety by Group and Individual Treatment[1]

Richard M. Suinn

Test-anxiety affects many students whose competence in coursework is judged through written examinations. Such anxiety is experienced as an inability to think or remember, a feeling of tension, and difficulty in reading and comprehending simple sentences or directions on an examination. In severe cases, a sensation of nausea may occur. Unfortunately for many ordinarily capable students, the anxiety prevents them from performing up to capacity (Alpert and Haber, 1963; Paul and Erikson, 1964; Suinn, 1965).

Despite the prevalence and importance of this problem, few studies have been done on developing a means for treating test-anxiety. Wolpe's (1958) desensitization method would seem to be most adaptable to this type of anxiety since it has proven helpful in other forms of specific anxiety, e.g. anxiety over public speaking (Paul, 1966). However, only three studies have used desensitization for the treatment of test-anxiety (Emery and Krumboltz, 1967; Katahn, Strenger and Cherry, 1966; Paul, 1964). Of these, one was based on a case study (Paul) and one relied upon a mixture of desensitization, study-skill advising, biblio-therapy, and face-to-face counseling (Katahn, Strenger and Cherry). Emery and Krumboltz' study showed significant reduction in anxiety as reflected in anxiety test scores and self-ratings.

The study to be reported in this paper adds several dimensions to that of Emery and Krumboltz. Whereas these authors relied upon desensitizing all clients using the same items in the anxiety hierarchy, the current study encouraged the students being treated to develop items appropriate to their own lives. Whereas Emery and Krumboltz apparently used individual treatment sessions, this study added initial group meetings to speed up relaxation training. Finally, the other authors accepted results based on a 19 item scale "known to discriminate" test-anxious students and having a

[1]Reprinted from *Behavior Research and Therapy*, 1968, *6*, 385-387, with the permission of the Pergamon Press and the author.

reliability coefficient of 0.76, while the current study included a 50 item test-anxiety scale, the Sarason test-anxiety scale (TAS) having a reliability of 0.91 (Sarason and Mandler, 1952), and a modification of the Fear Survey Schedule (Wolpe and Lang, 1964).

Method

Subjects. Ss forming the treated group were students who volunteered for the desensitization program which had been announced in psychology classes and through the student newspaper. Of 16 students who appeared, 12 remained in the program.

The untreated group involved students who took the anxiety and phobia scales as part of the Introductory Psychology course requirement that students participate in experiments. Scores on the first 16 students were used for this study.

Procedure: the treated subjects. These students were first interviewed for 1 hour to determine their appropriateness for the program. Criteria for inclusion were: anxiety specifically related to testing situations, the absence of severe pathology, and the absence of health problems. Students who were receiving professional help from other T's or counselors were excluded.

The treatment program included three group meetings and several individual sessions. The group meetings were designed to: (1) discuss the idea that test-anxiety is learned and can hence be unlearned, (2) explain the desensitization procedure, (3) begin group training in deep muscle relaxation, and (4) begin eliciting items for the construction of individual hierarchies. The group training was used as a more efficient way of utilizing the T's time. Each of three T's, all advanced graduate students, met with no more than five clients during the group training sessions. Each therapist then continued in individual sessions with each member of his group. Individual sessions continued twice a week until all items on the client's hieararchy were desensitized. All clients were tested with the anxiety scales and phobia scale before treatment and immediately after treatment was concluded.

Procedure: the untreated subjects. These students were seen in a group in which they were given the anxiety scales and the phobia scale for "normative purposes." They were reconvened for retesting 5 weeks later. This time lapse was chosen as approximating the time required for the treated students to complete the treatment program. On retesting, the untreated students were encouraged to disregard their answers on the first testing and to concentrate on answering the tests in terms of their current feelings.

Scales. Two measures of anxiety and one of fears were used. The Suinn Test Anxiety Behavioral Scale (STABS) is a 50 item self-rating scale composed of statements describing testing situations. The subject indicates the level of anxiety aroused in him by each situation described: high scores indicate high anxiety. The Sarason Test Anxiety Scale (TAS) (Gordon and Sarason, 1955) is a 16 item true-false measure of anxiety about testing. The

Fear Survey Schedule (Phobia Scale) is a 98 item self-rating scale listing objects or situations. The subject indicates the level of fear aroused by each item; high scores indicate high anxiety about a number of different things, e.g. animals, noises, interpersonal situations.

Results

The treated students all completed the individual phase of the treatment program in an average of 7.77 sessions. The treated and the untreated students' anxiety scales and phobia scale scores on first testing were compared; analysis of variance (unequal sample size) showed no significant difference between the mean scores of the two groups. Inspection of individual scores indicated that nearly all of the treated Ss showed decreases in their test scores on the second (or post-therapy) testing. However, some of the untreated Ss also showed decreases upon second testing (Table 1). Therefore, in order to determine the significance of these changes in scores, the difference between the differences between mean scores was statistically analyzed. Results showed that the treated Ss' decreases on test scores were significantly greater than the decreases shown by the untreated Ss on all scales ($t = 3.47$, $p < 0.01$ on STABS, $t = 5.33$, $p < 0.001$ on TAS, and $t = 23.84$, $p < 0.0001$ on Phobia Scale).

TABLE 1

Mean scores of treated and untreated subjects.

Group	Suinn scale*		Sarason scale*		Phobia scale*	
	I	II	I	II	I	II
Treated	155.08	93.08	10.00	5.33	247.20	181.70
Untreated	168.93	152.81	9.43	8.12	227.77	234.25

*$I =$ first testing, $II =$ second testing.

Discussion and Conclusions

The data indicate that a combination of group and individual desensitization treatment is successful in reducing the reported anxiety of treated students. Some reduction also seems to occur in nontreated students. However, the reported decrease in anxiety as measured by test scores is significantly greater for the desensitized students than the untreated ones. Furthermore, although the desensitization was limited to test-anxiety, the treated students also experienced a decline in their overall fears. This suggests that the favorable treatment effects generalized to other areas in the students' lives.

It is difficult to determine whether the group training sessions significantly shortened the total number of treatment meetings for the clients. Other studies using desensitization for test-anxiety are not clear about the average length of treatment when the individual meeting method is used.

Emery and Krumboltz suggest that a *maximum* of 8 weeks was used in their study; in comparison to this, the addition of group sessions does not appear to contribute much savings of client time (the group plus individual meetings in our study totalled 7-8 weeks average). On the other hand, there is no question that group training saved *therapist* time, since he could meet with five clients for one group training session in one hour, instead of devoting one hour to each client. Since the treatment outcomes were successful, the group method would seem to be the more economical means for utilizing T schedules.

REFERENCES

Alpert, R. and Haber, R. (1963) Anxiety in academic achievement situations *J. abnorm. soc. Psychol. 66*, 207-216.

Emery, J. R. and Krumboltz, J. D. (1967) Standard versus individualized hierarchies in desensitization to reduce test anxiety. *J. counsel. Psychol. 14*, 204-209.

Gordon, E. and Sarason, S. (1955) The relationships between "test anxiety" and "other anxieties." *J. Personality 23*, 317-323.

Katahn, M., Strenger, S. and Cherry, Nancy (1966) Group counseling and behavior therapy with test-anxious college students. *J. consult. Psychol. 30*, 544-549.

Paul, G. (1964) Modification of systematic desensitization based on case study. Paper read at Western Psychological Association. Portland, Oregon.

Paul, G. (1966) *Insight versus desensitization in psychotherapy*. Stanford University Press, Stanford.

Paul, G. and Erikson, C. W. (1964) Effects of test anxiety on "real-life" examinations. *J. Personality 32*, 480-494.

Sarason, S. and Mandler, G. (1952) Some correlates of test anxiety. *J. abnorm. soc. Psychol., 47*, 810-817.

Suinn, R. M. (1965) Anxiety and intellectual performance: a partial failure to replicate. *J. consult. Psychol., 29*, 81-82.

Wolpe, J. (1958) *Psychotherapy by reciprocal inhibition*. Stanford University Press, Stanford.

Wolpe, J. and Lang, P. (1964) A fear survey schedule for use in behavior therapy. *Behav. Res. & Therapy., 2*, 27-30.

PART III
Cases

In this section are illustrated a variety of uses of behavioral methods in casework with clients typically encountered in counseling settings, such as the university counseling service or the mental hygiene clinic.

The first case is in a class by itself, since it illustrates a variety of behavioral interventions. Leventhal has shown how behavioral techniques can be interwoven into an overall case strategy that is not conceptually restricted to behavioral treatment. Leventhal used behavioral techniques to promote his client's readiness for subsequent and advanced phases of treatment. As a consequence of his behavioral efforts, the client was able to make accessible to her counselor, thoughts and feelings which she was unable to discuss, and hence unable to modify, earlier.

The next three cases (Geer and Katkin, Geer and Silverman, and Katahn) illustrate the use of the systematic desensitization method with three types of client problem. The Geer and Katkin case has the added twist of suggesting how sub-doctoral counselors might carry through on cases planned and initiated by more highly trained professionals. The Katahn case report goes into considerable detail with regard to the development of the anxiety hierarchy used in desensitization, as well as in describing its use in the counseling sessions.

The Migler and Wolpe report is significant because of its illustration of the potential for self treatment that behavior modification techniques possess. In the Migler and Wolpe case most of the desensitization itself occurred outside of the counselor's office, leading to a more economical use of both counselor and client time.

The Burgess and Keutzer papers illustrate the use of reinforcement and extinction methods in counseling with college students regarding a broad range of academic and adjustment problems. The methods described by Burgess and Keutzer are somewhat different from those used in systematic desensitization as described by Geer, Katkin, Silverman, and Katahn

183

earlier, and thus add another set of techniques for the counselor to consider in working with clients.

Finally, the series of papers from *Introduction to planned behavior change* (Ford; Urban; Wall and Campbell; Osipow and Grooms) show how behavior may be analyzed to make it accessible to the counselor, and thus make available a wide range of counseling interventions, each designed with a particular client's concerns and situation in mind, and, hence, potentially more effective than a general method.

While methods cannot be proven through case examples, the case reports described by these authors in this section encourage optimism with regard to the potency of behavioral and individually tailored counseling. Furthermore, they illustrate that aspects of behavioral counseling may be performed in the context of the counselor's office (and out of it) and with a variety of client concerns. Finally, behavioral concepts add to the degree of specificity with which client behaviors may be analyzed and case objectives developed and matched with available techniques.

Use of a Behavioral Approach within a Traditional Psychotherapeutic Context: A Case Study[1]

Allan M. Leventhal

Troublesome resistances arise in psychotherapy when the client confronts particularly anxiety-provoking thoughts. Such resistances might well be handled most satisfactorily by a therapeutic "shift of gears," borrowing techniques suggested by the behavior therapists to reduce or eliminate the anxiety which prevents the expression of these thoughts. For example, in establishing rapport, the clinician, as a social stimulus, acquires reinforcing properties (Dollard & Miller, 1950). He, thus, may utilize his value as a reinforcer in any model learning situation he might arrange to accelerate treatment at certain points or in relation to certain topics. Such strategy assumes a flexible approach on the part of the therapist, and its success will depend upon the imagination, ingenuity, and attention he brings to bear. The value of incorporating behavior-therapy techniques within a more traditional framework depends upon the inventiveness of the clinician in designing conditioning models shaped to the particular needs of the client, timed and applied in such a manner as to capitalize upon the reinforcing properties of the therapist which have accumulated in the therapeutic relationship.

Such an approach has recently been employed with striking success in the case of a young girl suffering from acute sex-anxiety, complicated by gross immaturity caused by maternal over-protectiveness which stifled any show of independence.

THE CASE OF JANET

The client, who when first seen at the university counseling center was an 18-year-old freshman, remained in treatment for weekly interviews over a period of about 2 years. At the time of the initial interview, Janet's dress was

[1]Reprinted from the *Journal of Abnormal Psychology*, 1968, *73*, 178-182, with permission of the author and the American Psychological Association.

185

disheveled, her hair uncombed, and she walked and sat in a slumped, childish attitude. Her appearance was in marked contrast to that of her well-dressed mother who, in a very domineering manner, had led Janet by the hand to the appointment. Janet was noted to be pathetically timid, hesitant in her speech, and highly anxious. Seen apart from her mother, she complained plaintively that she was unable to make decisions and had no friends of either sex. Although she was deeply dependent on her mother, they constantly fought.

Traditional Treatment

Counseling was arranged on a one session per week basis. The following synopsis of the treatment attempts to summarize trends by focusing on predominant themes viewed over time. During the first 4 months of treatment the counselor offered a relatively nondirective type of therapy, behaving in an accepting, supportive, benign fashion to win Janet's trust and confidence. Therapeutic interventions were completely reflective or supportive in nature. Much of the time was spent discussing the client's relationship with her mother and the conflict over whether to accede to mother's demands and keep mother's love, or make decisions for herself and thereby risk mother's rejection. The client described a counseling relationship in high school that had been terminated after a few months when Janet's mother insisted she stop seeing the counselor because she was becoming "disrespectful" at home. In this connection, it was learned that even minor differences of opinion with mother met with strong threats of loss of affection, which greatly distressed Janet since she had no other meaningful relationships. This period of treatment was culminated by a discussion of the absence of any pride in herself as a result of her failure to act at all independently, and led to some limited improvement in her personal appearance and a deeper involvement in counseling.

Another 4-month period ensued, the central theme of which was her many humiliations within the family (principally with mother and an older sister) and in social contacts which led her to withdraw from others, choosing not to interact even in the simplest of situations. Discussion of one incident in particular was not only illustrative of this problem but first suggested to the counselor the potential worth of behavior therapy. In this instance, Janet had left a favorite sweater in a classroom but later could not bring herself to ask the professor if he had seen it. Discussion of her great anxiety about initiating conversations with strangers resulted in a suggestion from the counselor that a graded series of experiences be devised which might gradually enable her to get to know others. This was frightening to Janet at first (as new ventures always were) but acceptable. When she found on two occasions that she successfully managed to begin a superficial conversation with some classmates, she began to see more directly the possibility of change. She subsequently divulged that there were other problems she had not discussed which she now believed ought to be broached.

A period of great distress followed as she struggled to express her secret thoughts and feelings, during which time much attention was paid to the conflict between self-hate and self-pity, which was interpreted in relation to her sado-masochistic relationship with her mother. Eventually, after struggling for several interviews and for more than 20 minutes of intense concentration in a particular interview, she emitted the word "sex" as the central feature to her distress. Immediately thereafter she warned the counselor that she could tolerate very little discussion in this area and during the next few sessions related a series of experiences to illustrate her feelings on this subject: mother would permit her to read no book or magazine article with any sexual content and Janet agreed that this was only right; 2 years previously, Janet had abruptly left a physician's office and had never returned when he began asking "personal questions"; an assigned paperback textbook of readings with a picture on the cover of a Greek male statue could only be read after she had blackened out the "middle part"; she objected vehemently to topics covered in a Health class because they "weren't nice"; she had been persuaded by mother that it was unwise to date boys because they were interested "in only one thing"; many ideas related to sex were "unspeakable"; etc. Nevertheless, over the next 5 months she struggled to describe her ambivalent feelings about sex and find a way to express the sexual thoughts that were so disturbing to her. It became quite clear from her inability to communicate that she felt extremely guilty about her sexual thoughts and feelings. In addition, her inhibitions plainly prevented her from gaining knowledge about either the normality of her interests or the positive aspects of sexual expression. It was surmised from the very veiled references to "certain actions" that part of the problem had to do with masturbation and that, as a result of the great restrictions that had always been placed on communication related to sex, she was lacking in normative information which might reduce her anxiety. Accordingly, the suggestion was made that she read *Sexual Behavior in the Human Female* (Kinsey, Pomeroy, Martin & Gebhard, 1953). She agreed to this plan, but only after very elaborate arrangements had been made to insure that no one could possibly know what she was reading. Although under these circumstances she was able to look at the book, she could bring herself to read only the table of contents. Nevertheless, this was a significant experience for her, largely because she had been allowed some exposure to sexual material without dire consequences.

As a result of this venture and because of her continued inability to discuss sex, she was persuaded to join in an attempt at relaxation and desensitization, as described by Wolpe (1958). With some reluctance she agreed to proceed with the relaxation exercises, she objected vigorously to the naming of any body part between shoulders and knees! Faced with this barrier, the counselor indicated that no further progress could be made until something was done to increase Janet's ability to tolerate words she associated with sex. A review of the past 6 months' effort provided convincing evidence that little or no further advancement was possible until she could communicate about her sexual feelings more directly and unambiguously. In fact, a link was interpreted between the growth of autonomy and the growth of sexuality so that she was in a position to understand the significance of the barrier we had come upon.

Through this stage of counseling, relying on reflective, interpretive, and information-giving techniques within a conversational mode of treatment, progress of a modest sort had been made. In general, Janet was somewhat more comfortable with herself, she had learned something about her neurotic relationship with mother, she had begun to question some of her invalid assumptions about herself and others, she had been able to maintain herself in school, and she had begun to hope for a more secure and meaningful life in the future. However, it was also clear that in approaching the sexual area she had come upon a hurdle that was endangering any further progress and which, in its confrontation, was stimulating intense anxiety and an impulse to leave treatment.

Behavioral Treatment

The major difficulty Janet was facing was formulated to her as an inability to use sexual words because of the anxiety which had become attached to them. To quiet Janet's fright at the prospect of having to use such a vocabulary, the counselor assured her that he had devised a simple, systematic procedure which she could manage because it was designed gradually but effectively to increase her verbal capacities. She was shown the materials and after examining the procedure and listening to a |description of its rationale, agreed to give it a try. The materials included a set of instructions, a list of 58 sex words taken from a table of contents of the Kinsey volume she had perused, and a set of 58 3 × 5 cards on each of which had been typed one of the words. The instructions read as follows:

1. You are to rate the attached 58 words according to your best guess as to how difficult it might be for you to say each word:
   (a) not too difficult
   (b) difficult
   (c) quite difficult

2. Make your rating by making a light check mark in the appropriate column.

3. Now go back and count the number of words placed in each category and enter your totals here:
   A. not too difficult = (14)
   B. difficult   = (30)
   C. quite difficult   = (14)

4. If your totals do not coincide with the numbers given above in

parentheses, you must change some of your ratings so that they do conform.

      Although this is not easy to do, it is necessary so that the words can be properly arranged. Do it now.

5. Take the deck of 3 × 5 index cards and sort the cards into three piles, according to the ratings you have made.

6. Take the cards in Category A (not too difficult) and sort them into two groups:

  A1 = relatively easy words   (6 cards)
  A2 = relatively difficult words (8 cards)
  Put a title card and rubber band around each set.

7. Take the cards in Category B (difficult) and sort them into three groups:

  B1 = relatively easy words   (9 cards)
  B2 = moderately difficult words (12 cards)
  B3 = quite difficult words   (9 cards)
  Put a title card and rubber band around each set.

8. Take the cards in Category C (quite difficult) and sort them into two groups:

  C1 = relatively easy words   (8 cards)
  C2 = relatively difficult words   (6 cards)
  Put a title card and rubber band around each set.

9. Good. You have now arranged these sexual words in a personally meaningful way and we can begin desensitizing your usage of them.

Completing the required judgments and sorting took Janet a full session, during which time the counselor was present in the room but working at his desk, only attending to her when she asked for some clarification. During the next session the desensitization procedure was explained to Janet. Beginning with Packet A1, a sequence of steps was to be followed. She was to: (a) read the words to herself three times, (b) write the words three times, (c) read the words aloud to the counselor three times, (d) hear the words read to her three times by the counselor, (e) write a sentence using each word, (f) read the sentence out loud, and then (g) hear the sentence read back to her by the counselor. In this manner, when A1 was completed, A2 would be attempted, and so on, until all seven packets had been mastered. Successful completion of all parts of the sequence was immediately and strenuously reinforced by the counselor by saying "good," smiling approvingly, congratulating her on her success, etc.

This procedure, which on the surface may seem elaborate and time consuming, was completed in only nine sessions and with striking success. In reducing sex anxiety, the materials allowed for frank discussion of Janet's fears concerning sex which, when later supplemented by role playing, led to the initiation of highly reinforcing behavior. Some of this behavior was only tangentially related to sex but had been inhibited previously by diffuse generalization of sex anxiety. A list of behavioral change during these nine sessions includes the following: (1) Janet spontaneously requested to return to the comfortable chair that had been rejected during the unsuccessful relaxation experience, a negative reaction which (unknown to the counselor) had been viewed by Janet as a failure. (2) She requested to attempt to use a sex word not on the list which she had never been able to use. (3) She discovered during a Criminology class that when a visiting lecturer used, in class, a word she had just practiced, she no longer was upset by it. (4) Upon visiting a physician at the Student Health Service for a mouth sore (the first visit to a physician since her fright 2 years previously), Janet made the equally startling discovery that she was not upset when he used the word "period." This was such a highly reinforcing event that she, herself, then found the nerve to use the word (which she had been urged to attempt if an occasion arose), and discovered that her own usage was not upsetting. (5) Much to her joy, she was able to inform a classmate that her mother was in the hospital for a hysterectomy, something she would have carefully avoided in the past as too upsetting.

In addition, within 3 months after completion of the procedure, the following gains were effected: (a) Janet found that she could tolerate a discussion about her masturbation with the counselor and was able to admit that she had been extremely concerned for a year and a half that she had inadvertently damaged the lining of her vagina during masturbation. (b) After role playing, the client was able to visit a gynecologist, describe the problem, and receive treatment for the slight damage she had done to herself. (c) Weekly visits to the beauty parlor were initiated to improve her personal appearance, with the result that she found herself for the first time being noticed as attractive by boys. (d) Regular group social contacts were initiated at a campus religious organization which gave her the opportunity to interact with both sexes in a controlled situation. (e) The statement was made: "I see now that my mother is from a different generation and I don't expect her to understand how I've changed." (f) Two months after the completion of the desensitization, the client requested additional practice on three words in List C2 so that she could more comfortably discuss some of her fantasies. Ten minutes of this rehearsal were successful in enabling her to broach the topics on her mind. (g) A highly pleased self-report was given of her "tangible achievements" and the "lifting of a great weight" of inhibition which had plagued her since early adolescence, with the growing recognition that she could "grow up after all."

About 6 months of counseling followed the completion of the behavioral procedure during which time the gains were integrated, and a good deal of insight and self-confidence were developed. For example, she spontaneously realized that her mother was using her as a replacement for her father and that smiling at a boy did not logically lead to a series of events ending in rape, as she characteristically had assumed. At the time of termination, while some problems remained, it was clear that Janet felt much more comfortable about herself, was now capable of effective independent living, and had begun to develop the skills and attitudes which would enable her to make further progress on her own.

Discussion

It has recently been stated that the problem in psychotherapy today is not to determine whether behavioral techniques will replace conversational methods, but to understand how the best elements of each can be combined for maximum usefulness (Kanfer, 1966). Of significance in the case of Janet is: (a) a relationship with the therapist which allowed the client to dare to use sexual words which acted to offset the anxiety elicited by the expression of sexual words and feelings (probably by facilitating experimental extinction and counterconditioning), and (b) the structuring of a technique which provided a vehicle for gradually introducing sexual language into the client's repertoire in a manner which could be accepted and tolerated. Thus, this case appears to represent a combination of conversational and behavioral techniques with a more successful outcome than would have been likely had either technique been applied alone.

The particular technique chosen for desensitization was derived from the principles of classical conditioning (Kalish, 1965) and was based on the following assumptions: (a) a wide spectrum of potentially anxiety-provoking stimuli should be employed, ranging from words evoking little anxiety to words evoking much anxiety; (b) the individual is capable of arranging these stimuli into a graded series meaningfully related to increasing levels of anxiety; (c) provided that the words having the lowest loading of anxiety are not far from neutral, early experiences with the list in the presence of the therapist will be possible; (d) toleration of these communications in this dyad will be reinforcing if the therapist makes use of the reinforcing properties he has accrued during treatment; (e) the positive effects of this reinforcement will generalize to words not as yet attempted, reducing the anxiety associated with them and thereby simplifying the task for the client; and (f) reduction of anxiety associated with sexual words will generalize from the therapeutic situation to the remainder of the individual's life, allowing more reasonable sexual behavior.

Anxiety becomes associated with sexual words in our culture, particularly within repressive families. As a result of generalization of this learned anxiety, many persons develop a conditioned inhibition to the use of terms having only a peripheral relationship to sex, as well as an avoidance of situations where sexual words (as components of ideas) are likely to arise. The pervasiveness and indiscriminateness of this process is enhanced by non-specific communications from parents and others promoting repressive sexual attitudes. In addition, the relief afforded by turning thoughts to other than sexual topics reinforces ideas relating to the evil nature of sexual thoughts and effectively prevents the individual from the extinction of anxiety which might follow from ordinary verbal expressions of a sexual nature. Sexual practices, of course, have an even higher loading of anxiety attached to them, with the result that autoerotic behavior, because of its privacy, represents the only outlet for sexual expression and is a great generator of sexual guilt. For this reason, providing a vehicle for the sexually repressed person to practice usage of sexual terms under appropriate reinforcing conditions can be a powerful tool for attitudinal and behavioral change.

REFERENCES

Dollard, J., & Miller, N. E. *Personality and psychotherapy: An analysis in terms of learning, thinking, and culture.* New York: McGraw-Hill, 1950.

Kalish, H. I. Behavior therapy. In B. B. Wolman (Ed.), *Handbook of clinical psychology.* New York: McGraw-Hill, 1965.

Kanfer, F. H. Implications of conditioning techniques for interview therapy. *Journal of Counseling Psychology*, 1966, *13*, 171-177.

Kinsey, A. C., Pomeroy, W. B., Martin, C. E., & Gebhard, P. H. *Sexual behavior in the human female.* Philadelphia: W. B. Saunders, 1953.

Wolpe, J. *Psychotherapy by reciprocal inhibition.* Stanford: Stanford University Press, 1958.

Systematic Desensitization and Counseling for Anxiety in a College Basketball Player[1]

Martin Katahn

The combined therapeutic approach, *systematic desensitization* (Wolpe, 1958) and personal counseling, (Katahn, Strenger & Cherry, 1966) has proven to be of significant value in the reduction of academically-related anxieties. The present paper reports the use of this approach with a varsity basketball player who requested counseling to reduce anxiety associated with his basketball playing and to eliminate extreme nervousness and vomiting before games—a problem he had had for eight years. Special attention was paid to interpersonal aspects of the counseling relationship since, as critics and reviewers have pointed out (Andrews, 1966; Breger & McGaugh, 1965), such aspects of counseling are often ignored in behavior therapy reports. Role playing and the practice of more effective psychophysiological attitudes were also included in the treatment program.

BACKGROUND

In October, 1965, the student, Mr. J., heard of Vanderbilt University's Test Anxiety Program and came to the writer in the hope that we might be able to help him with his somewhat different anxiety problem. He was dissatisfied with his current performance in his athletic specialty and was becoming so anxious and preoccupied with his game that he was not only playing poorly but also was finding it almost impossible to study.

Mr. J.'s nervousness before games had always been acute. His first experience with nausea and vomiting before a game had occurred when he was 12 years old when he had become sick while riding with a girl friend on a bus to a game.

He vividly remembered the incident and his great embarrassment; after the incident he had begun to vomit before all games.

[1]Reprinted from *The Journal of Special Education*, 1967, *1*, 309-314, with permission of the author and the *Journal of Special Education*.

His major interest had always been his basketball playing. He was a high school star and was at the university on an athletic scholarship. However, he had not, as he had hoped, been able to distinguish himself on the varsity team, where he was in the company of some of the best players in the Southeastern Conference including one All-American star. He did have considerable ability, however, and had to this point contributed to the team as a reserve player.

Mr. J.'s failure to distinguish himself, and the pressure that he felt from his mother's interest in his achievement, seemed suddenly to compound his anxiety as practice for the coming season began. He reported being especially nervous in the presence of his mother whenever the subject of basketball came up. He also reported that his parents were divorced and that his father did not seem to have the same degree of involvement with his playing as his mother did, nor did it make him nervous to talk with his father about the game. At the present time—a few weeks after the start of basketball practice—he felt that his game was falling apart. He said that his coordination was "shot" and that almost anything associated with the game set off a wave of anxiety followed by a period of depression. He felt tired, heavy and sluggish on the court and had lost eight pounds since returning to school the month before. He attributed his loss of appetite to his anxiety and depression.

Certain features of the case suggested that counseling and *systematic desensitization* would be the most appropriate approaches to helping this student. The time until the opening of the season was short (seven weeks), and anxiety was elicited by many cues related to the game, for which counter-conditioning procedures had proven beneficial (Grossberg, 1964).

TREATMENT

Mr. J. was seen 19 times between October 11, 1965, and February 28, 1966. Counseling was on a twice-a-week basis for the first two weeks and once a week thereafter.

As is customary (Katahn, Strenger & Cherry, 1966), the learning theory rationale of the methodology of *systematic desensitization*[2] was explained in the first session after determining that it was a suitable treatment for Mr. J.'s problem. The major portion of the next three sessions was devoted to the construction of an *anxiety hierarchy* and to training in deep muscle relaxation. Mr. J. had no trouble mastering the relaxation technique and in constructing the following list of anxiety-eliciting situations, in order from the

[2]The technique of *systematic desensitization* involves the pairing of a relaxation response with imagined anxiety-eliciting scenes (Wolpe, 1958). The subject constructs an *anxiety hierarchy* of such scenes and the relaxation response is associated with each, starting with the one eliciting the least anxiety. We typically work on about three scenes per session, advancing the hierarchy to scenes ordinarily eliciting greater anxiety as tension is either reduced or extinguished in preceding situations. Subjects are also instructed on how to use the relaxation response in "real life".

least to the most anxiety-producing:

1. He meets an assistant coach in the gym and the coach doesn't say "hello."

2. He is in the gym changing for practice and he notices his hands beginning to sweat.

3. He is trying to study and he can't get the day's practice out of his thoughts.

4. He finishes practice and some observers speak to the other players but ignore him.

5. He is on the court and he gets a tired, draggy, no-good feeling.

6. He is on the court and notices that the coaches are keeping a record of each player's performance.

7. He is visiting at home and his mother makes a remark about another player.

8. He is eating dinner with his mother when she asks him something about how his game is going.

9. It is time for the late afternoon pre-game dinner and he is on the way to the cafeteria.

10. He is in the cafeteria line and the sight of food makes him feel sick.

11. He is in the gym changing for a game and he is sick to his stomach.

From the fourth through 14th sessions, about one-half to two-thirds of each hour was spent in a general discussion of Mr. J.'s attitudes toward his sport, his mother and father, his studies and future plans. The final 20 to 30 minutes were given to the actual desensitization period and the following specially devised procedure.

Since the usual methods of combating an anxiety cue with the use of a relaxation response did not seem particularly appropriate for the tired, heavy, "bad" sensation bothering Mr. J. on the basketball court, he was asked to see if he could actually feel, sitting in the office chair, the sensation he felt in his body when he was in top form, moving and shooting well. He proved able to do this to a considerable extent. He was also able to imagine the "bad" feeling. Thereafter he practiced turning on the good and bad feeling alternately, three to five times each session just before the desensitization period. He—and the therapist—were amazed at the control he was able to achieve over this part of his functioning. He found that he could do this on the court and that it became all but impossible to make himself feel "bad." He did not like to turn on the bad feeling, even during the therapy hours.

By the third week of December, 1965, the anxiety hierarchy had been completely worked through, and the vomiting before games had disappeared. Mr. J. reported that he was eating "like a horse" at his late afternoon, pre-game meal. Similarly, the tired, sluggish feeling on the court had disappeared.

The counseling portion of each interview seemed especially important to Mr. J. He told the counselor how he had often felt like chucking the whole basketball business, yet if he didn't play he couldn't keep his basketball scholarship and stay at Vanderbilt. Basketball, without exaggeration, obsessed him at all times. He had been unable to study since the beginning of the term and had fallen far behind in his work. The counselor suggested instituting a relaxation response when he began to study and whenever a thought about basketball intruded itself. He was to try to set aside a period of time for study and a period for intentionally thinking about the day's practice. If thoughts about basketball became insistent while he was studying he was not to fight them but was to say to himself, "Okay, I will think about that for a while" and then think intentionally about the game for as long as he wished. Whenever he felt that a reasonable time had been devoted to thinking about the game, he was to use the relaxation procedure and go back to studying. He was gradually to increase his study time until he could go an hour without thinking about the game. Thoughts about basketball began to intrude themselves fewer and fewer times during his study hours, and by the time the anxiety hierarchy had been worked through, Mr. J. reported better than 90% success in reaching the goal of an hour's study without intrusive thoughts. He would then think about basketball, or something else, and return to studying. The counselor frequently expressed his feeling to Mr. J. that he was doing well.

The role of a sport in a person's life was often discussed during the sessions. The counselor freely offered himself as a model by expressing his own view, drawing upon his own (rather slight) experience in competitive tennis. That the counselor had an understanding of an athlete's problems seemed important to Mr. J.

Since Mr. J. had not thought about much in his life besides basketball, it seemed necessary to try to establish some clearly defined attitudes about his daily activities and future goals. As discussions continued, it became clear to Mr. J. that his true worth as a person, especially in the years to come after leaving school, when he would be entering a profession and heading a family, would not be determined on the basis of his basketball playing. He began to make plans for going to law school and he wrote for catalogs and application blanks. At the same time, he made better plans for the coming year in basketball. The previous summer he had played only informally and had been out of shape when practice began. This year he decided to enroll for a summer session at another university which would have in residence a group of good varisty basketball players from other schools.

Mr. J. seemed especially to desire and appreciate the therapist's suggestions and advice using him much as he would a benevolent father figure in this respect. Mr. J. indicated a deep affection for his father and regretted that their relationship was so distant. Their meetings seemed limited to two or three times a year, with a week or two together at the father's home in the summer. The extent to which the counselor had become important in Mr. J.'s life was suggested on one occasion when the counselor was leaving the gym after changing for a tennis match. He met Mr. J. and his father, who had just arrived to watch the basketball game that evening. It was obvious from the conversation that Mr. J. had talked considerably about the counselor, and the father parted with the remark, "Well, take care of my boy."

After the symptoms related to Mr. J.'s anxiety over basketball had abated, he asked to continue seeing the counselor for help in improving his study habits. The final sessions were devoted to this problem. Advice modeled after suggestions by Pauk (1962) was given, and Mr. J. reported that it was helpful.

FOLLOW-UP

Mr. J. dropped by the counselor's office for a few unscheduled visits during the spring of 1966. His performance in basketball had picked up and although he wasn't playing a more important role with the team he was feeling much more satisfied with himself. Furthermore, his grades seemed to be improving. A check of the records indicated that before the 1965-66 academic year he had been carrying a 0.68, or unsatisfactory record. In the 1965 fall semester, during treatment, his grade point average was an even 1.00 (C), and this continued to improve. In the spring of 1966 he obtained a 2.00 (B) average, which raised his overall cumulative average to 1.28. (Vanderbilt grades on a 3.00 system.)

In December of 1966, a week after the opening of the basketball season, Mr. J. dropped by the office to report that he had experienced a little discomfort before the first game but that it had not been serious and had not recurred before the following two games. He had followed through on his plans for summer school and was in good shape for the season. This had resulted in his playing a more important, although still a reserve role, on the team. His basketball activities were taking up several hours a day, however, and while he was no longer obsessed by the game, he felt that he was in grave danger of falling behind in his work. He asked for some further sessions of counseling to help him organize his studying and improve his efficiency. He was seen three more times in December, 1966, for which sessions he brought in his texts and notebooks for specific advice. In February, 1967, he came in to report that he had been accepted in law school.

Discussion

The combination of systematic desensitization with counseling procedures proved effective in eliminating the anxiety and vomiting associated with Mr. J.'s basketball activities. While all coaches of athletic teams realize the importance of mental attitudes toward performance, Mr. J.'s ability to practice a more beneficial attitude involving specific physiological correlates away from the court suggests the possibility that this method, practiced in much the same way, might also be beneficial in other interpersonal performance activities as well. Such an approach has an old and venerable place in therapy, but it seems to have been somewhat neglected if one judges from the part it plays in published case histories (e.g. Moreno, 1959).

Since most behavior therapy reports stress the role of procedures bearing the closest relationship to learning theory, an attempt has been made here to report other interpersonal aspects of the therapeutic relationship in as much detail as is commensurate with demands on journal space. As noted elsewhere (Katahn, Strenger & Cherry, 1966), students participating in the counseling and behavior therapy program for test anxiety generally report that while systematic desensitization is helpful, it is the suggestions, advice and the "getting to know a professor better" that play the greatest role in the reduction of their anxieties. In the present case, a relationship developed which might be classified psychoanalytically as "positive transference." However, past experience in dealing with specific anxieties suggests that changes in behavior as quick and as drastic as the ones reported here and elsewhere (Katahn, Strenger & Cherry, 1966; Paul, 1966; Paul & Shannon, 1966) would not have been possible without the use of systematic desensitization.

While suggestions, advice and other interpersonal aspects of the relationship may seem most important to the person being counseled, systematic desensitization may, in fact, remain the essential ingredient for anxiety reduction *per se*. Without a quick reduction in anxiety and the removal of associated physiological symptoms, the other aspects of the counseling procedures might lose in apparent value to the student as treatment progressed.

To shed some light on this issue, a research program is underway to determine the relative contributions of counseling and desensitization, and to explore the role of student attitudes and expectations regarding treatment. Since such concepts as attitudes, expectations and cognitions have had a small place in a behavior therapy rationale based on narrowly defined S-R learning theory (Breger & McGaugh, 1965), research efforts including such data may hopefully prelude the formulation of a more adequate and inclusive theory of behavior modification, ultimately leading to an incorporation of behavior therapy techniques with other tools of counseling practice.

REFERENCES

Andrews, J. C. W. Psychotherapy of phobias. *Psychological Bulletin*, 1966, *66*, 455-480.

Breger, L. & McGaugh, J. L. Critique and reformulation of "learning theory" approaches to psychotherapy and neurosis. *Psychological Bulletin*, 1965, *63*, 338-358.

Grossberg, J. M. Behavior therapy: a review. *Psychological Bulletin*, 1964, *62*, 73-88.

Katahn, M., Strenger, S. & Cherry, N. Group counseling and behavior therapy with test anxious college students. *Journal of Consulting Psychology*, 1966, *30*, 544-549.

Moreno, J. L. Psychodrama. In S. Arieti (Ed.), *American handbook of psychiatry*. New York: Basic Books, 1959.

Pauk, W. *How to study in college.* Boston: Houghton mifflin, 1962.

Paul, G. L. *Insight versus desensitization in psychotherapy: An experiment in anxiety reduction.* Stanford: Stanford University, 1966.

Paul, G. L. & Shannon, D. T. Treatment of anxiety through systematic desensitization in therapy groups. *Journal of Abnormal Psychology*, 1966, *71*, 124-135.

Wolpe, J. *Psychotherapy by reciprocal inhibition.* Stanford: Stanford University, 1958.

Treatment of Insomnia using a Variant of Systematic Desensitization: A Case Report[1]

James H. Geer and Edward S. Katkin

The treatment of behavior disorders by techniques derived from learning theory has been receiving increased attention in current psychological literature (e.g., Eysenck, 1960; Grossberg, 1964; Wolpe, Salter, & Reyna, 1964). Among these techniques, Wolpe's (1958) method of systematic desensitization has been among the most widely reviewed. Critics of systematic desensitization, while often acceding to the efficiency of this technique for the treatment of phobic disorders, claim that it suffers from being limited *solely* to the treatment of phobias. The major purpose of this paper is to describe a case history in which a modification of systematic desensitization was employed successfully in the treatment of a nonphobic disorder—insomnia.

Although insomnia has long been known to clinicians and their patients as a common symptom of behavior disorders, the literature concerning this problem is surprisingly sparse, and consists primarily of theoretical formulations, frequently from the psychoanalytic viewpoint. For example, Fenichel (1945) says of insomnia that

> the cathexes of repressed wishes. . . make sleep impossible. Also acute worries or affect-laden expectations, whether agreeable or disagreeable, particularly sexual excitement without gratification, make for sleeplessness. In the case of neurotic disturbances of sleep, the unconscious factors of course outweigh the others [p. 189].

Discussions of the treatment of insomnia have usually been limited to descriptions of the relative merits of drugs (McGraw & Oliven, 1959) or hypnosis (Wolberg, 1954). Psychotherapeutic intervention is usually directed to the psychodynamic basis presumed to underlie the symptom, and rarely to the symptom *per se*.

A second purpose of this paper is to demonstrate the unique possibilities that systematic desensitization offers for the training of psychotherapists.

[1]Reprinted from the *Journal of Abnormal Psychology*, 1966, *71*, 161-164, with permission of the authors and the American Psychological Association.

201

Geer (1964) has noted that trainees may observe therapy sessions without appreciably disturbing the course of treatment. In the present case, an observer in the early stages of therapy actually became the therapist in later stages. Thus, not only was a trainee able to observe treatment at first hand, but in addition he was able to become the therapist and subsequently be observed directly by a supervisor.

CASE HISTORY

The client (Miss H.), a 29-year-old, female, white, single, Roman Catholic, was self-referred to the Psychological Clinic of the State University of New York at Buffalo. Her complaint was severe insomnia. She reported that since she terminated her engagement some 12 months before coming to the clinic she had been suffering from sleeplessness. The client reported that she would typically have great difficulty in sleeping for 5 or 6 nights consecutively; then there would usually be 1 night of 6-7 hours of sleep, presumably in response to physical exhaustion, followed by another week of sleeplessness. Miss H. stated that this general sleep pattern had been persistent for the past 12 months. The client was a registered nurse, who had recently returned to college for a BS degree, and she felt that her insomnia was interfering markedly with school performance as well as with most other aspects of her daily life. She felt that she was generally quite irritable as a result of her extensive sleep loss.

Clinical interviewing revealed no evidence of severe psycho-pathology, nor the presence of any symptoms other than insomnia. An MMPI was administered, and it too was interpreted as revealing no evidence for severe psycho pathology; all of the clinical scales were well within the normal range, and the validity scales showed no evidence of dissimulation.[2] Attempts to fit the client into any of the traditional nosological categories were difficult; thus no diagnostic label was attached to her.

Two factors suggested that this case be accepted for behavior therapy. First, the client reported that in 6-weeks time she would be leaving on an extended vacation; thus it appeared that traditional psychotherapeutic procedures would not be feasible because of time limitations. Second, it was felt that a specific symptom reaction such as hers, with its relationship to excessive tension, would be amenable to systematic desensitization. The client was fully informed about the exploratory nature of the procedures to be used, and about the use of the case as a training situation. She consented to enter treatment under these conditions since her insomnia posed an immediate and severe problem from which she desired relief.

[2]The client's MMPI was coded by the Hathaway (1956) system as follows: '4987—*136* (51) 2:6:13. This configuration has been associated with insensitive, emotionally immature patients, who encounter great difficulty in establishing enduring interpersonal relations (see Dahlstrom & Welsh, 1960). Such patients are frequently seen as poor risks for psycho-therapy.

COURSE OF TREATMENT

A total of 14 sessions were conducted with Miss H. The first session—the initial interview—was conducted by both authors. At this time information concerning the details and background of the problem was gathered. Also, an attempt was made to assess the suitability of Miss H. for the type of treatment considered. Miss H. reported that three specific themes recurred during her sleepless nights. One concerned her former fiancé; she reported that she still felt an attachment to him and she ruminated over the implications and meaning of her decision to terminate their engagement. The second disturbing theme was concern for the future; for example, Miss H. would wonder if she should continue in school or return to full-time nursing. The third distrubing theme which filled her sleepless hours was concern over her inability to fall asleep. Miss H. would find that not falling asleep would start a vicious cycle in which concerns over falling asleep led to increased sleeplessness and so on. Apparently these three disturbing themes occurred with equal frequency, and appeared to be equally effective in eliciting negative affect.

Four training sessions followed the intake session. These were similar to those described by Geer (1964) in the treatment of a phobia. During the training sessions the client was instructed in relaxation, rehearsed in visual imagery, and asked to construct a hierarchy relating to insomnia (see Geer, 1964; Wolpe, 1958). With respect to this last point, one major problem became obvious; the client could not construct a fear hierarchy related to her insomnia. She reported that she did not feel anxious when anticipating going to sleep, nor did she report anxiety when preparing to retire. Her description of her feelings was that only after retiring would her mind begin to race with upsetting thoughts. It was decided to proceed with treatment, using the presentation of a single item for visualization since construction of a fear hierarchy, traditionally used in systematic desensitization, was impossible.

During the first training session the client became markedly upset. While attempting to relax in a reclining chair Miss H. became agitated, fearful, and tense. She sat up and said that she could not relax with both the therapist and the observer in the room. After some discussion, it was decided that the trainee should leave, and he did. Even then, however, the client remained unable to relax, so the session was terminated. At the second training session the client asked that the trainee not be present; thus, this session was conducted by one therapist only. Miss H. complained that ever since the breakup with her fiancé she had been unable to relax around men. After about 10 minutes of discussion of her concerns surrounding the therapy situation she decided to try to relax once again. This attempt was only moderately successful; however, the client did not become as upset on this occasion. The third training session did not evoke any emotional upset. On the fourth and final training session the trainee returned; Miss H. did not become upset during this session.

Nine therapy sessions directly followed the training sessions and were conducted twice a week. These sessions generally consisted of a brief interview concerning the sleeping pattern of the previous few days, followed by relaxation and the presentation of a single item to visualize—that of the client at home in bed, trying to fall asleep. This single item was presented throughout the therapy sessions with the following modifications: first, Miss H. was instructed to visualize herself lying in bed; then she was instructed to imagine that her mind was racing and that she was unable to fall asleep; finally, she was told to turn her attention away from her disturbing thoughts and to think only of relaxation. At the end of this sequence, the client responded, with a finger movement, to questions asking if the scene was clear, if she was able to experience the discomfort, and if she was successful in returning her attention to relaxation. As the therapy sessions progressed, Miss H. reported becoming increasingly able to perform these tasks.

After the trainee had observed two therapy sessions it was felt that he could act as therapist. Therefore, in the third therapy session the trainee became the therapist, and the original therapist became the observer-supervisor. If any supervisory comments became necessary, hand-written notes were exchanged. The client, whose eyes were closed, was unaware of these exchanges. After two supervised sessions both therapists agreed that the trainee was able to continue the procedure alone. Thus, after the fourth therapy session the trainee continued the procedures without an observer.

For the first six treatment sessions the course of therapy was uneventful. Miss H. reported no change in her sleeping pattern and was still quite disturbed by insomnia. However, at the beginning of the seventh therapy session the client reported some change in her sleeping pattern. She reported sleeping more during the period between the sixth and seventh sessions. At the beginning of the eighth therapy session Miss H. gave a similar report, and at the beginning of the ninth therapy session she reported that she had slept well each of the previous nights. Because of final exam pressures and preparations required for her vacation trip, the client decided to terminate treatment at the end of the ninth therapy session. She was asked to return just prior to leaving on her vacation. At that time, $1\frac{1}{2}$ weeks after the final therapy session, she reported a continuation of good sleep. An interview by both therapists revealed no evidence of symptom substitution.

The next contact with the client was approximately $1\frac{1}{2}$ months following termination. At that time, she noted on a postcard from her trip that her sleeping problem had not returned, and that she was "having a wonderful time." A final follow-up interview was conducted 8 months after the final therapy session. At that time the client reported being quite satisfied with her sleeping pattern. She said that she had occasional nights when sleeping was delayed 2-3 hours; however, these nights never occurred more than once a week and often occurred only once in 2 weeks. She also noted that the sleepless nights did not fall consecutively and that they were not anxiety provoking—

that is, she did not worry or experience anxiety even though she might not fall asleep for several hours. Miss H. also reported that she felt her general disposition had improved as a result of reduced fatigue. Her response to the question, "How would you characterize the way it used to be with the way you are now?" was, "I had a constant feeling of anxiety and being upset and not being able to think clearly. Now. . . it is entirely different now. I feel relaxed and I am in control of the situation. I am more cheerful now." A detailed and careful inquiry was unable to uncover any evidence for symptom substitution. Indeed, there has been a positive spread of therapeutic effect in that her general feeling of well-being has improved as a function of regular sleeping.

Discussion

This case demonstrates several interesting points relevant to behavior therapy. First is the extension of a behavioral technique to a class of disorders usually considered in the province of more traditional techniques. With respect to this point, it is important to note that Jacobson's (1938) classic work with the technique of "progressive relaxation" bears some resemblance to the techniques employed in the present case. With specific reference to the treatment of insomnia, Jacobson (1938) noted: "Years of observation on myself suggested in 1910 that insomnia is always accompanied by a sense of residual tension[3] and can always be overcome when one successfully ceases to contract the parts in this slight measure (p. 29)." In discussing the general psychotherapeutic advantages of progressive relaxation Jacobson noted: "Accordingly, present results indicate that an emotional state fails to exist in the presence of complete relaxation of the peripheral parts involved (p. 218)." It should be noted also that the techniques employed in the present case are different from Jacobson's in some respects. Jacobson did not conceptualize the insomniac's difficulties in terms of tension associated with specific conditioned fear responses. Furthermore, Jacobson's technique required that the patient practice relaxation over a much wider range of muscle groups, and for a considerably longer period of time; some of his patients practiced relaxation at home for 1-2 hours per day. Finally Jacobson did not employ the technique of visualization. It is possible, of course, that visualization of the scenes was irrelevant, and that the client simply learned to relax; however, it appears that this alternative hypothesis is testable, and should be subjected to empirical investigation.

A second point of interest is the unique training opportunity offered by behavior therapy. In this case the trainee was able to observe at first hand the techniques employed and then take over the procedures without a serious setback in progress. In fact, the finding that only nine therapy sessions were required suggests that if the transfer was detrimental, the effects were transient. Obviously, only controlled studies can adequately answer this

[3]Residual tension as used by Jacobson refers to fine, tonic muscular contractions.

question. The successful transfer of the client from one therapist to another supports the suggestion that because of its reduced emphasis upon the patient-therapist relationship behavior therapy is relatively "therapist free" as compared with usual approaches to psychotherapy.

This paper also demonstrates the flexibility of behavior therapy. In the present case no fear hierarchy was utilized; thus it appears that in appropriate circumstances a hierarchy is not necessary. In summary, this case illustrates the successful use of a variant of systematic desensitization both for the treatment of a common symptom of behavior disorders and for the training of a psychotherapist.

REFERENCES

Dahlstrom, W. B., & Welsh, G. S. *An MMPI handbook*. Minneapolis: Univer. Minnesota Press, 1960.

Eysenck, H. J. (Ed.), *Behavior therapy and the neuroses*. New York: Pergamon, 1960.

Fenichel, O. *The psychoanalytic theory of neurosis*. New York: W. W. Norton, 1945.

Geer, J. H. Phobia treated by reciprocal inhibition. *Journal of Abnormal and Social Psychology*, 1964, *69*, 642-645.

Grossberg, J. M. Behavior therapy: A review. *Psychological Bulletin*, 1964, *62*, 73-88.

Hathaway, S. R. A coding system for MMPI profile classification. In G. S. Welsh & W. G. Dahlstrom (Eds.), *Basic readings on the MMPI in psychology and medicine*. Minneapolis: Univer. Minnesota Press, 1956.

Jacobson, E. *Progressive relaxation*. (2nd ed.), Chicago: Univer. Chicago Press, 1938.

McGraw, R. B., & Oliven, J. F. Miscellaneous therapies. In S. Arieti (Ed.), *American handbook of psychiatry*. New York: Basic Books, 1959.

Wolberg, L. R. *The technique of psychotherapy*. New York: Grune & Stratton, 1954.

Wolpe, J. *Psychotherapy by reciprocal inhibition*. Stanford: Stanford Univer. Press, 1958.

Wolpe, J., Salter, A., & Reyna, L. J. *The conditioning therapies*. New York: Holt, Rinehart & Winston, 1964.

Treatment of a Recurrent Nightmare by Behavior-Modification Procedures: A Case Study[1]

James H. Geer and Irwin Silverman

This paper presents the case history of the treatment of a recurrent nightmare with an unusually long duration and frequency of occurrence, by behavior-modification procedures. The case attests to the adaptiveness of behavior-modification procedures in that they were applied to a unique problem for this type of treatment. The general assumption underlying the use of these procedures in this case was that the anxiety elicited by the nightmare was amenable to manipulation by the same variables that manipulate anxiety aroused in the waking state.

HISTORICAL AND CLINICAL DATA

The client was a 22-year-old, married, male undergraduate student at the State University of New York at Buffalo. He did not come to the attention of the authors via the usual referral sources. Rather, in the course of collecting data on the frequency of dreams, his report of a frequent recurrent nightmare was noted. He was asked by the experimenter if he was interested in attempting to deal with his recurrent nightmare. The client replied affirmatively, and an appointment was made for an initial interview with the senior author. The following history of the problem was gathered during that first interview. The nightmare in question had occurred repeatedly for the past 15 years, and at a frequency of from three to five times per week. The nightmare was essentially the same in all instances and consisted of the following sequence. The client would be in bed for his night's sleep. As he was falling asleep, he would imagine that he saw some shadows in his room, then that there were some sounds, then a shadowy figure would become apparent. This figure would move toward the client, and the face would become bathed in light. At that point a knife would be seen in the figure's hand; he would come

[1]Reprinted from the *Journal of Abnormal Psychology*, 1967, *72*, 188-190, with permission of the authors and the American Psychological Association.

toward the client, about to attack. The client would try to resist by kicking out, and at this point he would wake up, often on the floor as a result of his "struggle." The individual in the dream would differ from time to time and was not a person that the client knew. This dream normally occurred shortly after falling asleep, although upon some occasions it did occur later during sleep or in the early morning.

The client noted that he often suffered from insomnia which he felt might be related to concerns that he had about falling asleep and having the nightmare. He was not certain that the insomnia was related to the dream since the insomnia was a relatively recent phenomena. In the course of this first session a rather complete diagnostic interview was undertaken, and there were no indications of any other behavioral disturbances. The client was a veteran, and the only concern he voiced was about being successful in school after having been away from academic work for several years. The client reported a mutually satisfactory marital relationship. He had never sought psychiatric or psychological help, and he had never had the suggestion made to him that he should. An MMPI was subsequently administered; and all scales were below a t score of 70, indicating a normal pattern. By stringent standards, the client would be considered normal with the exception of this severe recurrent nightmare.

TREATMENT PROCEDURES

The second interview, at which both authors were present, consisted of discussing with the client the highly experimental nature of the procedures to be involved, and the fact that there was no guarantee of success. The client was given a description of the theoretical underpinnings of the technique of systematic desensitization by reciprocal inhibition, originated by Joseph Wolpe (1958), and its application to phobias, and he was told that to the best knowledge of the authors this would represent the first application of this technique to a nightmare problem.

Five training sessions were undertaken, in which the client was taught deep muscle relaxation, and he practiced visualization of neutral scenes. Reference to an article (Geer, 1964) by the senior author will describe the training procedure involved. It was not possible to construct a fear hierarchy directly since the client did not experience anxiety at the simple thought of the dream, nor did he experience anxiety when anticipating going to bed. Therefore, it was decided that the hierarchy would consist of the inclusion of successive parts of the dream in temporal order. That is, the lowest item on the hierarchy would be imagining a few shadows in the room. Gradually, more of the dream would be included until the top item would be experiencing the complete dream.

The first two therapy sessions consisted of the client relaxing and being given instructions to begin imagining the dream. After each visualized scene, when the client was asked to respond with a finger movement if he experienced anxiety, he responded positively. At the end of the initial two therapy sessions, the client reported that he experienced considerable anxiety whenever he visualized the dream scenes, and he was unable to maintain his relaxed state. During the first two sessions, he was unable to relax while visualizing the first item in the hierarchy. During the third session a different technique was used. The client was instructed to relax, and to visualize the scene. When the client felt anxiety, however, he was instructed to say to himself, "It's just a dream," and then to continue visualizing the scene while trying to stay relaxed. The client reported that he was able to do this successfully. This procedure was continued for the third session and all remaining sessions. At the beginning of the fourth session, the client reported that the dream had occurred only twice that previous week. At the beginning of the fifth therapy session, the client reported that he had had the dream just once during the 4 days preceding. Two more therapy sessions were held, and at the last meeting he reported that he had not had the dream for over 2 weeks. A decision to terminate therapy was made at that time, and an appointment was made for approximately 3 weeks later. At that time the client reported again no recurrence of the dream.

Six months following the termination of therapy another follow-up interview was held. At this time the client reported dreaming only the ordinary "garden variety" types of dreams, pleasant in nature. One dream during the 6 months involved a shadow; but it did not make him anxious, nor did he wake up. A check was made to determine if anything that resembled symptom substitution had occurred, and nothing apparent of this nature had developed. At that time the client felt that the recurrent nightmare had been eliminated and that nothing of either a positive or a negative nature has taken its place.

Discussion

An explanation of how the behavior-modification procedures attenuated the nightmare must, of course, be rather speculative in nature. For example, it was possible that we were not dealing with more of what has been described by Foulkes (1962) as a hypnagogic dream; that is, a dream that occurs while falling asleep because it occurred so rapidly after going to bed, and most investigators (Tart, 1965) suggest that from 1 to 2 hours of sleep precede vivid dreaming. However, the clarity of the imagery is not consistent with the picture of a hypnagogic dream. Regardless of the actual label that one might apply to the particular piece of behavior involved, there can be no question that it was a recurrent and disturbing event, and it is apparent that it did disappear at the time when behavior-modification procedures were employed. The possibility that the dream still occurs, but that it does not wake the client and that he forgets that he had it, requires speculation that is beyond the authors.

A possible explanation of what occurred lies in a simple discrimination notion. That is, the client simply learned to discriminate that this event was not reality, and thus was not something of which to be afraid. This interpretation is supported by the fact that positive results occurred only after the client began to instruct himself, "It's only a dream." Another possible explanation is that the relaxation training procedure permitted the client to relax much faster than before and to rapidly pass the stage at which the nightmare was elicited. Thus, the dream simply did not occur since the conditions for its elicitation were never completely present.

The psychoanalytic theory of dream functions (Freud, 1942) does not seem to be contradicted by the present findings. As was noted, there was no symptom substitution and one might anticipate from psychoanalytic theory that the client should have developed another disturbing dream, or perhaps substituted some other maladaptive behavior if the dream was helping discharge excitation. However, the dream in question was not fulfilling the function of preserving sleep. Thus, it could be argued that little excitation was being discharged by the dream; and its removal would not necessarily be followed by another symptom, or dream, since there was no increase in build-up of libidinal energy previously discharged by the dream. Freud's discussion of the traumatic dream as being relatively independent of the underlying dynamic causes would also seem to suggest that no symptom substitution would occur. It is not at all clear, however, that this case was a traumatic dream. The client, to the best of his knowledge, had not been attacked prior to or subsequent to the dream. With regard to psychoanalytic theory, however, it should be noted that there is no aspect of that approach to dreams that would account for how the procedures used here eliminated the nightmare. It is also clear that psychoanalytic theory would not have suggested using the particular procedures that were employed in this case.

The problem presented by this client may be considered typical of those problems most successfully dealt with by behavior-modification procedures. That is, the disordered behavior is fairly well defined. For example, Lang, Lazovik, and Reynolds (1965) reported success when dealing with relatively well-defined snake phobias; and Paul (1966) found that systematic desensitization was successful with fears of public speaking. These data may suggest that where the S-R model is easily applied, behavior-modification techniques are particularly successful. An alternative interpretation of these findings is that behavior-modification techniques are most successful when the disordered behavior is either (a) not central to the personality or (b) not a way of coping with life. Evaluation of this alternative explanation is very difficult and probably cannot be attempted until an objective definition of "central to the personality" or "a way of coping with life" is available.

If one accepts the premise that desensitization procedures were directly responsible for the disappearance of the dream, then what has been established is that the content of the dream elicits fear or anxiety and that when the anxiety is eliminated, the dream disappears. This does not suggest why fear becomes manifested in recurrent nightmares nor why it is maintained over extended periods of time. It must be acknowledged that the use of the procedures described in this case could not be directly ascribed to any well-founded body of knowledge or theory concerning dreaming or the manipulation of dreams. Further study of an experimental nature is necessary, providing an adequate sample with this rather unique problem can be obtained, to specify the precise procedures that were relevant to the present case.

REFERENCES

Foulkes, D. Dream reports from different stages of sleep. *Journal of Abnormal and Social Psychology*, 1962, *65*, 14-25.

Freud, S. *The interpretation of dreams.* (Trans. by A. A. Brill) New York: Macmillan, 1942.

Geer, J. H. Phobia treated by reciprocal inhibition. *Journal of Abnormal and Social Psychology*, 1964, *69*, 642-645.

Lang, P. J., Lazovik, A. D., & Reynolds, D. J. Desensitization, suggestibility, and pseudotherapy. *Journal of Abnormal Psychology*, 1965, *70*, 395-402.

Paul, G. L. *Insight vs. desensitization in psychotherapy.* Stanford: Stanford University Press, 1966.

Tart, C. R. T. Toward experimental control of dreaming. *Psychological Bulletin*, 1965, *64*, 81-91.

Wolpe, J. *Psychotherapy by reciprocal inhibition.* Stanford: Stanford University Press, 1958.

Use of Therapy Time as a Reinforcer: Application of Operant Conditioning Techniques within a Traditional Psychotherpy Context[1]

Carolin S. Keutzer

The effective control of behavior was expanded beyond the animal laboratory to human behavior when Lindsley (1956) successfully adapted the
methodology of operant conditioning to the study of psychotic behavior.
Though many recent reports have shown that a wide range of behavior, in
both children and adults, can be controlled by explicitly arranging the
consequences of a specified response, the present report appears to contribute
to this growing body of literature in two respects. First it demonstrates the
effectiveness of reinforcement applied systematically to strengthen a response
already present in the behavioral repertoire (as opposed to extinguishing a
particular habit or symptom) of a *neurotic outpatient adult*. The latter qualifications distinguish this work from the bulk of operant conditioning research
which has dealt either with normal or autistic children or with psychotic or
other severely disturbed adults treated within the controlled environment of
an institution. Secondly, this case-study presents for consideration the contingent *allocation of therapy time* as a novel and specific type of reinforcer available within the framework of every psychotherapeutic relationship. Employing the conditioning procedure concurrent with, and within, the structure of
more or less traditional psychotherapy adds a further distinguishing characteristic to this case and is directly responsive to the frequent call for a rapproche-
ment between the implicitly and explicitly dichotomized "traditional" and
"behavioral" approaches to therapy.

Case Resume

The patient, an attractive 38-year-old widow and the mother of four children, had been seen by several different therapists on both an individual and
group therapy basis over a 3-year period. The present experimenter had been
seeing her for 2 hours a week in individual psychotherapy over a 5-month

[1]Reprinted from *Behavior Research and Therapy*, 1967, *5*, 367-370, by permission of the author
and Pergamon Press Ltd.

span before the initiation of this conditioning program. A positive and markedly dependent transference relationship had developed over the course of these 5 months.

A summary personality description of the patient would include references to an "introverted neurotic" personality classification as measured by the EPI Form A ($N = 18$; $E = 6$); a high level of intelligence; an acute sensitivity to slights and criticisms together with a marked self-esteem deficit; an extremely high anxiety level (IPAT Anxiety Scale normalized sten of 10); a passive-dependent mode of relating to others; and a generally flattened affect with periodic severe depression.

At the behavioral level, the most maladaptive features seemed to be the traditional concomitants of anxiety and depression. In the patient's daily life these took the form of an inability to concentrate; a lack of motivation and energy; incapacity to perform the routine duties of running a household; the escape from depression through inordinately long periods of sleep (up to 20-30 hours at a time); and the failure to make even minimal advancement in her personal, educational, and professional goal of completing the final year of university work—despite an extraordinarily high level of demonstrated academic ability. It was the subjective importance of the study problem as well as its assumed amenability to quantifiable manipulation which determined its selection as the behavior to be conditioned.

Procedure

After a brief explanation of the principles underlying the procedure, the conditioning proposal was presented to the patient. Initial resistance by the patient notwithstanding (suspiciousness of the therapist's motives, resentment at being "treated like a child," etc.), a contract was negotiated whereby the patient agreed to (1) keep a detailed record of her own study time during the following week; (2) keep a corresponding record of her own feelings and emotional responses both to the studying behavior and to the conditioning procedure; and (3) receive time in therapy if, and only if, it was earned according to a consistent "pay-scale" to study time. The initial rate of therapy-time for every 2 hours of study time, with an arbitrary earning capacity ceiling set a 2 hours of therapy-time.

The desired and anticipated outcome of this operant conditioning procedure extended somewhat beyond a simple increase in weekly study behavior; it was further predicted that as the response (studying) upon which reinforcement (therapy-time) was contingent was strengthened, there would concurrently develop an *increase* in positive feelings about studying and a *decrease* in negative feelings about the nature of the manipulative technique used.

Results

This program of reinforced study time yielded three different observations of change over the 16 week period: (1) the gradual increase in time (hours per week) spent in studying; (2) the decrease in negative comments about the nature of the procedure; and (3) an increase in verbal indications that the study behavior *per se* was becoming the primary reinforcing agent, with the time in therapy being seen more as a "bonus."

The increase in study-time can be seen from the two graphs presented below. Figure 1 depicts the total hours spent studying each week, and the line graph is characterized by moderate to severe weekly fluctuations within a gradual and consistent trend of increased weekly study rates. Figure 2 represents the cumulative number of hours spent in study. Clearly, there was a marked and significant increase in studying over time during the course of this conditioning procedure.

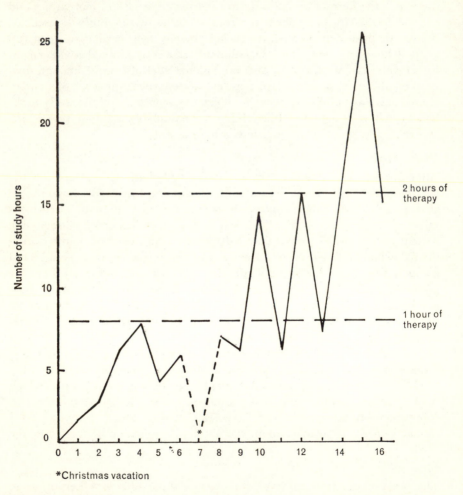

Figure 1. Weekly totals of hours studied

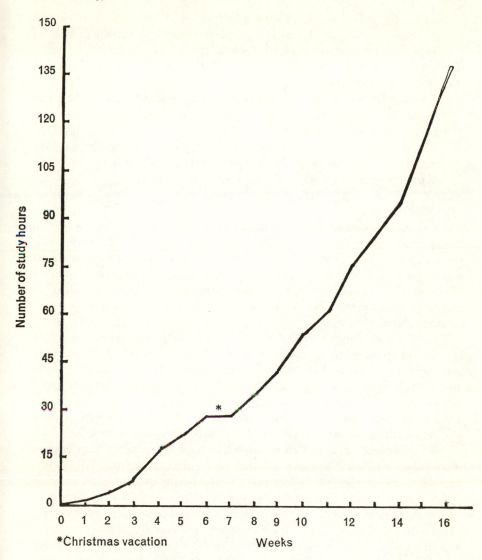

Figure 2. Cumulative number of study hours over a 16-week period

The mitigation of antipathy, resistance and resentment toward the program and the change in attitude toward the study behavior itself are much less easy to assess and demonstrate than is the change in study behavior. The entries in the patient's log, however, are consistent with the predicted changes in attitude. The following statements were representative of the first few weeks of the conditioning regimen.

"I am motivated to get the 2 hours in because I do not want to give up any time with you. I am embarrassed because it takes this kind of maneuver to make me work." (Week 2.)

Toward the end of the 16 weeks, however, more positive statements typified the patient's study commentary.

"Needing the time with you has encouraged me to get busy and study at times I might have failed to do any studying. These times have proved very rewarding." (Week 13.)

"I did not feel that I was buying time with you when I accumulated so much time because the study itself needed that much time devoted to it. It pleases me that I did study quite a lot." (Week 15.)

Discussion

The consistent increase in study behavior over time seems to indicate that, in this instance, spending time with the experimenter in a therapy relationship was an effectively reinforcing event for the specified behavior upon which it was contingent. Further, the gradual evolution in the direction of acceptance of the procedure, positive feelings toward the study activity, and a more favorable self-appraisal can be discerned from a perusal of the patient's written reflections.

In so far as the potency of a reinforcer in maintaining behavior is a function of its importance to the organism, the patient's established dependent relationship with the therapist and her great need for approval were probably of major significance in bringing this behavior under experimental control. However, with respect to this procedure in general, the nature of the influence of such assumedly relevant variables as length of time in therapy and personality characteristics of the subject need yet to be determined.

The deliberate manipulation and exploitation of a positive transference relationship might be repugnant to the more orthodox of the "dynamic" therapists; admittedly such a technique would hardly qualify as an instance of Rogerian "unconditional positive regard." Yet in this case, such a procedure seems not to have adversely affected the therapist-patient relationship nor significantly altered (for better or worse) the ongoing therapy process. Not only was a desirable habit strengthened effectively, but also the vicious circle of which it was part (inability to study—feelings of unworthiness—depression—inability to study) was interrupted. It seems not unreasonable to expect, therefore, that the changes in this one area of behavior will precipitate other desirable behavioral changes.

REFERENCES

Lindsley, O. R. Operant conditioning methods applied to research in chronic schizophrenia. *Psychiatric Research Reports*, 1956, *5*, 118-139.

Applications of Behavior Modification in a Student Counseling Center[1]

Elaine Burgess

Many college students seek the services of a university counseling center with symptoms or complaints similar to individuals who obtain out-patient treatment from community clinics. Reports from behavior modifiers in university counseling centers, however, have been primarily devoted to the modification of study behaviors, and to the reduction of test anxiety. It is the purpose of this paper to report on the application of behavioral techniques for the modification of other maladaptive behaviors which plague college students as well as members of the community. A brief analysis and summary of treatment for the following cases will be described: 1) depression, 2) homosexuality, 3) persistent vomiting. All cases were treated individually in an ordinary counseling setting without benefit of special equipment. The conditioning variables used to modify behaviors were stimulus control, reinforcement, and extinction.

Depression

Ferster (1966) has described depression as the consequence of decreased reinforcement. For a variety of reasons the source of reinforcement, reinforcement frequency, or amount of reinforcement may be reduced for an individual, producing extinction of certain responses, or reduction of response rate in that individual. Opportunities for reinforcement, therefore, are reduced, which results in fewer and fewer emitted responses, and fewer and fewer reinforcements. The writer suspects that concurrent with response extinction, is the acquisition of "depressive" behavior responses such as a woeful facial expression, slowed motor, speech and other responses, mournful verbalizations, etc. As the "performing" responses dwindle, the very absence of these behaviors becomes the occasion for reinforcement from the individual's environment. Facial expression, slowness, and sad verbalizations ("depressive" behaviors) are also attended to quite systematically. How many

[1] Previously unpublished material, printed with permission of the author.

220

times have many of us noted the sorrowful look expressed by another and paused to inquire, "What seems to be the matter?" Depressive behaviors are thus reinforced by generous amounts of consoling attention which only serve to increase the frequency of those behaviors.

In the treatment of depression with behavior modification it is necessary to identify the reinforcers past and present for that particular individual. A system of reinforcements for performing responses can be built into the client's environment, and arrangements can sometimes be made for the extinction of "depressive" responses. It is more easily said than done.

To date three depressed cases have been treated by the writer with the use of reinforcement and extinction. In all three counselor attention was used as one reinforcer, but other, more natural reinforcers need to be mobilized.

A 26-year-old male reported the onset of depression to be eight months prior to the first interview. His depression had grown steadily worse until he could no longer work, had slowed motor and verbal responses, no sexual response, and the classic "depressed" posture and facial expression. His wife's aid was immediately enlisted; she was instructed to reinforce with her attention and praise a broad class of performing responses, no matter how small an effort was required by each, and to extinguish the depressive class of responses with inattention. The writer met with the client three times the first week. The latter was instructed to begin only those tasks which he could complete successfully. Interview time was spent in the reporting and reinforcing of activities which he had undertaken and completed, and with anticipating a progression of activities to be performed between appointments. The client was not allowed to enter into discourses about how badly he felt and how difficult life was for him after the first interview. Acceleration of self-initiated performing responses was evident after the third session, along with a noticeable livening of motor and verbal responses. Response acceleration continued over the next two weeks as evidenced by his wife's report on numerous activities undertaken (letter writing, friends called and visited, etc.) for the first time in many weeks. After three weeks of treatment a traumatic family circumstance caused the client and his wife to move abruptly out of the state. Although the client's behaviors were not characteristic of a depressed individual at the time of departure, his restored response rate had not stabilized, nor was it maintained naturally by his environment. For all practical purposes he lost his wife as a primary source of reinforcement, for she was attending to her own family problems. Both were without counselor reinforcement, and they found themselves in a different community which offered few occasions for appropriate reinforcement. In a letter written three months later, the client reported having suffered a relapse, and had been subsequently hospitalized.

Another depressed client was found to have lost a vital source of reinforcement when, for the first times in his life, he experienced difficulty in grasping concepts in a mathematics course. This very bright 21-year-old student was a math major in his junior year whose primary reinforcers were: 1) satisfaction with intellectual mastery of material, and 2) grades. His math professor was not in the habit of grading until the term's end. The math course was advanced and theoretical enough so that the student could not engage in a discussion of the subject's intricacies with anyone in his immediate environment because of its unfamiliarity to them. A math student from the class provided a temporary reinforcer when the client arranged to meet with him for study and socialization three times a week, according to instruction. In two weeks the student was able to reestablish regular class attendance, his ability to make decisions was reinstated, excessive introspection and rumination had ceased, and he resumed his generally energetic approach to life. A three month follow-up indicated that his behavior had stabilized.

A very passive student had been depressed for three months at which point it dawned upon him that a girl in whom he was interested showed signs of being uninterested in him. This was not the first depression he had suffered, but he described it as the worst and longest. Two aspects of the client's behavior were undertaken for modification, partly owing to limited possibilities accessible from the environment. This college senior lived alone in an apartment, and managed to obtain reinforcements for depressed behavior from many individuals, including the girl. First, the client's weak and infrequent assertive responses and reports of responses were invited, then systematically and massively reinforced. Secondly, when the client became assertive enough to decide in the third session to compete for the girl, instead of accepting "his fate," he was instructed in a few behavior modification principles which might make the girl responsive to him. It was suggested that he date a second girl in an effort to provide a model for girl number one. The other reason for the suggestion was of course to enlist another opportunity for positive reinforcement, and to establish an alternative in case the young man should fail his first course in behavior modification. In the process of this planning, his ruminations turned from morose rehashing of the past to action oriented planning for the future.

At the fourth interview he shook his finger at the counselor and demanded to know whether behavior modification had been used with him, because he noticed changes in his behavior. He reported incidents in which he had behaved in an uncharacteristically assertive fashion, and noted, "everyone there sat up and took notice." In three weeks he was much less depressed, as evidenced by his improved manner of dress, return to classes and study, and by his almost jovial manner.

Homosexuality

A homosexual student with whom the writer had been working in a traditional manner for nine months showed some improvement with respect to insight, but no behavior change. Evaluation of his situation suggested that part of the reason for lack of change might be attributed to an overall restriction of social abilities and responses. Few, if any, interactions alternative to homosexual interactions were available to the client. Using herself and many cups of coffee as reinforcers, the writer initiated a program designed to widen the client's response repertoire. Client and counselor took coffee repeatedly at several campus installations, always inviting others to join them. The client was encouraged to attend campus meetings and was accompanied to one of the first by the counselor. Behaviors which increased the probability for successful social encounters were reinforced on the spot and during interviews. Gradually the counselor lessened her presence as natural reinforcers began to operate. When social behavior was established and self-maintaining, the writer refused to give interview time for the discussion of male acquaintances. In addition "time with counselor" became contingent upon frequency of formal interactions with females between sessions. Counseling time was devoted to discussion and reinforcement of appropriate behaviors during those interactions. After six months of this behavior shaping, the client had established several healthy social relationships, and had steadily decreased homosexual contacts. A year later the client reports absence of homosexual behaviors for the past three months.

Vomiting Behavior

A female student who had been vomiting frequently for several weeks was thought to have acquired the behavior as a result of classical conditioning. The first instances of a date-sleep-vomit sequence were perhaps brought on by physiological circumstances such as drinking or fatigue. During a two-month period she had experienced the date-sleep-vomit sequence a total of eight times. She had not vomited at an interval when date-sleep did not precede it, but she had, during the first month, experienced dates with the absence of the vomiting response following sleep. All dates for the last four weeks, however, had been followed by sleeping and morning vomiting. She had undergone examinations by doctors on two occasions, and had been hospitalized once for a thorough check. Results were negative.

The vomiting behavior could not be classified as an avoidance response, and a maintaining reinforcer could not be identified. Treatment was therefore designed using a classical conditioning paradigm in which the goal was to divest any and all stimuli surrounding the date-sleep sequence of their control over vomiting behavior.

After a simple explanation of the writer's analysis, the student was instructed to follow a dating program designed to assist her in "unlearning" a behavior she had learned quite by accident. Where she dated only once or twice a week, she was now to date nightly. The program consisted of successive approximations to her normal dating behavior with many stimulus elements eliminated in the beginning, and added back gradually. Early evening dates of an hour's duration began the program. This scheme produced a time and activity interval between the date-sleep-portion of the sequence, and with other modifications, differing stimuli surrounding the date itself. During the two-week treatment period prior to the semester's end, dating time gradually increased to $2\frac{1}{2}$ hours. No vomiting occurred. The student continued the successively approximated steps after she returned home, and experienced only one incidence of vomiting. Follow-up done at four months and at nine months indicated only one further incidence of vomiting, which the client attributed to the flu. She was leading an active life, and enjoying normal dating at the rate of two or three a week.

Conclusion

The wide variation of maladaptive behaviors which plague university students is probably representative of behaviors exhibited by individuals in the community at large. The bulk of research from counseling centers, however, concerns itself with the modification of study behaviors and test anxieties. It would seem appropriate, if not indeed mandatory, that counseling centers address themselves also to the investigation and refinement of behavior modification techniques for treatment within their own communities as well as for the wider community.

It appears that applications of behavior therapy in the traditional counseling situation can be effective, not only for the client, but also economical with respect to counselor time invested. In two of the depression cases less than ten counseling hours were invested, while the vomiting case required only four counseling hours. The success of behavior modification treatment for depression has been as exciting for the writer as it has been satisfactory for the client. One of the advantages of behavior therapy for depression came to light quite by accident when the writer was called away and requested that a colleague meet with a client. It was a simple matter to describe what needed to be accomplished!

It remains to be seen whether "non-depressed" behavior will stabilize for long periods of time. Does the client learn a new way of responding to a sudden decrease in reinforcements which will be available to him in the future? The question arises as to whether all depressions can be appropriately treated with the type of technique outlined, or are alternatives required for different types of depression? Another problem is one of classification or diagnosis. The vomiting behavior reported would probably be classified as an hysterical reaction, which indicates little with regard to implied treatment. The writer is presently treating a case which could be classified as a mild character disorder under the traditional system. Upon analysis, however, the difficulty seems to be that of the individual having been conditioned to short-term reinforcements. The treatment indicated, then, is the shaping of continued responding under conditions of successively longer inter-interval reinforcement.

It is the writer's intention that the material just presented will not only be the occasion for the emission of critical behaviors directed toward the foregoing data, but also a partial stimulus for systematic investigations by counselors of procedures and parameters applicable to the modification of maladaptive behaviors which are disruptive to a wide range of individuals.

REFERENCES

Ferster, C. B., Animal Behavior and Mental Illness, *The Psychological Record*, 1966, *16*, 345-356.

Automated Self-desensitization: a Case Report[1]

Bernard Migler and Joseph Wolpe

The technique of systematic desensitization (Wolpe, 1954) is effective in the treatment of conditioned fear, as both individual case studies (e.g. Wolpe, 1962; Wolpin, 1965) and reports of series of cases have indicated (e.g. Wolpe, 1958; Lazarus, 1963). In addition to these clinical studies, the effects of desensitization have been studied experimentally. Paul (1966) found systematic desensitization to be superior to traditional "insight" therapy, to "attention-placebo" therapy, and to no therapy, in the treatment of public-speaking fears. Cooke (1966) also found it superior to no therapy. Lang and Lazovik (1963), using subjects with strong avoidance and fear reactions to harmless snakes, found desensitization using snake scenes more effective than the hierarchical presentation of irrelevant topics. Davison (1965) and Rachman (1965) have shown the importance of relaxation during desensitization. Subjects visualizing scenes without relaxation did not progress at the rate of subjects who were relaxed during the visualizations.

On the other hand, there is evidence that the maneuvers of systematic desensitization are not effective under all conditions. In the first place, it is necessary for the training of the therapist and his experience in systematic desensitization to be adequate, or such mediocre results as reported by Marks and Gelder (1965) may be expected. Specific factors that can impotentiate the technique are—*a* poor relaxation; *b* poor visualization of scenes; *c* absence of autonomic responses to visualized scenes; *d* inaccurate reporting of autonomic responses and *e* incorrect identification of the stimuli controlling the conditioned fear and avoidance behavior. But even though systematic desensitization has proven itself in the clinic and in the laboratory, there is room for innovations that would minimize negative factors and improve the reliability and efficiency of the technique.

In this paper we report two innovations utilized in the treatment of a

[1]Reprinted from *Behavior Research and Therapy*, 1967, *5*, 133-135, with permission of the authors and Pergamon Press, Ltd.

single case. The first of these was the use of a specially modified tape-recorder to carry out the relaxation and desensitization procedures. The second innovation followed from the first. The patient took the tape-recorder home and administered the desensitization sessions to himself. The behavior problem concerned was eliminated in seven treatment sessions.

The Problem

What most immediately brought the patient for treatment was his inability to attend an important staff-meeting at his place of employment as a result of his fear of public-speaking. He had avoided the meeting because of the possibility that he might be called upon to speak. At the previous staff-meeting several other persons had been called upon, and believing that his turn would come, he had felt very strong autonomic reactions (heart-pounding, sweating, lightheadedness), i.e., "anxiety." On past occasions the patient had sometimes spoken in public but always with anxiety in varying degrees. He was greatly concerned at what the audience might think of him (e.g. "he's wasting our time;" "he doesn't know what the hell he's talking about;" mocking laughter, etc.). On some occasions he would feel only a little autonomic response while speaking, but a great deal immediately afterwards, when the audience might be assumed to be thinking unflattering thoughts about him.

Treatment

Desensitization was selected as the appropriate treatment for the case. Some of the weak items of the hierarchy were: sitting in the conference room before anyone else has arrived; the room filling up with people before the meeting has started. Some of the middle items were: people are being called upon to speak in turn according to where they are sitting, and there are ten speakers ahead of you (9,8,7,. . . .1); your heart is pounding while you wait to speak; you are asked for your opinion; you give your opinion which is contrary to what everyone else has said. Some of the strong items were: some people in the audience make faces of disgust; two people laugh openly at what you are saying; one person says to another, "he doesn't know what the hell he's talking about."

As described below, relaxation training, and the administration of scenes from the hierarchy with the patient relaxed were carried out at home, entirely by the patient, using a specially modified tape recorder.

Apparatus

The Wollensak T-1600 tape recorder has two features that make it suitable for use in automated desensitization. (The Uher Universal 5000, a more expensive recorder, also has these features.) First, it has a pause switch by which the tape motion can be instantly stopped. This switch was connected to a microswitch which the patient could hold in his hand, and, as desired, stop the tape motion at any time, for any duration. Second, the recorder has two metal-sensing strips on each side of the recording heads. When a metal foil which has been placed on the tape makes contact with the two sensing guides on the right side an internal circuit is closed, and the tape recorder automatically switches from *playback* to *rewind*. These two metal sensing guides were bypassed by the tape and a push-button was wired in parallel with the two sensing guides, so that momentary depression of the push-button switched the recorder from *playback* to *rewind*. The second pair of sensing guides, to the *left* of the recording heads, functions to stop the rewinding and return to *playback* when a metal foil reaches these guides. This was not altered. The push-button and the microswitch were held together by adhesive tape, to make a combined remote control unit that the patient could hold in his hand. Depression of the microswitch (hereafter called the *pause switch*) stopped the playback for as long as it was depressed. Momentary depression of the pushbutton (hereafter called the *repeat button*) produced the following sequential effects: the tape recorder stopped playback and switched to rewind; rewinding continued until the metal foil was detected by the sensing guides to the left of the recording head; and when rewinding had stopped playback began again.

Preparation of tape for desensitization

A tape recording was prepared, using the patient's voice throughout, with the following instructions: (1) Relaxation instructions*: "Relax your toes, arches, calves, thighs, hands, forearms, upper arms, shoulders, back, behind, stomach, chest, neck, jaws, mouth, tongue, cheeks, eyeball muscles, eyebrows, forehead, scalp." (In using this section of the tape the patient was instructed to press the pause switch after each anatomical part was named and concentrate on that part until it felt free of muscular tension, then to release the pause switch and let the tape continue.)

(2) A metal foil was attached to the tape at the end of these relaxation instructions.

(3) Just beyond the metal foil (and before the first scene), were a few brief relaxation instructions: "Relax your arms, legs, stomach, chest, neck, and all your facial muscles. Now pause until you feel relaxed." (The patient was instructed to press the pause switch at this point until he felt relaxed.)

(4) Following these relaxation instructions, the tape contained instructions to visualize the first scene in the hierarchy: "Now imagine (*first scene*). Pause." The patient was instructed to press the pause switch at this point until the visualization was clear, and then to let the tape continue.

(5) Ten seconds of recorded silence followed the instruction to pause, permitting 10 seconds of clear visualization. The silence was terminated by the words, "Stop visualizing it. Press the repeat button if that scene dis-

---

*A relaxation training tape with instructions to contract, then relax, various muscle groups had been used for several sessions of preliminary training.

turbed you at all." If the patient felt any negative emotional response to the scene he was to press the repeat button, which would rewind the tape back to the metal foil (step 2 above) so that the brief relaxation instructions, the scene, and the remainder of the sequence would recur. If the repeat button was not pressed, the tape-recorder continued to the next metal foil, which, like the first, was followed by relaxation instructions, but after these came scene 2 of the hierarchy—and so forth.

Results

Seven desensitization sessions were required to accomplish desensitization to all the scenes in the hierarchy.

A week after the final session the patient attended a staff meeting, was called upon to speak, and delivered a long speech disagreeing with all the previous speakers. He experienced no anxiety—in fact, felt elated and proud of himself. He subsequently found that the desensitization had generalized to other public speaking situations. He reported that now these caused little or no anxiety. When autonomic responses were felt, they were mild.

Follow-Up

Eight months after completion of desensitization the patient reports that he is continuing to speak in public without anxiety or avoidance behavior.

Discussion

This is not the first case to have been the subject of automated desensitization. Several individuals with phobias for harmless snakes have been treated in this manner by Lang (1966), using rather elaborate apparatus, with several tape-recorders and electronic switching circuits. The special features of this report are (1) the use of automated desensitization in the treatment of a clinical case; (2) the simplicity of the apparatus, and (3) the administration of desensitization by the patient using his own voice. These procedures made the therapist quite remote from the therapeutic situation, and thus further diminished the force of the possible contention that non-specific processes corresponding to "transference" or interpersonal interaction could be the real basis of change. By itself, of course, the success of this case does not do away with that possibility, against which controlled studies such as Paul's (1966) provide a much more cogent argument.

A more important implication of the case is that it is one more step in the direction of therapeutic economy. The demand upon the time of the therapist is minimized *both* during the preparation of the tape *and* during the scene preparations. Of course, this is a true economy only if the results of automated desensitization are comparable with those of therapist desensitization. Preliminary comparisons made by Lang (1966) in the context of snake phobias, have shown, if anything, a slight superiority for automated desensitization! It is quite likely, however, that for many patients the presence of a therapist facilitates change. How to sort them according to their requirements will be another subject for research.

REFERENCES

Cooke, G. The efficacy of two desensitization procedures: an analogue study. *Behavior Research and Therapy*, 1966, *4*, 17-24.

Davison, G. C. The influence of systematic desensitization, relaxation, and graded exposure to imaginal aversive stimuli on the modification of phobic behavior. Ph.D. Dissertation, Stanford University, 1965.

Lang, P. J. Personal communication. 1966.

Lang, P. J. and Lazovik, A. D. Experimental desensitization of a phobia. *Journal of Abnormal and Social Psychology*, 1963, *66*, 519-525.

Lazarus, A. A. The results of behavior therapy in 126 cases of severe neurosis. *Behavior Research and Therapy*, 1963, *1*, 69-79.

Marks, I. M. and Gelder, M. G. A controlled retrospective study of behavior therapy in phobic patients. *British Journal of Psychiatry*, 1965, *111*, 561-573.

Paul, G. L. *Insight versus desensitization: an experiment in anxiety reduction.* Stanford, Calif.: Stanford University Press, 1966.

Rachman, S. Studies in desensitization-I: The separate effects of relaxation and desensitization. *Behavior Research and Therapy*, 1965, *3*, 245-251.

Wolpe, J. Reciprocal inhibition as the main basis of psychotherapeutic effects. *Archives of Neurology and Psychiatry*, 1954, *72*, 205-226.

Wolpe, J. *Psychotherapy by reciprocal inhibition.* Stanford, Calif.: Stanford University Press, 1958.

Wolpe, J. Isolation of a conditioning procedure as the crucial psychotherapeutic factor: a case study. *Journal of Nervous and Mental Disorders*, 1962, *134*, 316-329.

Wolpin, M. and Raines, J. Visual imagery, expected roles and extinction as possible factors reducing fear and avoidance behavior. *Behavior Research and Therapy*, 1966, *4*, 25-37.

Introduction to Planned Behavior Change[1]

Donald H. Ford

Within the scope of its broadly conceived counseling program the staff of the Division of Counseling at The Pennsylvania State University is faced with the full range of human hopes, strivings, and difficulties present with the special urgency one finds in young people. The feeling has been growing among us that the current theories upon which clinical and counseling practice is based are too narrow for the scope of the task we have set for ourselves. Hugh Urban and I, in particular, have spent the last few years taking a fresh look at the theories and techniques available to us. Each theory seems to have focused on some aspects of human behavior and its situational determinants and to have given relatively little emphasis to other aspects. Some theories are broader than others, but all seem to have serious limitations in scope, while at the same time making some important contributions. Confronted with our own dissatisfaction, the alternative available seemed to be to try to build upon the central elements of existing theories a broader conceptual base for our work. Although our thinking is not yet sufficiently formalized to warrant a systematic presentation, a brief discussion of some of the notions guiding our thinking may illustrate that the developing approach represented in the case examples which follow is not eclectic in nature but a step toward developing a systematic view based on the best psychological knowledge and theories currently available.

First of all, we have decided we must develop and learn to use a conceptual language which enables us to utilize the extensive findings in the basic discipline of psychology as well as the clinical findings and theories which have grown from naturalistic observation. At this stage, we think it is awkward and limiting to try to study behavior in terms of large, inclusive concept units such as "ego," "dependency," and "relationship." We think we will progress more rapidly at the moment if we try to get closer to the

[1] From *Planned Behavior Change: Illustrations of an Approach* (unpublished monograph, Div. of Counseling, Pa. State Univ., 1963), with permission of the authors and D. H. Ford and H. B. Urban, Editors.

"data level" of behavior, so to speak, and talk about specific kinds of response events such as thoughts, emotions, speech, and motoric acts. We think larger concept units can be rendered more understandable and precise if represented in terms of kinds of responses, kinds of situational events, and their interrelationships.

Second, we have concluded that effective understanding and analysis of an individual's behavior must be based on the assumption that behavior occurs in a continuous stream within the context of constantly changing patterns of situational events. Such a view leads one to think in terms of behavior sequences and patterns, to look for the antecedents to and the consequences of particular behaviors in which one might be interested, and to look for both of these in situational as well as response determinants.

Third, we recognize that a counselor or therapist cannot deal with the entire behavior stream at the same time. Therefore, he is selective. We need ways of determining which responses to deal with at a particular moment. We know that a therapist or counselor can only work with behaviors as they occur *in the present*. For example, it is not childhood experiences or traumas which disturb the adult, but presently occurring memories and related emotions which do so. Therefore, when certain behavior continues to occur over time, one may assume that something is going on *in the present* to keep eliciting it. For example, protracted grief, recurrent anger, or persistent fears must have identifiable antecedents either in the environment or in the person's responses.

Fourth, when one thinks in terms of different kinds of responses and situational events occurring in a continuous stream, it becomes apparent that one must attend to the various ways in which different kinds of events may become interrelated. A variety of interrelationships is possible. One event may interfere with another, elicit it, increase its intensity, and so forth. Different theorists have suggested that responses may be incongruent, in conflict, facilitating, or inhibiting. These represent propositional statements as to the ways in which responses can come to be interrelated with one another.

Fifth, it follows that if one wished to modify or enlarge a particular situation-behavior pattern or unit, one might intervene at any one of several points in an ongoing pattern or sequence. Where to intervene involves a decision by the therapist. For example, an anger pattern may be terminated by modifying the antecedent thoughts which elicit it. Or, perhaps it may be extinguished by altering the consequences which follow from it. This also leads to the notion that a counselor proceeds in steps, focusing first upon one result and then another. This, too, requires a decision as to the order or sequence in which particular results will be sought.

Sixth, this raises the possibility that different procedures may be needed to achieve different results with different responses in different situations. Therefore, we have decided not to adopt the assumption found in some learning theories that all responses operate according to the same laws.

Rather, we wish to remain open to the possibility that different kinds of responses may be learned and modified according to different principles, or with different procedures. For example, perhaps emotions follow the principles of conditioning; thoughts on the other hand may not.

Finally, we recognize the critical role played by situational factors in developing, maintaining, and modifying behavior patterns. In fact, it now appears that behavior will cease to occur in any but the most rudimentary forms if stimulation from the environment is removed for extended periods of time. An effective counselor or therapist must attend to the situational factors involved in the behaviors with which he is concerned. This will help him to understand how a particular pattern came to be learned, why it continues to occur, and how it might be modified. Counseling itself represents the application of situational events (the counselor's behavior, e.g. speech) to the patient's behavior. Situational modifications may elicit new behaviors and produce permanent modifications in old ones.

Verbal Procedures in the Modification of Subjective Responses[1]

Hugh B. Urban

David was in real academic difficulty from the start of his college career. His high school pattern of "falling apart" in examinations was continuing to plague him and threatening to spoil his budding career. He explained that he expected to fail every test. His fear was manageable until the exam started. But when he read the initial test items, he became agitated; his heart would pound, his hands would tremble and perspire, and his "mind would go blank." The thoughts relevant to the test items would not occur. Instead, thoughts such as "Oh, my God—I can't do it—I'm sure to fail" came in their place. He used a number of habits to compose himself, such as smoking or looking around until he saw another student who appeared equally frightened. Gradually his agitation would subside until he could proceed. However, he typically could not complete the test and left the exam aware of his omissions and certain he had failed. After the test, he would experience a progressive recall of answers. For example, he would begin to remember the formulae which had eluded him during the test. Obviously, he knew the answers and could recall them under some conditions, but not under others. Moreover, his difficulty was progressive, with each failure increasing his expectation of future failures. The intense fear pattern apparently interfered with clear thinking and recall. But the question remained: Where did the fear come from? What was producing it? Apprehension about failing a test seemed reasonable but being victimized by such terror seemed quite inappropriate.

With this problem, one can start with the knowledge that a major source of fear is the anticipation of punishing consequents. Since *people* do the punishing, one may ask: of *whom* was he afraid, and what was he afraid, *they* would do? When questioned, Dave revealed that he feared being disparaged and rejected by a great many people. Tracing his anticipations in detail re-

[1] From *Planned Behavior Change: Illustrations of an Approach* (unpublished monograph, Div. of Counseling, Pa. State Univ., 1963), with permission of the authors and D. H. Ford and H. B. Urban, Editors.

vealed the following general thought sequences: "Here is a test—I may fail it —if I fail the test, I'll fail the course—if I fail the course, I'll probably flunk out of college—if I flunk out of college, I'll never be able to get a decent job and will be doomed to a meagre income for the rest of my life—moreover, my parents will lose all respect for me, and will reject me—so will my girl-friend, since she will not want to associate with someone who is not a college graduate."

Laying these thoughts out in explicit fashion made several things apparent. First, David's fears were related to his anticipations of what would happen in the future. Such consequences would be dire indeed, and warrant concern. Dave was convinced they *would* happen. Secondly, each event could occur, but Dave's conclusion that one must follow from the other was incorrect. The thoughts were potentially valid—it was the way they were hooked up in sequence which was at fault. Moreover, each thought elicited further anxiety and *augmented* the overall fear pattern.

As long as David thought in this fashion, the disruptive fear would persist. Thus, it was decided treatment would focus upon the troublesome thought sequence.

Dave was encouraged to ask himself: "Are the terrible events I anticipate at all likely to occur?" He quickly recognized that he had been over-generalizing (from failing a test, to failing a course, to flunking out of college) without being aware of it. He formed a discrimination: the occurrence of one failure would not inevitably lead to another.

Next in the sequence were his anticipations of the consequences of failure. Dave was helped to see that a college degree was not an absolute prerequisite for a meaningful career. Finally, he was led to question his prediction that the persons he cared about really would reject and disparage him. In successive stages he recognized that they had never said so explicitly, and that his conclusion was based on *his* inferences about *their* private thoughts and feelings. He agreed that the only way to verify these inferences was to question them and judge their reaction to the hypothetical event. Hesitant to find out, yet unwilling to remain in doubt, he called them. His girlfriend was explicit, and satisfied him that he was wrong and had imputed a set of feelings to her which she did not have.

Encouraged, he called his parents. Here things were not so clear-cut. He thought that their words belied their feelings. They assured him that he need not fear their disrespect, but he persisted in believing that they would privately disparage him, although unwilling to say so.

The basis for this conviction was explored. Again David had no concrete evidence. But his statements that he could hardly blame them if they did, and that he could see how they could feel otherwise, suggested the source of his conclusions. A series of questions established that Dave was the person who would despise himself if he flunked out, and by an act of assimilative projection, he assumed that others would judge him the same way. Another instance of an inappropriately generalized response had been encountered. A brief discussion helped Dave to remind himself that he and others did not necessarily think and feel in precisely the same way. His general stock of discriminations between himself and his parents came into play, and he concluded that they were more tolerant of people than he was. This left him with the question of his own self-evaluations. By rendering his self-rejecting thoughts explicit, he could recognize how discrepant they were with other views of himself as an adequate person. He finally concluded that it was ridiculous to accept or reject someone on the basis of a college diploma.

After this Dave completed three tests with little if any distress. The thought that he might fail continued to occur, but now other thoughts followed, such as "If I do, I'll do better on the next one," or "It's only a course—it doesn't mean the end of the world." These new thoughts did not elicit concomitant anxiety. Two terms later he was still free of test panics, experiencing mild fear only when he knew he was unprepared.

June's situation, although superficially different, had many features in common with that of David. She had been fretful and depressed for two and a half weeks when she first reported to the Counseling Office. She had sought help not so much to learn what was troubling her, but rather because of its effect upon her academic situation. She knew why she felt depressed and cried, why she slept fitfully, had lost her appetite, and could not study effectively. Her brother had recently died, and the loss was particularly acute since he was the only son and a family favorite.

Careful analysis suggested that June's problem was a grief pattern, protracted and continuous over several weeks, but the question was: What made her grief persist so long, and how could it be interrupted so that she could resume her work?

It seemed clear that something had to be happening to continue eliciting the grief pattern. Inquiry revealed that June had remained preoccupied with her brother's death. Repeatedly she thought of him, remembering his appearance, manner and actions in a hundred situations; she and her mother wrote letters daily commiserating with one another; and she sought to remain with her mother, only reluctantly agreeing to continue in college.

The antidote became evident: a way must be found to help June to discontinue all the daily acts which perpetuated her grief. With explanation, she quickly recognized the relationship between her thoughts and the feelings they produced, which in turn led to her misery and behavioral incapacity. She agreed that to overcome her grief she must stop reinstating it. She wanted to try. Controlling these feelings required controlling her thoughts, and she was shown two ways to control the kind of thoughts she had. First, by *selective inattention* or avoiding the situations likely to elicit the unwanted thoughts (e.g. by avoiding weekend visits and phone calls to her mother, and by removing mementoes from her dresser top). Secondly, by *response substitution:* that is arranging for other thoughts to occur whenever the grief-producing thoughts began. Talking to friends, attending the movies, and reading her lessons could elicit thoughts which would displace the grief-producing ones. During the next several days, June tried but said she couldn't implement the prescription. Could it be that the principles we had reviewed were still too unclear to be effectively applied? No! A series of questions established that she understood what to do and why, but could not carry through. For example, she recognized that she cried when she saw her brother's picture on her dresser. Rather than put it away and distract herself with other activities, she lay on the bed with her face next to the picture and spent an hour "grieving" over her dead brother.

What was producing this? She said she "could not" perform the responses, and yet this was not strictly true—she agreed she had the capability to do so. A collaborative search for another reason began. She could not account for it, other than to suggest that for some reason it didn't seem right. Did it seem wrong? Well, yes it did in a way. Then it gradually unfolded: a network of implicit ought-statements. She was continually reminding herself of her brother because she felt she ought to. It was a way of keeping him "alive," if not in reality, at least in the thoughts of those left behind. Why was it necessary to go to such lengths to keep his memory alive—wouldn't that occur in the natural course of events? No, she was afraid he would be forgotten. What led her to fear that? Since the family had known him intimately for many years, was it really likely that she or her parents would forget? Only if they wanted to. Did her parents want to? Oh, no. Then, it was she herself who might forget—because she wanted to? Ruefully, she agreed.

There followed a recitation of her feelings of jealousy toward her favored brother and her own yearning for the favorite role. Her behavior as a grief-stricken daughter was seen as an additional way in which to earn parental favor.

Following this third discussion, the problem was solved. A follow-up call 15 months later confirmed the fact that the behavior change had been permanent. Her natural thoughts about her brother brought a feeling of regret and sadness, but little more.

Jim, a junior in Chemistry, was referred to the Division of Counseling by the University Psychiatrist. Jim complained that he was being victimized by his fellow students. He was angry and agitated over their continual harassment and ridicule, and their labeling of him as a homosexual because of his difficulty in urinating in public. He acknowledged a chronic problem with urination, for which he wanted help, but vehemently denied its relationship to his sexual situation—this he protested was more than adequate (and indeed a check upon this proved him to be correct). He had already been materially helped by arranging for a change in his housing, authorizing a move out of the dormitories and into a room downtown. He was referred to us for help with his urination problem, and the associated effects upon his morale.

The analysis of Jim's difficulties was extensive—the kind for which intensive psychotherapy is often recommended. The analysis of the antecedents was considerably more intricate than in the two cases we have just cited. Portions of the work on his case have been abstracted, however, to illustrate the utility of close, detailed analysis of specific, concrete response events as they occur, identifying which occur in what order, so that differential procedures of modification can be employed depending upon which kinds happen to be involved.

Jim was so angry that he was considering verbal and physical retaliation; he felt that things had passed the point of tolerance. Attacking others in a fit of rage would have been clearly inappropriate, and something which had to be dealt with initially. This entailed establishing what was causing the anger, what its antecedents were.

Inquiry established that what was happening was really a recurrent sequence of events. Jim said certain events occurred in the situation. Other people were whispering and snickering behind his back, sending relays of students through the toilets in order to time him at the urinal, calling him "queer" and the like. He was identifying these behavior events in others, reaching conclusions as to what they meant, and this in turn led to intense anger and thoughts of violent retaliation. Where in this sequence of events lay the difficulty? Were such things happening, or was he *misperceiving* the situations as they occurred? Were both his *perceptions* of what was happening and the *conclusions* he drew about the thoughts of others essentially correct? If so, perhaps the fault was an excessively intense anger pattern, which in turn would trigger off aggressive acts.

It was necessary to determine where in the behavioral sequence attention should be focused. Thus, Jim was asked to report very carefully: precisely what did he see and hear, what did he observe other people doing, did he ever actually hear the word queer used in reference to himself?

Jim's answers provided the data necessary to determine where the difficulty lay. It developed that there was nothing wrong with his identification of what was happening—students *were* whispering, walking through the toilets and the like. However, he had not actually heard anyone call him queer or whisper his name. Although he had no concrete evidence of what others thought, he was confident that they considered him homosexual, nonetheless.

It seemed clear that where the sequence was going wrong was in the connection between what Jim saw and heard on the one hand and the conceptions he developed on the other. There seemed to be nothing wrong with the way he was perceiving events, and the anger would make sense if his thoughts were essentially correct. Instead it was the way he was thinking which was producing the problem, and to effect a beneficial change in this behavioral sequence required a change in the way he thought. It was decided to operate on this part of the sequence.

One of the troublesome thoughts was: hesitancy in urination indicates homosexuality. Clearly wrong, it was also clearly implicit in Jim's thinking. To change such a symbolic equation, one must first make it verbally explicit. The therapist did so by saying, "As I understand it, you believe others think this and have concluded you are homosexual?" Jim acknowledged the thought.

The next step was to establish in whose thought sequences this conclusion was occurring—Jim presumed it occurred in others' and did not recognize it was implicitly in his own. The therapist registered surprise that others would think such a thought, and reminded Jim that he had never actually heard anyone say such a thing. He acknowledged that he had not. If no one he had met mentioned such an idea, where might it have come from? To whom had such a possibility occurred? By a Socratic procedure, then, Jim was led to recognize that there was only one person in the situation left—Jim himself. He must implicitly accept such an equation.

Initially he denied that such was the case, but he did see the logic of it and agreed to consider it further. With urging he became able to recall some relevant thoughts to the effect that he must be sexually deviate if he could not urinate in public, since this was a masculine activity. Similarly, he began to recall his adolescent fears of lack of virility and his fears that others would consider him homosexual because of his general timidity and two adolescent experiments in multiple masturbation. He then saw that he had indeed been construing his problem as indicative of homosexuality. He himself was convinced that he was a homosexual.

Once this notion was made explicit it was possible to operate on it and to help Jim see that it was ridiculous to judge a person's virility in terms of how fast he could initiate a stream of urine. There might be other bases for thinking he was homosexual, but the difficulty in urinating was a very inadequate one.

A break in this conceptual organization was definitely made, and Jim began to consider his urination problem in other terms. On two subsequent occasions his paranoid conceptions recurred. He thought he heard his landlady speaking to others and protesting that her boarder didn't seem so queer. On another occasion he chanced upon a visitor at the house and concluded that he was a University representative assigned to keep records of his urinary schedule surreptitiously. Having once learned to correct his errors of projection, however, he was able to dismiss these two subsequent sets of thoughts —the first with help in a treatment session, the second on his own with self-correcting thoughts. Subsequently, he was no longer plagued with ideas of persecution by others.

With this aspect of the problem resolved, it was necessary to move on to the next features, and these were managed in order—first his judgments of masculine inferiority, and secondly an exploration of the causes for the inhibition of the urinary pattern. In this latter instance, we moved through a collection of sixteen specific barriers to relaxed urination—a series of responses of disgust, revulsion, guilt, shame, fear of assault, and the like. The series was concluded after the sixteenth session when not only his inappropriate conceptions of his problem were corrected, but also the urination problem itself. This was judged to have occurred when he was able to join a group of peers in a downtown apartment, without fear of social derogation, and with the capacity to urinate effectively.

In all these cases, we were concerned with feelings, thoughts, and perceptions—all of which are responses occurring "within the skin" and accessible only to the observations of the person in whom they occur. They are not *directly* accessible to the observation and the manipulation of the therapist or counselor. Access to them is by indirection. Either the subject must label them verbally, or the therapist must guess at their occurrence from some other behavioral event. Being highly dependent upon the person's self-report, the therapist must seek some degree of correspondence between the response and the person's report of it, for example, between a thought and the person's verbalization of it. Similarly, any method of modifying these subjective responses must also be by indirection, since the therapist cannot directly touch, see, or manipulate subjective responses.

The complaints presented by these students involved intense affective patterns of behavior (fear—despondency—anger) and their consequences. They were unable to study, eat, sleep, take tests, or urinate effectively because of interfering patterns. To change the consequents, the affective response patterns had to be modified.

The modification of a response entails the control or modification of its antecedent. Thus, the first step in the solution of such a problem is to establish the conditions under which the troublesome behavior begins to occur. The individuals were unable (or unwilling) to verbalize the reasons why they felt as they did. Knowing what to look for permits the psychologist to proceed, however, since the data is typically there in the form of raw observations if only the right questions are asked.

In these cases, the troublesome affective responses followed upon various sequences and patterns of thoughts. The antecedent thoughts were rendered explicit and verbalized, and then it became evident that the problem was "located" in the person's conceptual habits. This became the logical place to try to effect a change.

There is still much we do not know about modifying thought responses. However, modifying the way a person talks has some generalizability to modifying the way in which he thinks. The verbal statements which are at fault must first be spoken in specific and explicit form. This follows the dictum in general psychology that a response must first occur if it is to be modified and entails techniques for eliciting the necessary responses. Once these have occurred, procedures for their modification come into play, and these will vary depending upon what is judged to be wrong with the responses. They may be overgeneralized responses; then discriminant learning is involved. It may be just the opposite; inappropriate discriminations between essentially the same conditions may be occurring. In this case, effecting a generalization may be involved.

What changes occurred in the responses of the people discussed? They appeared to be new thoughts, but strictly speaking none of them was. They had been ideas which each subject had been capable of thinking and *did* think in other contexts. Apparently the change was not so much one of introducing new responses into a person's habit structure, but rather of rearranging the interrelationship between the ones which were already there. The subjects had "learned" to think differently about specific events; their thought sequences went along a different progression, and this time it led to constructive and effective action rather than intense and disorganizing affective states. A different set of antecedents led to a different set of consequents, illustrating once more that behavior is a function of the conditions under which it occurs.

The Alteration of Overt Instrumental Responses by Verbal Methods[1]

Harvey W. Wall and Robert E. Campbell

The Division of Counseling often encounters students whose poor grades, unhappy relations with others, loneliness, or possibly ill-health are due to the use of inappropriate or poorly developed overt instrumental responses. That is, the students respond to a routine or troublesome event in a way which creates new or unnecessary difficulty. Furthermore, their ineffective instrumental responses and resultant failures may increase anxiety, negatively affect their confidence, or undermine their feelings of well-being. Frequently, this is a particularly puzzling situation to the person involved because the troublesome instrumental behaviors were once reasonably effective; that is why they were learned. Thus, the individual often does not think to examine such responses as potential troublemakers in his current life.

For example, the exhausted fraternity pledge whose daily routines of sleeping and eating defy physiological logic, may be inattentive to lectures, may fall asleep at his studies, and thus fail his examinations. The lonely, naïve coed, who overfeeds on starches and carbohydrates and who practices poor personal grooming, may show alarm at her failure to make friends. The enthusiastic freshman, who practices study techniques which were once successful in high school but are now ineffective in college, may unwittingly approach his examinations ill-prepared, thereby inviting examination panic and probable failure. In each instance, there are present inappropriate, inadequate, or perhaps complete absence of essential instrumental response patterns which may produce consequences, such as failure, which in turn elicit more troublesome responses such as disordered thought sequences, anticipations of rejection, excessive fear or anger, and related physical symptoms.

Such students often are not suffering from chronic emotional or personal disturbances, though sometimes their symptoms might suggest such an

[1] From *Planned Behavior Change: Illustrations of an Approach* (unpublished monograph, Div. of Counseling, Pa. State Univ., 1963), with permission of the authors and D. H. Ford and H. B. Urban, Editors.

inference. They are basically well-adjusted young people, using habitual responses which are self-defeating. With such people, direct modification of inappropriate instrumental behaviors using verbal procedures is often quite successful. This does not imply that such procedures are inappropriate for persons with severe or chronic adjustment problems. Quick, successful resolution of problems which in and of themselves may be aggravating an already tenuous adjustment, may make more intensive treatment procedures more effective. Such successes may also directly produce personal satisfaction and increased self-confidence, which in turn could lead to additional therapeutic gains.

Needless to say, before deciding on a counseling procedure, careful diagnosis is essential. Problems of fatigue, unhappiness, inadequate achievement, and interpersonal failure are often symptomatic of serious emotional or physical disturbances requiring other treatment. However, even when such serious disorder is present, there seems to be no reason to avoid trying to modify ways of dealing with troublesome events, as long as such modifications are used as judicious supplements to psychotherapeutic, medical, or other treatment.

The approach being discussed can be described in terms of three phases. First, the psychologist and individual work together to identify and evaluate the problematic behaviors. Here, the individual is being helped to see that his responses in dealing with his problem have been ineffective and often self-defeating. The second phase is primarily teaching. The individual is helped to discover and to implement new instrumental responses and to discard ineffective ones. When the staff of the Division of Counseling lacks the training or skill for dealing with a particular problem, consultation or treatment is requested from other University agencies such as the Health Service, or the Speech and Hearing Clinic. Finally, the student is encouraged and supported in trying out the new ways of behaving. He begins to understand why his old established responses to problems were ineffective and circular, and why through the fact of failure, his original anxieties became more intense and his problems compounded. If the new instrumental responses result in the predicted consequences, not only does the person learn to deal more effectively with immediate troublesome events, but also the positive consequences often produce a modification of the antecedents of his problem. For example, he may become less anxious, more self-confident, and more aware of how his own behavior may produce positive or negative consequences.

The following examples illustrate this approach. A 20-year-old coed was referred by a University physician after her insomnia reappeared whenever medication was discontinued. When not taking sleeping pills, she could not fall asleep directly and thus slept only four to five hours nightly. She reported having periodic attacks of insomnia since the age of 15, but that they were controlled through sedatives prescribed by her family physician.

Four weeks after the beginning of her junior year, the insomnia was appearing almost nightly, creating constant fatigue and related inattention to her instructors and studies, and indifference to social activities.

Prior medical examinations ruled out neurological or physiological malfunctioning. Her adjustment was diagnosed as satisfactory in all other respects. Her insomnia appeared to be primarily the result of a pattern of inappropriate preparations for sleep. For example, rather than tapering off her day, she remained tense and alert, studying and completing her assignments up to bedtime. She reported that her assignments often created a sense of stimulation, sometimes in the form of excitement when she was learning new and interesting ideas, and sometimes in terms of mild anxiety evoked by thoughts of approaching examinations and possible failure. After getting into bed, she would read novels or perhaps write letters to her parents and friends back home, an activity which generated reminiscences and related alerting emotional responses. Her habit of drinking soft drinks in late evening might have also delayed drowsiness and consequent sleep, as the result of the ingestion of sugar concentrates. In short, she seemed to be engaging in a series of responses, and exposing herself to situational events which had the effect of maintaining a state of alertness and excitement, which interfered with a normal sleep pattern.

The counseling procedure decided upon was a direct and relatively simple one. She was taught to adopt responses which would encourage a normal sleep pattern and to discontinue those habits which kept her awake. For example, she was instructed to taper off her evenings and not to plunge into bed directly after studying. She was to take a warm bath and soak for 15 minutes prior to retirement. She was to forego sugar concentrates such as pop and instead fill up on warm milk and crackers of which she was fond. After getting in bed, she was to read only that material which made her drowsy, and to do her pleasure reading and letter writing earlier in the day. Discussion of her habits of thinking produced recognition that some of her thoughts created drowsiness, and other wakefulness. She could then try to exercise control of her thought sequences by substituting the former for the latter.

Two weeks later, the girl reported success in quickly falling to sleep and of "never sleeping more soundly." As a result, she was experiencing less fatigue and tension, and was more enthusiastic and attentive to her studies and social responsibilities. At the end of the year, three terms later, she was earning above average grades.

Thus, a troubled person can be taught to identify and discontinue inappropriate interfering behavior and to adopt more effective responses resulting in resolution of a problem.

Treatment of a more extensive behavior pattern is illustrated by the case of a 21-year-old student who initially came in for counseling the early part of his senior year complaining of conflicts, fear of failure in school, and an intense apprehension about attending a ten-week student teaching practicum in another city the following term.

The time limit (six weeks) before he started his student practicum, ruled out the possibility of extended treatment. Therefore, the treatment focused on the most immediate problem: that of dealing with his many fears in anticipation of the ten-week practicum—fear of being alone in a strange community, the possibility of failure as a student teacher, feeling overwhelmed by the details in preparation for the trip, etc. The counselor helped him develop overt instrumental behaviors such as the following to deal with these fears:

1. Develop a calendar to allow supportive visits from his family, friends, and girlfriend.
2. Have in his possession a list of professional persons to call in a crisis.
3. Make a reconnaissance trip to the area (visit his practicum supervisor, become familiar with the area, etc.).
4. Check public transportation schedules to reassure opportunities to return home with ease.
5. Communicate with roommate to reduce ambiguity of living arrangements.
6. Organize a schedule of preparatory tasks in anticipation of the trip to avoid feeling overwhelmed or panicky.

A follow-up eight months later revealed that he not only was able to start his practicum, but also completed it with a straight A average. His girlfriend reported that he adjusted very well and has had no further problems. His brother described him as currently very happy, having more self-confidence. After graduating, he took a very responsible position in a large eastern city. The latter is especially significant since, prior to counseling, he panicked at the thought of ever leaving his home town. Eight months after the first interview, the parents also noted improved family relationships.

A final example concerns a third term freshman. The referring physician in the Student Health Center described the student as "very tense;" tranquilizers were prescribed. During the initial interview, the student complained of general anxiety symptoms, *e.g.* shortness of breath, tightness in his chest, butterflies in his stomach, headaches, dizziness, restlessness, and difficulty studying. He added that similar symptoms had occurred often in high school. He reported having previously visited several physicians, who arrived at the same diagnosis, *i.e.* no organic impairement, but excessive anxiety. Further inquiry revealed that the student experienced the symptoms most often while he was studying and was very fearful of failing. His anxiety became so intense that it was interfering with his academic performance, which compounded the anxiety. The psychologist and student agreed to work together in establishing techniques to (1) reduce anxiety while preparing for examinations, and (2) deal with test anxiety. In seven sessions, instrumental behaviors such as the following were developed:

1. Organize a study schedule to demonstrate that he had control over his assignments and to be better prepared for examinations.
2. Learn to see the cause-effect relationships between his anxiety and above mentioned symptoms.
3. Employ relaxation techniques, *e.g.* breathing exercises, rest, pauses, etc.
4. Establish occasional physical recreation to tap off tension.
5. Improve his examination-taking skills.
6. Avoid getting to his examinations too early to reduce and prevent ruminations while waiting for the examination.

The student responded very favorably. He reported improvement in his overall adjustment and his grades rose from C+ to B+ during the term of counseling. Four months later, his parents also reported that he appeared much more relaxed. Follow-up reports showed that he continued to function above a B for three subsequent terms and in his most recent term, he earned academic honors.

In summary, persons whose difficulties stem from the use of poor instrumental responses can be helped to overcome their problems through a procedure in which the ineffective and self-defeating instrumental responses are replaced by new and more appropriate ones. Although this alternative of overt instrumental responses by verbal means may be most effective with basically well-adjusted young people, people with chronic emotional and adjustment problems can also be helped to develop better habits and ways of dealing with specific problems. However, here the procedure should be used judiciously and as a supplement to more intensive and appropriate treatment.

The value of this approach lies in its apparent simplicity and effectiveness. Patients see it as directly and immediately related to their concerns. If successful, the effects of subsequent satisfying events may not only increase the occurrence of new instrumental responses, but may also alter distressing thoughts and feelings which were antecedents to the problems. Perhaps herein lies the greatest value of the approach. The individual discovers that there are concrete instrumental responses which he can employ successfully to cope with his problems. The experience of analyzing his difficulties and planning the use of new, more effective behaviors may begin the creation of new habits of handling future difficulties on his own, without the aid of a therapist.

Behavior Modification through Situational Manipulation[1]

Samuel H. Osipow and Robert R. Grooms

The influence of situational factors on human behavior has long been recognized by psychologists. The psychology of learning has, for years, been very much concerned with arranging situational variables so that learning is facilitated. It is a short step from recognizing the importance of situational variables in learning to realizing that the manipulation of the situational context of a human being will result in modifications of his behavior. In fact, there are often circumstances when such manipulations are especially well suited to deal with the problems of humans, particularly in an academic setting. Frequently, by the time students seek counseling they are already in such great difficulty that some immediate action is necessary in order to preserve enough of their way of life in which to make treatment possible. This occurs often in a university setting, where students must cope with the academic matters at hand, or, because of university academic standards, lose their educational opportunity and, as a result, be lost to the facilities of the counseling agency entirely.

Very often modifications in the situation of a student can bring about behavior changes more quickly than the traditional methods of verbal counseling or psychotherapy. However, one problem involved in manipulating situational factors to bring about behavior changes lies in identifying the cases where such methods are appropriate. Situational manipulations inappropriately applied can lead to errors in treatment and unfortunate consequences.

Cases illustrating two types of situational manipulation will be described. In the first type, the student is led to expose himself to some situational contexts while avoiding others; in the second type, the counselor or therapist directly manipulates the situational events in certain parts of the student's life.

[1] From *Planned Behavior Change: Illustrations of an Approach* (unpublished monograph, Div. of Counseling, Pa. State Univ., 1963), with permission of the authors and D. H. Ford and H. B. Urban, Editors.

The first case describes a student capable of accomplishments beyond his aspirations. Counseling led him to expose himself to a more demanding academic program, resulting in his recognition that he could achieve higher goals. Harry was seen for preregistration counseling at a Commonwealth Campus, where he planned to enroll in a two-year engineering program. It was evident to his psychologist that Harry had the potential to succeed in a four-year program, despite the fact that he lacked certain mathematics and English high school courses. Using the test results as a vehicle, the psychologist pointed out to the student the implications his abilities had for a four-year program. When the student showed interest, the psychologist, because of his knowledge of University structure and policies, his awareness of the availability of programs, and his familiarity with administrative officers of the University, was able to help the student make some rather drastic changes very rapidly. Thus, the student was transferred from one campus to another, and from an associate to a baccalaureate degree program. He went on to graduate with a B.S. in engineering, and eventually earned an M.S. in engineering. It is conceivable that Harry might have eventually found his way to a four-year degree program independently, but probably with considerably less efficiency. By helping the student more accurately assess his capabilities, by recommending a change of program more in keeping with those possibilities, and by implementing that change, the psychologist enabled the student to begin his studies in an entirely different situation than he originally thought himself capable of, leading to more advanced career possibilities.

The case of Martin shows how a student apparently headed for failure in an inappropriate program was led to expose himself to an exploratory curriculum in which he could experience success, develop new interests, and discover his limitations in the field of his original choice. The student, failing to meet the entrance requirements of the College of Engineering, enrolled in the Division of Counseling, hoping he might thus gain admission to engineering by qualifying through an exploratory program in counseling. His high school performance, below average for Penn State freshman, had resulted in a self-derogatory attitude; he attributed his poor performance to attacks of test anxiety. This, and other data, suggested he was unlikely to succeed in an engineering program. A series of interviews might have been used to lead the student to give up his goal of engineering. This would have been time-consuming and expensive. Open disagreement with his aspirations and self-appraisals might have been used, but this sometimes produces a bitter and ineffective student. Besides, tests can be wrong. After one interview, Martin selected an exploratory schedule including psychology and engineering mathematics the first term and a complete engineering schedule the second term. He liked his psychology course and did well, and his test panics apparently decreased as he discovered he could earn satisfactory grades. By the second term he discarded the idea of engineering entirely and substituted biological science teaching for psychology. For the remaining two terms of his freshman year, his grades were above average. A recent follow-up showed the student continuing toward a degree in secondary education with above average grades through three years of study. The counseling procedure used in this case was two-pronged. The nontechnical courses showed the student that he could succeed in and enjoy fields outside of engineering, and the engineering mathematics course allowed him to experience in part the difficulties he would encounter in an engineering program, without seriously damaging his academic record. The counselor correctly predicted that this combination would end the student's desire for an engineering program before the second term.

Douglas illustrates the effects of direct situational manipulation on student behavior. Frequently we find students with considerable academic ability making poor progress toward a degree. Many of the colleges at Penn State refer such students to the Division of Counseling hoping the student will discover a new and more appropriate curriculum or that counseling might help the student identify and change the factors causing his inefficiency and ineffectiveness. Douglas was doing poorly after four terms in engineering, was apparently getting worse, despite the fact that he appeared to be a capable student, and was referred by the College of Engineering. The student insisted that he wanted to be an engineer and requested an engineering program. The Director of the Division of Counseling, however, feeling that this would contribute to the student's problem, refused to approve an engineering schedule, but offered Douglas the opportunity to schedule a nontechnical program of his choice. Douglas agreed, asking that he be given an opportunity to try engineering courses again if his academic performance improved. Blocking the student from his goal led him to realize the extent to which his behavior was interfering with the attainment of his goals. Working extremely hard to regain the opportunity to return to an engineering curriculum, he raised his grades from a D average to nearly an A average the next term. This warranted another try at engineering the following term, which resulted in his best engineering average to date, a strong C+. Controlling his curriculum raised the stakes high enough to make Douglas realize how strong his commitment to engineering really was, thus raising his academic motivation and improving his scholastic achievement.

Sometimes a student can be taught to avoid some situations which adversely affect him and to seek others which are helpful. A freshman student complaining of depression, irritability, disinterest in his studies, and thoughts of quitting college was referred by the University Psychiatrist. Careful interviewing revealed only one specific source of dissatisfaction. Russell did not like the fraternity he was pledging, but preferred another one that had not offered him a "bid." His psychologist pointed out that periods of excessive irritability seemed to follow active participation in fraternity affairs and suggested a temporary reduction in fraternity participation. On a second visit, Russell reported that he felt considerably better since becoming less active in his fraternity. He raised the issue of depledging his fraternity and attempting to gain acceptance into the one of his choice. It became apparent that his rejection by the fraternity of his choice was the result of a misunderstanding and not a reflection of their disinterest in him. Russell depledged his fraternity, with the assurance that the desired one would reconsider him later, and gained immediate relief from his symptoms through removing himself from a situation which generated constant disappointment and anger within him. Although other factors might have been involved in the student's complaints, his symptoms were terminated quickly and effectively by focusing his attention on the immediate antecedents of his complaints, revealing that these antecedents were a series of situational events. The counseling procedure, then, was to alter the situation instead of the traditional procedure of attempting to modify the student's subjective responses to the situation through verbal psychotherapy. The latter would undoubtedly have required a lengthy series of interviews and might never have reduced the student's irritability and depression.

Sometimes, in the course of modification of situational factors, a student realizes that he has misperceived the way that significant people in his life view him. This was evidently important in the case of Susan, a sophomore coed who had transferred to Penn State from a small junior college. She presented symptoms like those of a person in an agitated depression, the bases of which were apparently unknown to her. Immediate intensive psychotherapy might have been implemented. However, interviewing revealed several situational stresses related to what appeared to be an academic overload in an inappropriate curriculum coupled with the feeling that she was under great pressure from her parents to earn high grades. A change of curriculum and a reduction in credit load (situational manipulations) in the context of other treatment procedures quickly reduced her agitation and, further, forced Susan to discuss her situation with her parents frankly for the first time. To her surprise, she found her parents to be very understanding and tolerant of her academic difficulties, and the resulting parental support was in itself an important therapeutic agent. This aspect of the treatment was accomplished quickly enough to permit Susan to avoid irreparable damage to her academic status at Penn State, allowing her to work on the more long term aspects of her problem under less pressure. Her psychologist chose to manipulate the particular situational variables reported because he felt that the foremost objective was to reduce her agitation quickly.

The effects of interpersonal misperceptions on behavior are even more clearly illustrated in another case. Roger, a bright young man with a poor high school record, was continuing his habits of poor academic performance at college, and was failing. He would not enter into a counseling relationship to seek and plan a remedy for this longstanding pattern of behavior. As an alternative, it was proposed that he withdraw to avoid dismissal and to protect his future, enter the military service or work for a couple of years to give himself time to mature, and then return. Although this had some appeal, he adamantly refused to consider it. The psychologist hypothesized that the history of academic underachievement and his unwillingness to withdraw from college grew out of feelings resulting from the belief that his parents cared much more for an older brother, who was a highly successful student. A joint interview with the parents and Roger was arranged. A series of indirect questions by the psychologist led the parents to talk about their feelings toward the boy. Their honest affection for him became apparent and he was deeply touched. They talked frankly with one another about their feelings and opened new channels of communication. By the end of the interview, he felt free to withdraw without fear of loss of their love. He is now back in college and an adequate, though not brilliant, student.

The implications of the type of situational manipulations applied in these cases seem clear. The ultimate objective of all counseling and psychotherapy is to change behavior in situations outside of the interview. Situational manipulations in counseling can provide a quicker, more direct way of reaching this objective in some cases. The recognition of this and the use of situational manipulations give the psychologist another tool with which to bring about behavioral changes and, when properly applied, may result in more efficient and effective treatment. This implies that psychologists must sharpen their ability to make judgments about when such procedures are appropriate, a problem necessarily approached through research.

Name Index

Acker, C. W., 241
Alexander, S., 106
Allen, D. W., 81, 98, 99
Allen, K. E., 79, 160–167
Alpert, R., 178
Andrew, B. V., 62
Andrews, J. C. W., 194
Apostal, R. A., 11
Auld, F. W., 8

Baer, D. M., 2, 64–74, 81, 160–167
Ban, T. Z., 55
Bandura, A., 85, 98, 127, 147
Bartelme, P., 104
Beck, J. C., 83
Bendig, A. W., 106
Berezin, A. G., 11
Berle, B. B., 103
Bernstein, A., 47, 170
Bijou, S. W., 27, 161
Blinder, M. G., 55
Bookbinder, L. J., 103
Bordin, E. S., 11
Boyd, R. W., 103
Braceland, F. J., 103
Brawley, E. R., 160
Brayfield, A. H., 21, 27
Breger, L., 175, 194, 199
Brown, P., 103
Buell, J. S., 160 162
Burgess, E., 183, 220–226

Callis, R., 2, 4–13
Cameron, D., 47
Campbell, R. E., 184, 243–247
Carkhuff, R. R., 83, 91, 93, 94, 95
Castell, D., 103
Cattell, R. B., 106

Cherry, N., 81, 168–177, 178, 194, 195, 199
Chestnut, W. J., 168, 174
Combs, A. W., 103
Cooke, G., 227
Cooper, J. E., 103
Cowen, E. L., 103

Darley, J. G., 11
Davison, G. C., 227
Delatil, P., 33
Dengrove, E., 57
Distler, L., 147
Dollard, J., 8, 185
Duncan, G. M., 55, 58
Dymond, R. F., 103

Elkes, C., 83
Emery, J. R., 178, 181
Endler, N. S., 106
Erikson, C. W., 178
Eysenck, H. J., 36, 49, 122, 168, 175, 201

Fairweather, G. W., 104
Farquhar, W. W., 84
Farson, R. E., 99
Feldman, P., 127
Fenichel, O., 104, 201
Ferster, C. B., 51, 57, 58, 220
Fiske, D. W., 103, 104
Fleming, R. E., 160
Flint, A. A., 83
Ford, D. H., 184, 232–234
Foulkes, D., 210
Frank, J. D., 48, 103, 121
Freud, S., 56, 211

Gardner, G. G., 48

Gebhard, P. H., 187
Geer, J. H., 183, 201–207, 208–213
Gelatt, H. B., 19, 133, 146
Gelder, M. G., 103, 227
Gelineau, V. A., 83
Gibb, B. G., 18
Gliedman, L. H., 48, 120
Goldiamond, I., 36, 50
Goldstein, A. P., 50, 122
Goodman, G., 103, 104
Gordon, E., 179
Greenspoon, J., 134, 146
Grooms, R. R., 184, 248–252
Grossberg, J. M., 168, 195, 201
Gundlach, R., 103

Haase, R. F., 79, 83–102
Haber, R., 178
Haring, N. G., 33
Harris, F. R., 81, 160–167
Hart, B. M., 160, 161
Hathaway, S. R., 55, 202
Hendrick, I., 104
Henke, L. B., 81, 160–167
Hobbs, N., 28
Hunt, J. McV., 104, 106
Husek, T. R., 105

Imber, S. D., 103, 121
Ivey, A. E., 79, 83–102

Jacobson, E., 205
Jaffe, J., 170
Johnson, C. J., Jr., 19
Johnston, M. K., 160
Jones, M. C., 31
Jones, R., 160

Kagan, N., 85
Kalish, H. I., 191
Kanfer, F. H., 2, 45–53, 191
Kantor, D., 83
Katahn, M., 79, 81, 168–177, 178, 183, 194–200
Katkin, E. S., 183, 201–207
Kelley, C. S., 160
Kelly, G. A., 53
Kennedy, D. A., 84

Keutzer, C. S., 183, 214–219
Kinsey, A. C., 187
Kogan, L. S., 104
Kora, T., 61
Krasner, L., 36, 37, 47, 104, 122, 136, 146
Krathwohl, D. R., 79
Kraude, W., 104
Krumboltz, J. D., 2, 16–20, 21–29, 79, 80, 81, 83, 84, 133–145, 146–159, 178, 181

Laffal, J., 170
Lang, P. J., 104, 121, 127, 179, 211, 227, 230
Lazarus, A. A., 2, 46, 55–60, 79, 121, 127–132, 168, 176, 227
Lazovik, A. D., 104, 121, 127, 211, 227
Lennard, H. L., 47, 170
Lesse, S., 122
Leventhal, A. M., 183, 185–193
Lindsley, O. R., 214
Llewellyn-Thomas, E., 147
London, P., 45
Lorr, M., 103
Loucas, K. P., 62
Luce, R. D., 33

McCulloch, M., 127
McDonald, F. J., 98, 99
McGaugh, J. L., 175, 194, 199
McGraw, R. B., 201
McKinley, J. C., 55
McLuhan, M., 93
McNair, D. M., 103

Maccoby, E. E., 147
MacQuiddy, R. H., 18
Maddison, D., 55, 58
Mandler, G., 179
Marks, I. M., 103, 227
Marsden, G., 31, 47
Martin, C. E., 187
Maslow, A. H., 5, 6
Matarazzo, J. D., 47, 83, 88, 134
Mattoon, C. U., 2, 30–34
May, P. R. A., 104, 123
Mees, H., 160

Migler, B., 183, 227–231
Miller, C. D., 79, 83–102
Miller, J. G., 11
Miller, N. E., 185
Moreno, J. L., 199
Morrill, W. H., 79, 83–102
Mussen, P. H., 147

Nash, E. H., 103, 121
Newman, R. G., 83
Normington, C. J., 79, 83–102

Oliven, J. F., 201
Orme, M. E., 98, 99
Osipow, S. H., 2, 75–78, 184, 248–252

Pascal, G. R., 27
Patterson, G. R., 160
Pauk, W., 198
Paul, G. L., 37, 38, 79, 80, 103–126, 127,
    174, 178, 199, 211, 227, 230
Pavlov, I., 31
Pepinsky, H. B., 6, 11
Pepinsky, P. N., 6
Peterson, R. F., 160
Phillips, E. L., 2, 30–34
Pinsky, R. H., 103
Pomeroy, W. B., 187
Pope, B., 47
Poser, E. G., 83

Rachman, S., 46, 168, 175, 227
Raimy, V. C., 35
Reyna, L. J., 45, 46, 201
Reynolds, D. J., 211
Reynolds, N. J., 81, 160–167
Rickard, H. C., 149
Riess, B. F., 103
Rioch, M. J., 83
Risley, T. R., 2, 64–74, 160
Rogers, C. R., 11, 98, 103
Rosenstein, A. J., 106
Ross, D., 147
Ross, S. A., 147
Roth, L., 103
Rothney, J. W. M., 133
Ryan, T. A., 19, 79, 80, 133–145, 149

Sager, C. J., 103
Salter, A., 45, 46, 201
Samler, J., 21
Sarason, I. G., 82, 169, 179
Sargent, H. D., 103, 104
Saslow, G., 47, 49, 83, 88
Schmidt, E., 103
Schofield, W., 45, 48
Schroeder, W. W., 18, 146, 147, 150, 152
Shannon, D. T., 105, 174, 199
Sidman, M., 64, 68
Siegman, A. W., 47
Silber, E., 83
Silverman, I., 183, 208–213
Simon, R., 104
Sinett, E. R., 103
Skinner, B. F., 56, 64, 84, 88, 89
Spielberger, C. D., 168, 174
Stafford-Clark, D., 93
Stenstedt, A., 55
Stevenson, I., 41, 122
Stimput, W. E., 103
Stoller, F. H., 99
Stone, A. R., 48, 103, 121, 122, 123
Straight, E., 103
Strenger, S., 81, 168–177, 178, 194, 195,
    199
Strupp, H. H., 47
Sturm, I. E., 127, 131
Suinn, R. M., 79, 82, 178–182

Tart, C. R. T., 210
Thompson, I., 84
Thoresen, C. E., 18, 79, 81, 84, 146–159
Truax, C. B., 83, 89, 91, 93, 94, 95
Trumbo, D., 47
Tuma, A. H., 104

Ullmann, L. P., 2, 35–44, 104
Ulrich, L., 47
Urban, H. B., 184, 233–242
Usdansky, B. S., 83

Varenhorst, B. B., 18, 84
Voeks, V., 172

Wall, H. W., 184, 243–247
Walters, R. H., 85, 98, 147

Watson, J. B., 31
Weitz, H., 168, 174
White, A. M., 8
White, R. W., 22
Whittier, J., 160
Wiener, D. N., 33
Wiens, A. N., 83, 88
Wiener, I. B., 11
Williams, J. H., 47
Williamson, E. G., 11
Wishner, J., 22
Wolberg, L. R., 201
Wolf, H. E., 103
Wolf, M. M., 2, 64–74, 160, 165

Wolf, S., 103
Wolpe, J., 41, 42, 45, 46, 49, 57, 104,
   121, 127, 168, 170, 171, 175, 178, 179,
   183, 187, 194, 195, 201, 203, 209,
   227–231
Wolpin, M., 227
Wrenn, C. G., 83
Wright, M. A., 160

Yates, A. J., 39, 42
Young, H. H., 103

Zax, M., 27

Subject Index

advice, 127–132
anxiety, 57
  control of, 32–33
  hierarchy of, 178, 195–196
  introduction of instrumental responses to deal with, 245–246
  test, 79, 81
    alleviation of associated physical symptoms, 175
    and behavioral counseling, 168–177
    desensitization of, 178–182
    hierarchy of, 170
    treatment of, 235–237, 246–247
attending behavior, 81
  and control of hyperactivity, 160–167
  and microcounseling, 83–102
  use as reinforcer, 160–167
attention-placebo therapy, 227
attention span, 160
awareness, 142–143

behavior, analysis of, dimensions of, 64–74
  attending, and control of hyperactivity, 160–167
  change of, via advice, 127–132
    via behavior rehearsal, 127–132
    by extinction, 30
    generality of, 72–73
    by interference, 30
    via non-directive therapy, 127–132
    by skill acquisition, 30
behavior, continuous stream of, 233
  decision-making, generalization of, 141–142
  learning of, 24–25
  and reinforcement counseling, 133–145

frequency of, 152
goals, consequences of, 26–27
information-seeking, and counseling, 146–159
maladaptive, 211
  alteration of, 23–24
modification of, in counseling center, 220–226
  through situational change, 248–252
overt changes in, 21
overt controls of, 33
problems, prevention of, 25–26
rehearsal of, 80, 127–132
repertoire of, 4, 6–12
  definition of, 7
  development of, 6–9
  treatment of inadequate, 9–12
technique of reversal, 68–69
types of, 152
variety of, 152
behavior therapy, 48
"behavioral engineers", 49
behavioral counseling, use in traditional therapy, 185–193
Beta hypothesis, 31
bibliotherapy, 178

catharsis, 31
character disorder, treatment with behavioral techniques, 225
conditioning, techniques of, implications for counseling and therapy, 45–54
counseling, behavioral, 1
  applications of, 220–226
    in combination with traditional therapy, 185–193, 214–219
    effects of group work on information seeking, 146–159

effects of individual work on information seeking, 146–159
  ethical dilemmas of, 75–78
  goals for, 21–29
  and modeling, 35–36
  and nightmare elimination, 208–213
  rationale for, 14–20
  and stereotype as mechanistic, 35–44
  training for, 200–207
client-centered, ethical dilemmas of, 65–68
cognitive, 1
criteria for, 15, 22–23, 26–27
decision-making, 24–25
definition of, 16
differential, 4–13
directive, 1
goals of, 76-77
group-reinforcement, 149
group model-reinforcement, 150
group, with test anxious students, 168–177
individual-reinforcement, 148
individual model-reinforcement, 149
counseling, limits of, 16–17
  microcounseling in training for, 83–102
  model-reinforcement, 147
  non-directive, 33, 127–132
  planned reinforcement, effects of, 133–145
  preventative, 25–26
  strategy, 185
  techniques of, search for, 26
  training in reflection of feeling, 89–93
  training in summarization of feeling, 94–97
  treatments in, interference vs. extinction, 30–34
counselor, training of, and microcounseling, 83–102
Counselor Effectiveness Scale, 84
  scores on, 84–103
counterconditioning, 191
criteria, training to, 151–152
criterion, use of grade point average as, 169

decision-making, 24–25, 81
  effect of reinforcement counseling on, 133–145
decision responses, 19, 140–141
  definition of, 134
deliberation responses, 19, 137–140
  definition of, 134
dependency, 232–233
depression, antecedents of, 57
  decrease through extinction, 221–222
  endogenous, 55, 58
  exogenous, 55
  psychogenic, 56
  treatment of, 58, 59–62
    based on learning theory, 55–63
desensitization, 31, 37–39, 57, 80–81, 103–126, 168, 172–173, 176
  of anxiety in athlete, 194–200
  of anxiety to sexual words, 189–192
  as result of suggestion, 104
  mixed with other procedures, 178
  of test anxiety, 178–182
  through automated procedures, 227–231
  in treatment, 209–210
  use in reducing insomnia, 201–207
diagnosis, 11, 49–50, 57–58

ego, 232–233
emotional life, 1
environment, manipulation of, 59
ethics, 75–78
experimental extinction, 191
extinction, 136

fear, hierarchy of, 203
  failure to develop, 209
Fear Survey Schedule, 179
feeling, reflection of, 84, 97–100
  summarization of, 84, 97–100
friendship therapy, 48

generalization, 136
grief reaction, treatment of, 237–238

Hawthorne Effect, 147
hierarchy, of anxiety, 178
homosexual, thoughts, treatment of, 238–241

homosexuality, elimination through behavioral counseling, 222–223
hyperactivity, control of, 160–167
hypnagogic dream, 210

information-seeking, 81
insight, 45, 103–126
insight therapy, 227
insomnia, reduction through desensitization, 201–207
treatment of, 244–245
Instigation Therapy, 50–51
IPAT Anxiety Scale, 106, 215

learning theory, and treatment of depression, 55–63

mental disorder, Kraepelinian classification of, 55
microcounseling, 79, 83–102
minimum goal, use of in behavioral counseling, 171
MMPI, 202, 209
model, disease analogy, 104
modeling, use of in anxiety reduction, 197
Morita Therapy, 61–62
motivation, 4–6
"multiple baseline technique", 69–70

needs, Maslow's list of, 5–6
nightmare, treatment of, through behavior modification, 208–213

operant, 136
operant procedures, use within traditional therapy, 214–219
operant responses, 56

paranoid, thoughts, treatment of, 238–241
phobic reactions, 168
Pittsburgh Social Extroversion–Introversion Emotionality Scales, 106
positive transference, 199, 218, 230
problems, prevention of, 25–26
progressive relaxation, 205
psychoanalytic, theory of dreams, 211

psychotherapy, follow-up, 103–126

reciprocal inhibition, 209
reflection of feeling, 84
relationship, 232–233
reinforcement, 40–41
of information-seeking, 18
positive, 59
and social control, 160–167
verbal, 133
reinforcement counseling, 80–81, 133–146
relaxation, deep muscle, 209
instructions for, 229–230
progressive, 205
relaxation training, 170–171
use in case, 187–188
repression, 31
research, applied versus basic, 65–66
response deficit, 48
responses, decision, definition of, 134, 140–141
deliberation, 137–140
definition of, 134
operant, 56
overt instrumental, alteration of verbally, 243–247
self-defeating, 244
training of assertive, 58
use of verbal procedures to modify subjective, 235–242
reversal technique, 68–69

selective inattention, 237
self-acceptance, 21
Self-Concept Scale, 91
self-understanding, 21
sensory deprivation, 61
sleep therapy, 62
situational manipulation, implications of, 252
spontaneous remission, 122
S–R Inventory of Anxiousness, 106
strategies, for therapy, 51–52
study skill advising, 178
subjective states, 21–22, 235–242
Suinn Test Anxiety Behavioral Scale,
summarization of feeling, 84

symptom, 47
  substitution, 115–122

test anxiety, and behavioral counseling,
    168–177
  desensitization of, 178–182
Test Anxiety Scale, 169, 179
tests, interpretation of, 18
  training in, 100
testwiseness, 18
therapist, as generalized reinforcer, 122
therapy, attention-placebo type, 104
  behavior, and test anxious students,
    168–177

training for, 200–207
  treatment of nightmare, 208–213
therapy, behavioral, stereotype as mech-
    anistic, 35–44
  insight-oriented, 104
  non-directive, 127–132
therapy time, as a reinforcer, 214–219

unconditional positive regard, 218
uncovering, 31

verbal reinforcement, 133
vomiting, elimination through extinction,
    223–224